GEORGE WASHINGTON
& the Founding of a Nation

GEORGE WASHINGTON
& the Founding of a Nation

ALBERT MARRIN

Dutton Children's Books
New York

A NOTE ON THE ILLUSTRATIONS

The drawings in this book, which capture so vividly the texture of George Washington's America, were made by leading American artists of the last century. They were taken from these sources: Edward S. Ellis, *The Youth's History of the United States* (New York, 1887); Edmund Ollier, *Cassell's History of the United States* (London, 1875); and these books by Benson J. Lossing: *Our Country: A Household History* (New York, 1877); *George Washington's Mount Vernon* (New York, 1870); *Mary and Martha: The Mother and Wife of George Washington* (New York, 1886); *Pictorial Field Book of the Revolution* (New York, 1855). Washington Irving's classic 1859 biography, *The Life of George Washington*, contains many engravings. The Library of Congress and National Archives in Washington, D.C., house countless valuable illustrations, as does the New York Historical Society.

Text copyright © 2001 by Albert Marrin

PHOTO CREDITS: page *ii* courtesy of Washington-Custis-Lee Collection, Washington and Lee University, Lexington, Virginia; page *iii* reproduced by permission of The Huntington Library, San Marino, California; pages 10, 19 (top), 43, 44, 46, 60, 64, 66 (bottom), 72, 74, 77, 79, 85, 98, 99, 100, 106, 110, 112, 113, 114, 115, 121, 127, 134, 145, 146, 149, 150, 161, 170, 177 (bottom), 223, 234, 235, 236, 237, 256, 257 courtesy of the author; pages 11, 13, 15, 18, 19 (bottom), 23, 24, 38, 39, 49, 50, 55, 63, 65, 66 (top), 67, 70, 71, 86, 89, 90, 92, 93, 108, 120, 124, 132, 154, 164, 166, 179, 188, 205, 207, 208, 216, 218, 224, 227, 238, 239, 240, 243, 250, 251, 254, 255 courtesy of the Library of Congress; pages 75, 78, 80, 84, 87, 88, 96, 104, 105, 107, 111, 118, 126, 131, 135, 148, 158, 173, 178, 181, 182, 184, 197, 206, 212, 226 courtesy of the National Archives; page 82 courtesy of Yale University Art Gallery, the Mabel Brady Garvan Collection; pages 136, 249 courtesy of the National Gallery of Art, Washington, D.C.; page 165 courtesy of the Chicago Historical Society; pages 214 (by Thomas Rossiter), 230, 231 courtesy of the Independence National Historical Park; page 245 courtesy of the White House Collection.

Library of Congress Cataloging-in-Publication Data

Marrin, Albert.
   George Washington and the founding of a nation / Albert Marrin.—1st ed.
      p. cm.
  Includes bibliographical references and index.
    ISBN 0-525-46481-6
    1. Washington, George, 1732–1799—Juvenile literature. 2. Presidents—United States—Biography—Juvenile literature. 3. Generals—United States—Biography—Juvenile literature. 4. United States—History—Revolution, 1775–1783—Juvenile literature. 5. United States—Politics and government—1783–1809—Juvenile literature. 6. United States—History—French and Indian War, 1755–1763—Juvenile literature. [1. Washington, George, 1732–1799. 2. Presidents. 3. United States—History—Colonial period, ca. 1600–1775. 4. United States—History—Revolution, 1775–1783.] I. Title.
E312.66.M28 2001 973.4'1'092—dc21 [B] 00-034088

Published in the United States by Dutton Children's Books,
a division of Penguin Putnam Books for Young Readers
345 Hudson Street, New York, New York 10014
www.penguinputnam.com

Designed by Amy Berniker
Printed in China   First Edition
1 3 5 7 9 10 8 6 4 2

For Bruce McMahan,
my Irish brother

Contents

Prologue   A MAN FOR HIS TIMES   *3*

1   A MAN OF GOOD QUALITY   *17*

2   THE WORLD ON FIRE   *32*

3   A KIND OF DESTINY   *62*

4   WAR AND WASHINGTON   *95*

5   POUNDS OF SORROW   *138*

6   GREAT WASHINGTON'S ADVANCE   *168*

7   THE THING IS DONE   *199*

8   THE SACRED FIRE OF LIBERTY   *220*

9   THE FIRST AND THE LAST   *248*

Notes   *259*

More Books About Washington and His Times   *265*

Index   *270*

"*Washington is the mightiest name of earth. . . . On that name, [a] eulogy is expected. It cannot be. To add brightness to the sun, or glory to the name of Washington, is alike impossible. Let none attempt it. In solemn awe pronounce his name, and in its naked deathless splendor, leave it shining on.*"   —ABRAHAM LINCOLN, FEBRUARY 22, 1842

George Washington
& the Founding of a Nation

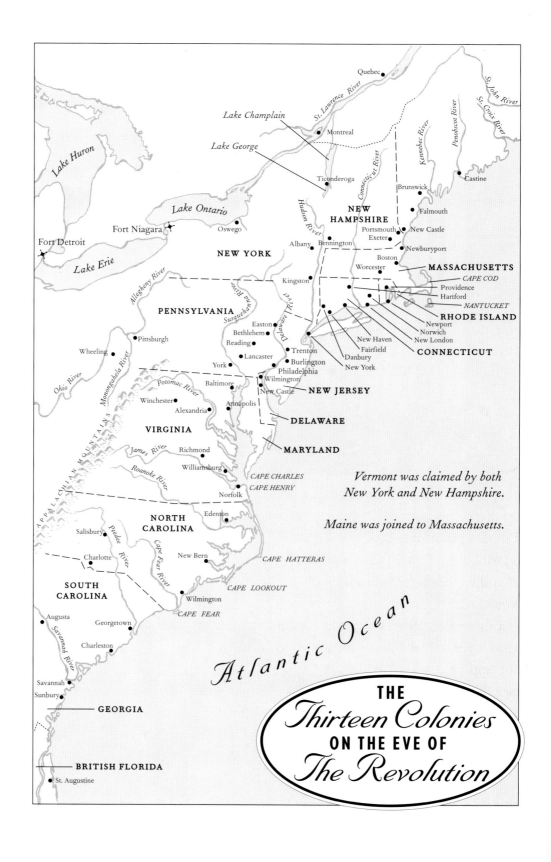

THE
Thirteen Colonies
ON THE EVE OF
The Revolution

A MAN FOR HIS TIMES

Mighty Washington!
Words fail to tell all he has done!
—ANONYMOUS POEM, 1789

The United States of America is an accepted reality in the world today. Other governments seldom go ahead in any key foreign policy matters without first considering how the United States might react, for no nation can match its present economic and military power. The United States owes its place in the world, in part, to George Washington. Yet, in his day, the "Father of Our Country" could not have imagined what his country would eventually become, or how long it would take.

Little more than two centuries ago, our country did not exist. Nobody knows for sure who invented the name *United States of America*. It does not appear in print anywhere before January 1777, as far as I know. Six months after the Declaration of Independence (July 4, 1776), a writer named Thomas Paine used it in a pamphlet titled *The American Crisis*. "The United States of America," Paine wrote, "will sound as [importantly] in the world or in history as the kingdom of Great Britain."[1]

If we could go back, say, to the year 1760, we would find not a single nation, but thirteen colonies set along a narrow strip of shoreline bordering the Atlantic Ocean. From north to south, the colonies were: Massachusetts, New Hampshire, Rhode Island, Connecticut, New York, New Jersey, Pennsylvania, Delaware, Maryland, Virginia, North Carolina, South Carolina, Georgia.

All were part of the British Empire. From its capital in London, England, Great Britain ruled the mightiest empire in all of human history. Besides its North American colonies, the empire had colonies in places stretching from the islands of the West Indies to South Africa, India, and Australia. Its subjects took pride in the slogan: "The sun never sets on the British Empire."

During the eighteenth century, George Washington's America looked very different from how it looks today. For one thing, America was still mostly wilderness. "The country is one vast wood," a French traveler wrote. He did not exaggerate. Although each year settlers cleared thousands of acres for planting, they barely made a dent in the forests. If the wind blew from the land, sailors approaching the New England coast from far out at sea could smell the pine forests. Colonists claimed that a squirrel might leap from treetop to treetop for a thousand miles and not touch the ground.[2]

The land teemed with game. Deer and wild turkey seemed as plentiful as when the first English settlers arrived in the early 1600s. Flocks of passenger pigeons might break the thickest tree branches when they landed. Although now extinct, these birds once numbered in the hundreds of millions. When a flock of passenger pigeons took flight, it blotted out the sun at noontime. Now and then, farmers shot bears and wolves in the long-settled areas.

In 1760, the thirteen colonies had about 1,600,000 people, white and black. Everyone who made the voyage to the New World faced a life-threatening ordeal. Even with good weather, you could not cross the Atlantic in under six weeks; in bad weather, it might take three months. For enslaved blacks, the horrors of the "middle passage" from Africa often killed half those crowded into a ship's hold.

Although they were not kept in chains or beaten, white immigrants could suffer dreadfully, too. Gottlieb Mittelberger, a German musician who left home in 1754, described his voyage:

During the voyage there is on board . . . terrible misery, stench, fumes, horror, vomiting, many kinds of sea-sickness, fever, dysentery, headache, . . . constipation, boils, scurvy, cancer, mouth-rot, and the like, all of which come from old and sharply salted food and meat, also from very bad and foul [drinking] water, so that people die miserably. . . . The lice abound so frightfully, especially on sick people, that they can be scraped off the body. . . . Children from 1 to 7 years rarely survive the voyage. . . . I witnessed such misery in no less than 32 children in our ship, all of whom were thrown [dead] into the water.[3]

Of those who reached the colonies, or were born there, fewer than one person in ten lived in a town or city. The rest lived on farms or, like George Washington, on tobacco plantations. We cannot be sure how many Native Americans there were. All we can say is that foreign diseases and colonists' guns steadily reduced their numbers.

Towns were small, usually with fewer than fifty families. By today's standards, even colonial cities were tiny. In 1776, Philadelphia had 40,000 people, making it the largest city, next to London, in the English-speaking world. New York City, the colonies' greatest seaport, came next with 20,000 people. Boston, Massachusetts, had 16,000 people; Charleston, South Carolina, 12,000; Newport, Rhode Island, 11,000.

Towns were widely separated and hard to reach by land. Washington once described colonial roads as "infamous." He was right. Since there were no paved roads, travel was always slow and uncomfortable. It could be dangerous, too, especially in the rainy season. Sometimes, after a downpour, travelers drowned on the public roads. A man might fall off his horse, be knocked unconscious, and land with his face in the mud. Travelers also needed patience. It took a week to go by stagecoach the two hundred miles from Boston to New York. It took another three days to cover the ninety miles from New York to Philadelphia. It was worse in the South. A Virginian once complained that five out of the eight streams near his place had neither a bridge nor a ferry. No wonder colonists made their wills and said their prayers before setting out on a journey.[4]

Still, the colonies were places of opportunity—*if* you were lucky, free, and a white man. Each colony had plenty of poor people struggling just to eat and stay warm in the winter. In 1737, when Washington was five years old, a letter appeared in a New York City newspaper. The writer described a homeless street child as "an Object in Human Shape, half starved with Cold, with Clothes out at the Elbows, Knees through the Breeches, Hair standing on end." Now and then, the poor rioted to protest their poverty.[5]

Despite widespread poverty, you might gain more in a few years of hard work than generations of your ancestors had in Europe. Town dwellers' chief occupations were manufacturing, shopkeeping, shipping, foreign commerce, the building trades, law, and medicine. In New England, men from the coastal towns went to sea to fish and hunt whales; melted whale fat fueled the lamps in most colonial homes. In addition, every port city had its dealers in "black ivory," a polite term for people captured in West Africa and sold into slavery. In Washington's day, all colonies held black people in bondage. So did he.

The frontier acted as a magnet, attracting people who wanted to improve themselves. Land was so plentiful that families constantly left the older settlements in search of better opportunities. Their willingness to pull up stakes amazed foreign visitors. "Wandering about seems engrafted in their nature," one noted. "They forever imagine that the lands further off are still better than those upon which they are already settled."[6]

Each colony had its own assembly, or legislature, elected by men (but not women) of property; the poor seldom had the right to vote. According to the royal charter that created each colony, its assembly could vote to collect taxes and decide how to spend the money. Moreover, every colony had a governor appointed by the King of England, who could veto laws passed by the assembly. Governors rarely used their veto power, however, because the assembly paid their salaries. If they acted against the colonists' wishes, they did not get paid. Thus, each colony was really a tiny self-governing republic within the empire.

Yet the colonies were far from independent. Parliament, Britain's own lawmaking body, controlled their dealings with the outside world. Starting in the 1650s, it passed a series of Acts of Trade and Navigation to regulate the colonies' overseas trade. By these laws, colonists had to send their products to England aboard English ships and sell them only to English merchants. They had no choice in the matter, although foreigners might offer better prices. And if Britain went to war with another country, its colonies went to war, too. The enemy might then seize their ships on the high seas and invade their territory. France posed the worst threat. From its colony in Canada, it sent its soldiers and Indian allies to raid English settlements.

British control could be annoying, but not enough to make the colonists want to form their own country. Colonists took pride in their heritage, calling themselves the "overseas English."

Although living in the New World, they brought England with them in familiar place names: *New* England, *New* York, *New* Jersey, *New* Hampshire, *New* London, *New* Britain, Plymouth, Portsmouth, Boston. When speaking of England, they called it the "old country," the "mother country," or simply "home." Colonists prayed to God in English; some said the Lord *was* English. They spoke English with English accents. A visitor wrote, they used "better English than the English do."[7]

English law guaranteed to colonists the "rights of Englishmen." Thanks to that law, in 1760 they enjoyed more freedoms than any people on earth. Freedom of the press. Freedom from arbitrary arrest. Trial by jury. These rights belonged not only to the nobility and the wealthy, but to all English people. A song, "Virginia's Hearts of Oak," captured colonists' feelings toward the mother country:

> *Though we feast and grow fat on America's soil*
> *Yet we owe ourselves subjects of Britain's fair isle;*
> *And who's so absurd to deny us the name*
> *Since true British blood flows in every vein.*[8]

Colonists lived in America, but they did not see themselves as Americans. In 1760, America was a name on a map, not a country. America did not command your love or respect, much less your sense of pride. You identified yourself either as English or by the name of your colony. Not an American, you were a New Yorker, a Pennsylvanian, a Virginian— and so on. You owed your loyalty to Britain and to your colony, not to "America."

This seemed right because different people had settled different areas, at different times, for different reasons. New Englanders, for example, were mostly Puritans; that is, Protestants who had fled religious persecution in the 1600s. Virginians, however, belonged to the Church of England, the official national church. Most Virginians had come to get land; others were convicts sent to work off their prison terms in the colonies. Little better than slaves, they hated their masters. Sometimes they joined the slaves in uprisings against wealthy landowners. Thus, each colony had its own history and economic interests.

Each colony also thought itself better than the others. John Adams expressed that attitude best. A future president of the United States, he thought Boston the finest place in America. "Philadelphia," he wrote in his diary, "with all its Trade and Wealth . . . is not Boston. The Morals of our People are much better, their Manners are more polite, and agreeable— they are purer English. Our language is better, our Persons are Handsomer, our Spirit is greater, our Laws are wiser, our Religion is superior, our Education is better."[9]

Colonies were rivals rather than allies. New York taxed cargoes passing through its port bound for New Jersey. Maryland did the same for goods bound for Pennsylvania. When Massachusetts appealed to its neighbors for aid against Indian raids, they refused to give a penny. Massachusetts was like a foreign country to Pennsylvanians, let alone Virginians and other southerners. What happened to it was nobody's worry but its own. Colonies even exchanged shots in quarrels over boundary lines.

It seemed that the colonies would remain disunited forever. Writing in 1765, a respected Boston lawyer named James Otis said: "Were these colonies left to themselves tomorrow, America would be a shambles of blood and confusion." Most thoughtful people agreed with Otis. Few, if any, believed the colonies could unite to form a separate, independent nation. They felt that the colonies needed Britain to prevent them from tearing each other apart.[10]

Yet there came a time when the mother country began to change the rules. In London, Parliament tried to tighten its control over the colonies. It began to pass laws to bypass the colonial assemblies and tax their people directly. Those new laws sent waves of protests rolling across the colonies.

Colonists accused Britain of betraying its own traditions of freedom and justice. Many were both disappointed and angry, agreeing with John Adams that "there was no more Justice left in Britain than there was in Hell." If they did not stop Britain, they felt, it would make them slaves in their own land. Like Adams, many "wished for War" against the mother country.[11]

Their wish came true. War came. We call it the American Revolution or the Revolutionary War. Out of the struggle grew the United States of America. Still, that did not happen easily or cheaply. Although the colonies became states, their people's loyalties remained unchanged. For the majority, the idea of being a citizen of a united country seemed strange, almost unnatural. Worse, within each colony rich and poor still feared and despised each other.

The Revolutionary War lasted eight and a half years (1775–83), or the length of the Civil War (1861–65) and World War II (1941–45) combined. Only the Vietnam War (1962–73) lasted longer. School textbooks and the media often portray the struggle as a mass uprising of devoted patriots. Driven by an unshakable faith in the justice of their cause and in its inevitable victory, patriots gladly bore every hardship—or so the story goes.

It is a fairy tale. Most men in the colonies never fired a shot during the Revolution, much less rushed to enlist in the army. Those who did, as we will see, quickly lost whatever illusions they had when they joined up. War is not a glorious adventure. It is a real and cruel teacher, and those who fail to learn its lessons early do not get a low grade. They die.

The Revolutionary War showed people at their best and worst. Yes, there were countless acts of courage, self-sacrifice, and humanity. Set against these were also countless acts of bigotry, brutality, and ignorance. No enemy killed more colonists, or treated them worse, than fellow colonists.

Historians agree with John Adams, who estimated that one-third of the colonists favored independence, one-third opposed it, and one-third stayed neutral. Those divisions ignited a civil war within the Revolutionary War. Wars between nations are bad enough; civil wars are worse, because they set communities to fighting among themselves.[12]

Hatred not fellowship, division not unity, ruled during the war years. A

New England minister put it this way: "Everywhere distrust, fear, hatred and abominable selfishness were met with. Parents and children, brothers and sisters, wife and husband, were enemies of one another."[13]

Like all wars, the Revolutionary War saw frightful bloodshed. The patriot side lost about 25,000 soldiers in battle or to disease. Seen in terms of today's population, this figure would translate into 2,500,000 deaths. The country felt the war's effects for years afterward. In certain areas, every building lay in ruins and every well had dead farm animals floating in it, a sure way to deprive the enemy of drinking water.

Even as the struggle raged, people called it "George Washington's War." Washington earned his reputation in two wars. For that reason, I must devote a good deal of this book to his military career. That career was the basis of his fame and later of his role in shaping the new nation. Thus, Washington the soldier prepared the way for Washington the statesman.

Washington was an active-duty soldier for a total of twelve and a half years. In 1754, he ambushed a French patrol on the frontier, an event that triggered a great war. During that war, he fought as a loyal British subject. Although the war lasted until 1763, he left the British service in 1758. In his second war, the American Revolution, he led rebel forces in alliance with France against Britain. That made him the leader of history's first anticolonial war—its first successful war against imperialism.

Washington was the one person it is impossible to leave out of the story of these times. We cannot imagine our history without him. If not Thomas Jefferson, another person would have written the Declaration of Independence, though not as beautifully. If not Benjamin Franklin, somebody else would have helped bring France into the war on the patriot side. Nobody could have filled Washington's boots. He played the key role in the winning of independence and in creating our system of government, the union of states under the Constitution.

The signature of G. Washington. He usually signed his name this way; only rarely did he spell the name *George* in full.

Washington was America's first hero. Before photography, most people knew what he looked like, thanks to crude drawings printed in newspapers and prints sold by roving peddlers. "Every American," a European traveler wrote, "considers it his sacred duty to have a likeness of Washington in his home, just as we have the images of God's saints."[14]

People expressed their love of Washington in countless ways. They celebrated his birthday and named their children for him. An expert on rear-

President-elect Washington received a gala reception when he passed through Trenton, New Jersey, on his way to his inauguration in New York City.

ing children advised parents to follow a simple rule: "Begin with the infant in his cradle. Let the first word he lisps be the name of WASHINGTON." "O Washington! How I do love thy name!" a college president gushed. To some Americans, he was not human at all. They glorified "godlike Washington," and capitalized "Him" in their writings, as if he were the Lord. They called him "our Savior," "our Redeemer," "our star in the east," "our cloud by day and our pillar of fire by night." A few insisted "Washington . . . is not a man but a God."[15]

Nowadays, we know Washington by his picture on the dollar bill and the formal portraits found in schoolbooks. One state, seven mountains, eight streams, ten lakes, nine colleges, thirty-three counties, and 121 towns and villages bear his name. The navy has a nuclear-powered aircraft carrier, the USS *George Washington*.

Yet he is a stranger to most Americans—a cold, distant figure, not a flesh-and-blood human being with strong beliefs and emotions. That is too bad. For he *was* a man, with all the faults and frailties of other men. In other words, he was no saint. Washington expected to get as much work as possible out of his employees and slaves. He liked money—lots of it. He had little appreciation of music or literature. Nevertheless, he was a great man.

Washington was blessed with a capacity for growth. Lord Fairfax, Virginia's largest landowner, had befriended him as a teenager. When Washington was sixteen, His Lordship described him as "a man who will go to school all his life." School did not mean classrooms and libraries. His knowledge, and thus his wisdom, came from experience in what he would have proudly called "the college of hard knocks." That is, it came from life. His genius was that he knew how to learn.[16]

Washington also knew how to fight. To those who saw him in battle, he seemed fearless. "A god of war," a stunned onlooker called him.

He led from the front, putting himself in harm's way just like any of his men. But what really won them over was the general's moral courage. In Washington, soldiers knew they had a leader who cared more for them and their cause than for himself.

Washington admired them, too. "To see men," he wrote in 1778, "without clothes to cover their nakedness, without blankets to lay on, without shoes, by which their marches may be traced by the blood from their feet, and almost as often without provisions as with, marching through frost and snow . . . is a mark of patience and obedience which . . . can scarce be paralleled." Finally, he led them to victory against the British army, an enemy who had defeated Europe's best troops.[17]

Yet Washington was no military genius. He fought nine battles during the Revolutionary War. Of these, he won only three. In a way, he resembled Joe Louis, the greatest heavyweight boxer who ever lived. Critics said Louis won because he fought "the bum of the month"—an inferior boxer who was no match for him. That judgment is unfair. There *may* have been better boxers than Louis. Yet he had to beat only those who stepped into the ring with him. So it was with Washington. At first,

In 1789, President-elect George Washington was rowed across New York Bay from New Jersey for his inauguration in New York City.

Britain's generals, all veterans of the European wars, pushed him around like a bumbling amateur. But he learned—painfully. He took their best shots, hung on, and came back for more. The point is, a champion boxer or a victorious general need not take on everyone, but only those who challenge him. Victory does not necessarily go to the best fighter, but to the fighter who can outlast his opponent.

Washington lost or fought to a draw the battles of Long Island, White Plains, Princeton, Germantown, Brandywine, and Monmouth. He won at Trenton, Harlem Heights, and Yorktown. He captured Boston not by fighting, but by threatening to blow the city to bits with his artillery.

As the first president, Washington embodied people's aspirations and fears. And, since there were no precedents for him, he was stepping into the unknown. Washington had to make decisions for a nation of former colonies that had little love for each other.

He believed the winning of independence was only a means to an end. That end, he said, was nothing less than creating a free government run by the people's elected representatives so that "our lives, liberties and properties shall be preserved." More, he hoped to see that form of government spread worldwide. For him, therefore, the American "experiment" was about a lot more than independence. "For with our fate will the destiny of unborn millions be involved."[18]

It is not always easy to learn about Washington. In a sense, we have both too much and not enough information. He wrote more than any other president in his own handwriting; he left at least 25,000 letters and several thousand diary pages. These writings deal with official business and everyday matters. Usually, they make for slow reading.

Washington was a private person who did not like to talk about himself or share his inner self with others. His wife, Martha, protected his privacy and their relationship. We know that they exchanged hundreds of letters during the forty years of their marriage. After he died, she burned all but two. What did the burned letters say? Was it embarrassing? Did her husband ask her to burn the letters, or did she do it on her own? These are interesting questions, but we will never know the answers. Realizing this tells us something about history. However much we may know about the past, much of it remains unknown and unknowable.

Our understanding of Washington is a blend of fact and myth. Still, myth can serve a good purpose. I especially like this example: In 1800, "Parson" Mason Locke Weems published his *Life and Memorable Actions of Washington*. To capture the public's interest, he invented stories about his subject. The most famous story has the young George chopping down a cherry tree and earning his father's forgiveness for confessing his "crime." Yet, although Weems got certain facts wrong and made up others, he got his subject right—that is, he portrayed Washington's basic honesty and decency.

Weems's *Washington* inspired countless young readers. Abraham Lin-

"Father, I cannot tell a lie." Young George Washington confesses to his father that he chopped down his favorite cherry tree and wins forgiveness for telling the truth. The only problem is that this is just a story, made up by Mason Locke Weems to illustrate Washington's unshakable honesty. From a copy of an engraving of 1867 by John C. McRae after a painting by G. G. White.

coln read it beside a fireplace in a log cabin in frontier Indiana. Years later, amid the crisis leading to the Civil War, he recalled how reading about the struggles of Washington and his fellow patriots had left an indelible mark on his mind—no, on his *soul*. "I remember," he told an audience, "all the accounts there given of the battlefields and struggles for the liberties of the country. . . . I recollect thinking then, boy even though I was, that there must have been something more than common that those men struggled for; that something even more than National Independence; that something that held out a great promise to all the people of the world to all time to come." Just as Washington was the founder of the Union, so Lincoln vowed to become the preserver of the Union.[19]

In writing this book, I have set myself a double task. Naturally, the book is a biography of George Washington aimed at giving readers a reliable factual account of his life. Yet it is more than that—it *must* be.

My larger purpose is to depict Washington in relation to the important issues of his time. Should the colonies break away from their mother country to create a new country? If so, what should the United States be? Should it have a weak central government, leaving the states to do pretty much as they wished? Or did the new nation as a whole have needs that were more important than those of each individual state? Washington and his fellow citizens struggled with these questions constantly. I hope that by seeing their struggle through their eyes, we may reach beyond our misconceptions and easy myths to a better understanding of who we are and how we came to be that way.

I also hope to turn a spotlight on a subject that many biographers find uncomfortable. Washington was a slave owner, a fact usually omitted or passed over quickly in books for young readers. Yet black people, both enslaved and free, played a vital role in American history. Throughout his life, Washington faced this question: Is it right for one person to own another as a piece of property? His changing views about slavery need to be examined here.

A MAN OF
GOOD QUALITY

"Associate yourself with men of good quality if you esteem your own reputation; for 'tis better to be alone than in bad company."

—GEORGE WASHINGTON'S COPYBOOK, C. 1742

*I*n colonial times, before local governments issued marriage, birth, and death certificates, the head of a household recorded these in the family Bible. The Bible served as a permanent record, passed from hand to hand, down the generations.

So it was with Augustine Washington, a blond giant of thirty-eight. "Gus," as everyone called him, owned Wakefield, a tobacco plantation along Bridges Creek in Westmoreland County, in the colony of Virginia, where it joins the Potomac River before it flows into Chesapeake Bay. On the night of February 11, 1732, Gus sat at an oak table, surrounded by darkness save for flickering candlelight. Slowly he dipped the tip of his turkey-quill pen into a silver inkwell and opened the big leather-covered book to a blank page at the front. Writing carefully, he noted that, at ten o'clock that morning, his wife had delivered a fine boy they called George. (February 11 was the birth date according to the Old—Julian—Calendar. The New—Gregorian—Calendar was adopted by England and its colonies in 1752. Eleven days were added to correct the errors in the old calendar, and to begin the new year in January rather than March. Thus,

Washington's birth date became February 22, "New Style," as we know it today.)[1]

George always imagined his birthplace as the best spot on God's green earth. Virginia was the largest of the thirteen colonies in area, population, and wealth. Here, between the Potomac River and Chesapeake Bay, is where British America had begun. In May 1607, a group of colonists sent by the Virginia Company of London had founded the first permanent English settlement at Jamestown, sixty miles south of where Wakefield was established.

George's family had grown up with the colony. John Washington, a preacher's son, had left England in 1657 to seek his fortune in the New World. While working as a ship's officer, he married, Anne Pope, the daughter of a tobacco planter. Back then, tobacco was a way to make a fortune quickly. Demand in Britain and the colonies for the "bewitching weed" rose yearly. Whether chewed, sniffed, or smoked in clay pipes, not only did tobacco become fashionable, but doctors recommended it for good health. "Drinking tobacco"—inhaling the smoke—warmed your insides, they said, preventing and curing a host of illnesses. Some doctors claimed smoking cured cancer!

George Washington's birthplace at Bridges Creek, Westmoreland County, Virginia. A colored lithograph published in New York City by Currier & Ives.

John Washington's sons, John Jr. and Lawrence, followed his example. They grew tobacco and married women who brought them more land, enabling them to grow still more tobacco. In time, they adopted a coat of arms and a family motto, *Exitus acta probat,* Latin for "By their deeds ye shall know them." As the family prospered, its influence in Virginia grew. Its menfolk became justices of the peace, church wardens, and burgesses—that is, members of the lower house of the Virginia Assembly, or legislature. The legislature met in Williamsburg, the colonial capital.

Lawrence's son, Gus, was a go-getter who planted tobacco and also built a small ironworks. Although business often kept him away from home for months, he managed to marry Jane Butler and start a family. In May 1730, Gus returned to find that his wife had died of a "fever," leaving him to raise their two sons, Lawrence and Augustine Jr. Like other men of his time, Gus probably mourned his wife's loss but took it as part of the natural course of events. Eighteenth-century wives died in higher proportions than their husbands. Poor diet, ignorance of hygiene, and the risks of childbirth took a dreadful toll of wives. About one in eight died in childbirth, called by women "the greatest of earthly trials." That figure becomes even more frightful when we realize that fewer than one in twenty soldiers died in battle. In any case, a typical man could expect to have two wives in his lifetime; John Washington had three.

Gus found that he could not run a family and a business alone. So, less than a year after losing Jane, he took another bride. In March 1731, he married Mary Ball, twenty-three years old, a tobacco planter's daughter. Family friends described the second Mrs. Washington as a solidly built woman with yellow hair, "like unto flax," and cheeks "like May blossoms."[2] Although she could scarcely write her name, Mary enjoyed galloping over the countryside on spirited horses and jumping high fences. Apart from a silhouette, an outline of her profile colored in black ink, no image of her survives. Her husband, Gus, it seems, never sat for a silhouette or portrait.

Mary's first child, George, arrived eleven months after their wedding. George's birth seemed a kind of miracle, the family always thought. Once, during Mary's pregnancy, a storm had burst just as friends arrived for dinner. Claps of thunder rattled the windowpanes. Lightning zig-

George Washington's bookplate showing his family's coat of arms and Latin motto, *Exitus acta probat,* which means "By their deeds ye shall know them."

A silhouette of Mary Ball Washington, the future president's mother. Her son thought her a strict, cold person and had as little to do with her as possible after he became an adult.

zagged across the sky. Suddenly, a bolt of lightning came down the chimney, killing a woman guest who sat across from Mary at the table. Mary was terrified, not knowing whether the experience would harm her unborn child. Popular belief held that if an expectant mother saw something horrible or a loud noise startled her, it would disfigure her child for life. When George was born healthy, his parents must have thanked God for the blessing. Nevertheless, Mary often trembled and hid behind the furniture during thunderstorms.

Within six years of George's birth, Mary had borne four other children. Elizabeth ("Betty") arrived in 1733, Samuel in 1734, John Augustine ("Jack") in 1736, and Charles in 1738. Mildred, born in 1739, died the following year. These siblings were private people who traveled little and played no role in their brother's career.

Gus's absences probably kept George from knowing him very well; in all the thousands of letters George wrote, he mentioned his father only twice. However, he knew his mother only *too* well. If he ever described his feelings toward her in a letter, it has not survived. Visitors described her as a tough, bossy lady who smoked a corncob pipe. "Of the mother," a playmate of George's recalled late in life, "I was ten times more afraid than I ever was of my own parents. . . . I have often been present with her sons, proper tall fellows too, and we were all as mute as mice; and even now, when time has whitened my locks, and I am the grandparent of a second generation, I could not behold that remarkable woman without feelings it is impossible to describe."[3]

We do not know if Mary ever hugged her children or told them she loved them. We *do* know that she never showed any interest in her eldest son's activities or pride in his accomplishments. For his part, George did his duty toward her, giving her the respect due from a son and some money when necessary. That was all. When he grew to manhood, he visited her as little as possible. He never invited her to his home or introduced her to his wife. In the few letters he sent, he addressed her formally, as "Honored Madam."

In 1735, Gus moved his family to Little Hunting Creek Plantation on the Potomac River fifteen miles south of the future city of Washington, D.C. The family moved again in 1738, this time to Ferry Farm on the

Rappahannock River, opposite the village of Fredericksburg. By then, Gus owned 10,750 acres of land. This may seem like a lot today, but it hardly compared to other Virginia planters' holdings. For example, William Byrd II and Robert "King" Carter owned upward of 330,000 acres of prime tobacco-growing land.

People like the Byrds and Carters lived like European nobility in red brick mansions with grand-sounding names like Westover and Nomini Hall. They sent their sons to exclusive boarding schools in England, not to learn a profession, but to become "gentlemen"—men of good family who did not have to do physical labor. Until their daughters married, live-in governesses taught them to read, write, and act like proper "ladies." The Washingtons, though they lived comfortably, were not in the same league as these "First Families of Virginia."

Unlike their two English-educated half brothers, Gus's younger children stayed home because money was tight. George got his schooling between the ages of seven and eleven. Just where he got it, and from whom, is something of a mystery. According to one story, his father hired a one-eyed ex-convict to give him private lessons. Another story has him attending a day school run by a minister in Fredericksburg.

Both stories may, or may not, be true. What is certain is that the boy learned to read and write. His writing, however, was not that of a person with a formal education. George spelled common words the way he pronounced them. For example, he wrote *blew* for "blue" and *oyl* for "oil." He usually spelled more difficult words correctly, probably because he used a dictionary. Yet he was a whiz with numbers. Throughout his life, he had a passion for counting, calculating, and measuring. He had a habit of counting the windowpanes in houses. Once he calculated the number of seeds—71,000—in a pound of red clover.

The Library of Congress has his boyhood notebooks. Totaling 218 pages, these contain arithmetic exercises and notes on the books he read. A practical youngster, George collected facts about geography, history, and the lives of famous people. He also recopied the *Rules of Civility and Decent Behaviour in Company and Conversation*, a collection of sayings to teach youngsters manners and morality. George seemed to find great content in them. Perhaps he wanted guidance, and they provided it. He strove to live by those sayings. They helped shape his character, becoming a code of conduct he followed throughout his life. Here is part of what he wrote in his best penmanship:

Be no flatterer. . . . Let your countenance be pleasant but in serious matters somewhat grave. . . . Show not yourself glad at the misfortune of another though he were your enemy. . . . Be careful to keep your promise. . . . When a man does all he can, though it succeed not well, blame him not. . . . Use no reproachful language against any one; neither curse nor revile. . . . Let your conversation be without malice or envy. . . . Speak not evil of the absent, for it is unjust. . . . Think before you speak.[4]

Lawrence Washington took his young stepbrother, George, into his house and helped him make the right social contacts. From an engraving of a portrait at Mount Vernon.

To George, his half brother Lawrence embodied these rules of behavior. Lawrence was a reserve captain in the British army and an officer in the Virginia militia. Since it cost the British taxpayer too much money to station many British troops in America, each colony saw to its own defense by raising a militia. Only the governor could call out the militia, and then only during emergencies.

Most militiamen were well off: small farmers, tradesmen, and skilled craftsmen like printers, who owned their own businesses. Since being away from work for more than a month kept them from making a living, a colony turned to the less fortunate when it needed soldiers for more than a month. It hired civilians and formed them into regiments, units of between four and five hundred men. Colonial soldiers enlisted for a fixed time, usually a year. These "hirelings," as they were called, were poor men who signed up mainly for the money, not because they believed in any cause.

In 1740, England went to war with Spain over a trade dispute. Lawrence Washington joined a regiment of Virginia volunteers to attack the City of

Cartagena, a Spanish fortress on the northwest coast of Colombia. The attack failed miserably, as tropical diseases and enemy bullets killed his comrades in droves.

Lawrence was lucky—or so it seemed. Returning home in 1742, he appeared happy and healthy, apart from a hacking cough. Night after night, he sat by the fire, telling stories of wild charges, savage sword fights, and roaring cannons. Although younger by fourteen years, George felt closer to Lawrence than to anyone else. We can imagine him listening to his brother's stories and wanting to have his own daring exploits. War was not only exciting; it paid off. As a reward for Lawrence's services, the governor named him adjutant general of Virginia; that is, the officer in charge of

George Washington's favorite place on earth, the mansion on his Mount Vernon estate overlooking the Potomac River in Virginia. From an 1800 aquatint by Francis Jakes, after a drawing by Alexander Robertson.

training the militia. It was an honorable position that involved little work other than checking equipment and supervising drills.

In April 1743, when George was eleven, his father, Gus Washington, died. By his will, the bulk of his estate went to Lawrence as the eldest son of his first marriage. Lawrence took over Little Hunting Creek Plantation and named it Mount Vernon in honor of his old commander, Admiral Edward Vernon. The Wakefield plantation went to Lawrence's younger brother, Augustine Jr. As the eldest son of Gus's second marriage, eleven-year-old George got Ferry Farm, which he had to share with his mother until his twenty-first birthday. She refused to leave and died there in 1789, soon after her son's inauguration as president of the United States. Gus's other children received smaller parcels of land, some cash, and their father's best wishes.

Lawrence now became the most important person in George's life. Seeing the youngster so unhappy under his mother's control, Lawrence invited George to visit Mount Vernon from time to time. Those visits were like sunlight flooding into the dark, dreary room of George's life. Gradually, the visits became more frequent and lasted longer. In 1746, at age fourteen, he moved in with his half brother for good. Mary let him go. No wonder George called Lawrence "my best friend."

George blossomed at Mount Vernon. Guided by his brother, he continued his studies and learned surveying, the art of measuring land and determining boundary lines, a vital skill for a landowner. In his spare time, he fished in the Potomac, shot deer in the forests, and rode horses. Ah, horses! The boy loved horses. He loved the feel of them, the smell of them, and the sheer power of them. Mastering

George Washington, at age fourteen, drew this surveyor's diagram of his stepbrother's turnip field at Mount Vernon.

the horse brought self-mastery, a growing sense of his own abilities. In time, he became a superb judge of horseflesh. Thomas Jefferson, no slouch on horseback himself, described the adult Washington as "the best horseman of his age, and the most graceful figure that could be seen on horseback."[5]

Meanwhile, Lawrence married Anne Fairfax, daughter of Colonel William Fairfax of Belvoir, the neighboring plantation. Anne was a real "catch." Not only was she smart and pretty, her family stood at the height of high society. In all the thirteen colonies, few families could match Fairfax wealth. A leading member of the governor's council, Colonel Fairfax had enormous political influence. When the governor needed the support of other influential men, he asked the colonel to speak to them first. That usually did the trick.

Lawrence's marriage became a turning point for his brother. Whenever the newlyweds visited Belvoir, they brought George along. Anne's family welcomed the gangling teenager as one of their own. So did their guests. And why not? Although shy and soft-spoken, the *Rules of Civility and Decent Behaviour* served him well. Always polite, he knew the right things to

George Washington, right, foxhunting with his neighbor and friend George William Fairfax. The Fairfax family was one of the richest and most powerful in colonial Virginia. From an engraving in Washington Irving's *Life of George Washington.*

say; nor did he hesitate to use flattery. He also had boundless energy for horseback riding and foxhunting, the favorite sports of Virginia planters. George so wanted to be part of that gay, sophisticated world. Guided by Lawrence, he honed his social skills. He took dancing and fencing lessons at Fredericksburg, learned to enjoy music, and became something of a dandy, wearing the latest clothing styles.

During one visit to Belvoir, he met a genuine English nobleman. Colonel Fairfax was the cousin of Thomas, Lord Fairfax, Virginia's largest landowner. His Lordship held over five million acres in the Northern Neck, a thickly forested area between the Potomac and Rappahannock Rivers. In 1747, Lord Fairfax arrived from England to supervise the surveying and sale of part of his domain. A childless bachelor, he took an immediate liking to the teenager. When he learned that George knew something about surveying, he invited him to join the exploring party, a group of local men hired for the purpose.

In March 1748, the party set out for the Blue Ridge Mountains and the Shenandoah Valley beyond. This was George's first time away from home—*really* away from home—and he intended to make the most of it. We know what happened, because he began a diary. Save for the most trying times during the American Revolution, he kept that diary all his life. He made the last entry the day before he died.

After leaving Belvoir, the party headed north, passing farms and plantations along the way. Before long, however, they saw only isolated log cabins surrounded by small plots of cleared land. For a few pence—pennies—settlers gave them food and a place to sleep. That was not as simple and convenient as it sounds. On their first night in a cabin, George's companions ignored the beds and lay down on the floor fully dressed. Old hands on the frontier, they knew what to expect. Not George. Until the invention of pajamas a century later, well-bred people slept nude.

Next morning, an itchy but wiser George Washington took up his diary. Although his spelling and punctuation are not perfect, his meaning is clear:

. . . We got our Supper and was lighted into a Room and not being so good a Woodsman as ye rest of my Company stripped myself very orderly and went in to ye Bed as they called it when to my Surprize I found it to be nothing but a Little Straw-Matted together without Sheets or any thing else but only one thread Bear blanket with double its Weight of Vermin such as Lice, Fleas &c. I was glad to get up (as soon as ye Light was carried from us) I put on my Cloths and Lay as my Companions. Had we not been very tired I am sure we should not have slep'd much that night I made a Promise not to Sleep so from that time forward, chusing rather to sleep in ye open Air before a fire. . . .[6]

Sleeping by a fire also had its dangers. One rainy night, he recalled, "Our Straw catch'd Fire that we were laying upon and [we] was luckily Preserv'd by one of our men awakening when it was in a [blaze.]"[7] Nevertheless, he enjoyed the company of these hired men. He liked sitting around the campfire listening to stories of grizzly bear hunts and Indian raids as they drank whiskey and smoked their pipes. George took a nip now and then, too—to keep off the chill, he said. Smoking made him dizzy.

After returning to Mount Vernon in April, the first thing George did was take a hot bath, eat a properly cooked meal, and crawl into bed between clean sheets. But he had been able to hone his surveying skills during the month-long trip. The following year, 1749, he helped in laying out the town of Belhaven (renamed Alexandria), a few miles north of Mount Vernon. We do not know how he got this job; most likely, the Fairfaxes spoke to the right people.

Each job led to the next, and before long, landowners were asking the youngster to survey their properties in northern Virginia. Surveying paid off in two ways. First, it put money in his purse. By his eighteenth birthday, George was earning £125 a year, more than most small farmers ever saw in a year. Second, it taught him self-reliance. Living in the wilderness was not just "camping out." For weeks on end, he and a few helpers wore the same clothes, slept on the ground, and braved all kinds of weather in unknown and unexpected terrain. The young man learned that if he could not discipline himself out there, he could not survive. A mistake might end with an Indian arrow in his chest.

George was doing pretty well, until tragedy struck. Three of

Lawrence's children had died soon after birth, leaving only an infant daughter named Sarah. Nor was Lawrence himself healthy. The cough he had brought back from South America was an early symptom of "consumption," a disease of the lungs now called tuberculosis. Night after night he lay awake, coughing and spitting blood. In desperation, he decided to go to the British West Indies, hoping to find relief in the warm climate. Since his wife must stay home with Sarah, George would have to go with him to keep him company and generally help him.

In October 1751, the brothers sailed for the island of Barbados. Al-

The youthful George Washington earned money as a surveyor in frontier Virginia. The frontier experience toughened him and made him self-reliant. From an engraving in Washington Irving's *Life of George Washington.*

though he did not know it then, this was to be George Washington's only trip outside mainland North America. The voyage, lasting four weeks, was an adventure. Each night, he wrote a summary of the day's activities in his diary. Most of the time, they enjoyed "fine pleasant breezes with fair weather and smooth seas." Sunlight played on the blue water, creating countless specks of light that rose and fell with the swells. "Dalphins"—dolphins— capered around the ship's bows. "We catchd" a small one and ate it for supper, he wrote proudly. Like everyone aboard, he dreaded sharks. In their spare time, sailors caught sharks, clubbed them to death, and tossed them back overboard, to be eaten by other sharks in a frenzy of snapping jaws and blood. Each night, the sun set with "extraordinary redness."[8]

During their first two weeks in Barbados, the brothers were happy. Lawrence seemed to improve a bit. Since they came from the mainland, the locals treated them as celebrities, inviting them to their homes to hear the latest news. George soon regretted all that attention.

One night, he awoke with a pounding headache and red pimples on his chest. He did not need a doctor to tell him what he had. "Was strongly attacked with the small Pox," he wrote in his diary.[9] Smallpox is highly contagious; it has killed more people over the centuries than any other infectious disease. Caused by a virus, its symptoms are a high fever and muscle aches, followed by pimples that break open, ooze pus, and finally form scabs. The pimples cover the body, particularly the face, often leaving survivors blind and disfigured by deep "pits" or scars. Luckily, for George, he recovered with only scars on his face. Yet those marks signaled a blessing in disguise. By getting the disease and surviving, George had gained a lifelong immunity to "the speckled monster."

Lawrence was not so lucky. Although he escaped smallpox, his coughing continued. Finally, he decided to try the climate of Bermuda, an island in the western Atlantic. Since George could do nothing else for him, he returned to Virginia. "If I grow worse," Lawrence said, "I shall hurry home to my grave."[10] And so it was. Six weeks after reaching Mount Vernon, in July 1752, Lawrence died. George was at his bedside and arranged for his funeral. By the terms of Lawrence's will, his widow, Anne, held Mount Vernon in trust for their infant daughter. If Sarah died without leaving children of her own, and if Anne agreed, the estate would go to George.

Just then, it seemed more important that Lawrence's death left open his militia post. Governor Robert Dinwiddie had recently split the adjutant general's post into four parts, each adjutant having the rank of major and a yearly salary of £100. Supported by the Fairfaxes, George applied for and got the post in the Northern Neck. It required no special qualifications; any intelligent person could have easily carried out the adjutant's duties.

George desperately needed the job. At twenty, he was no longer a boy. What would he do with his life? What would he become? How would he earn a living? Those questions nagged at him, as they do most people at that stage of life.

George wanted to be like his brother and the Fairfaxes—that was certain. Yet, wherever he turned, he found his way blocked. Ferry Farm was too isolated and unprofitable to support his ambitions; it produced only food for the table and some tobacco for sale locally. Besides, his mother still lived there. Surveying might give him a decent living, but not the social acceptance he craved. There seemed little chance of inheriting Mount Vernon; anyway, he did not want to inherit it over the bodies of his dear brother's family.

Only a military career seemed to offer a way out of his dilemma, not in the militia but in the British army. "My inclinations," as he put it in 1754, "are strongly bent to arms."[11] And for good reason. Officers in the British army wore gorgeous scarlet uniforms decorated with gold braid. Everyone admired them and showed them respect. Moreover, they enjoyed economic security. A disabled or retired officer received half pay for life. The problem, of course, was becoming an officer in the first place.

Until 1871, every British officer from the rank of lieutenant to colonel bought his commission. In Washington's time, a lieutenant's commission cost around £550, a colonel's £3,500. These were fabulous sums in the 1700s. A commission, and the salary that went with it, was as much a piece of property as a horse or a house. Its owner could sell it, trade it, and borrow against it to pay his debts. Since commissions were good investments, rich men bought them for their sons. As a result, an officer might be only a child of age six! As in any walk of life, some officers did better than others. The British army had no shortage of fools. It also had its share of brave, able battle commanders.[12]

Washington could not afford a commission. Yet there was another way to get one. He could earn it. In times of emergency, the British government gave a few of these prizes to colonial officers of exceptional ability. His militia post was a small start. With luck, he could use it as a springboard to fame and security. All he needed was a chance to prove his worth.

THE WORLD
ON FIRE

*"The volley fired by a young Virginian in the backwoods
of America set the world on fire."*

—HORACE WALPOLE, ENGLISH WRITER, 1753

George Washington was born into a violent world. Over the centuries, Europe seldom enjoyed more than a few years of peace in a row. England and France often battled for territory, glory, and to avenge past defeats. The opening of the New World to white settlers moved their struggle across the Atlantic Ocean. Used to seeing each other as natural enemies, England and France began a furious race to control North America. In time, their hunger for land would explode into full-scale warfare. The winner would shape the lives of millions of human beings right down to present time.

Canada lay at the heart of France's American empire. From settlements in the St. Lawrence Valley, the empire's boundary ran westward in a wide arc along the Great Lakes. From there, it turned southward into Louisiana, following the line of the Mississippi River to New Orleans, where the "Father of Waters" empties into the Gulf of Mexico.

France had no interest in large permanent settlements; in 1752, Canada had fewer than 80,000 white people. Canada existed for the beaver trade. Every fashionable European wanted a hat, coat, or cape trimmed with the beaver's silky brown fur. French trappers, to survive in the forests, had to be able to get along with the Indian tribes, whose ancestors had lived there for thousands of years. Many "went native," learning to dress, act, speak, and think like Native Americans. Often they married Indian women, who gave birth to children of mixed heritage.[1]

Apart from a few trading posts, the French left the land as they found it. By preserving the forest and its creatures, they protected their own livelihood. That suited the native peoples just fine. Their religion taught that the land belonged to all living beings equally, for all owed their existence to the Great Spirit. Humans could not own the land any more than they could own the air, the rain, or the sun's rays.

The English settlers disagreed. Like the Washington family, most immigrants wanted to own land and earn their living from it. To these people, the wilderness was an enemy, a barrier to progress. When settlers from the thirteen colonies came into an area, they cut down the trees to clear the land for farming, which drove away the game. By 1752, the thirteen colonies had about one million people, over twelve times the population of Canada. As their numbers grew, settlers moved further westward, threatening the Frenchman's trade and the Native American's survival.

English colonists hardly thought of Indians as fellow human beings, but as "children of the devil," "brutish savages," "hellish fiends," and "the very dregs, garbage and spawne of Earth." Along the frontier, the tribes well knew that in the older settled areas Englishmen had attacked Indian villages and massacred their inhabitants. In the 1620s, for example, Virginians nearly wiped out the Powhatan Confederacy. During the Pequot War of 1637, the Puritans set fire to a sleeping Pequot village in the colony of Connecticut, killing anyone who tried to escape. A soldier, an eyewitness, described the scene:

> Those that escaped the fire were slain with the sword; some hewed to pieces, others run through with rapiers [swords], so as they were quickly dispatched, and very few escaped. . . . It was a fearful sight to see them thus frying in the fire, and the streams of blood quenching the same, and horrible was the stink and scent, but the victory seemed a sweet sacrifice, and [the soldiers] gave the prayers thereof

to God who . . . [did] give them so speedy a victory over so proud and insulting an enemy.

The attackers used mastiffs, savage hunting dogs, to tear fugitives apart. A century later, Benjamin Franklin urged colonists to hunt Indians with "large, strong, and fierce" dogs.[2]

By the time George Washington turned sixteen, the French and the English had already fought three wars in North America. Colonists called them the French and Indian Wars, because the French fought alongside the Algonquian group of tribes, among them the Huron, Ottowa, and Shawnee. The Algonquians' enemies, the Iroquois, helped the English. Each war ended with a peace treaty signed by diplomats in Europe. In reality, the treaties were scraps of paper that settled nothing. Small wonder that people expected another, final, struggle for "ownership" of the continent! The only questions were where and when would it begin. The answers came soon enough.[3]

In the early 1750s, traders from the colonies of Virginia, Pennsylvania, and Maryland pushed across the Appalachian and Blue Ridge Mountains into the valley of the Ohio River, south of today's city of Pittsburgh, Pennsylvania. In exchange for furs, they gave the local tribes guns, ammunition, and whiskey. Although few in numbers, their coming was like tossing matches at kegs of gunpowder. The English colonies claimed the Ohio country as their western frontier. Frenchmen said they owned it by right of discovery in the 1600s. Only war, it seemed, could settle the dispute.

France made the first move. In June 1753, the Marquis Duquesne, governor of Canada, declared that his country owned the entire region and ordered trespassers to leave at once. To make sure they did, he sent Indian war parties led by Frenchmen to drive them out. Duquesne also built a chain of forts to bar the way. Fort Presque Isle went up on the southern shore of Lake Erie, followed by Fort Le Beouf (Fort Buffalo) twelve miles beyond, at the head of French Creek. Fort Venango rose a few miles downstream, where French Creek joins the Allegheny River.

All this worried Virginia's governor, Robert Dinwiddie. Although he had asked London for instructions, none arrived. Summer passed and, with each day lost, the French tightened their grip on the valuable territory. Finally, London ordered him to demand that they abandon their forts. If they refused, the governor should "drive them off by force of arms."[4] Yet London did not say who should bear those arms. Clearly, since Britain had so few troops in America, the colonies would have to act on their own. That was a big step, a *dangerous* step that might lead to war. Before taking action, Dinwiddie decided to send a stern warning to the French commander in the Ohio country.

Who would carry it? Washington learned of the governor's plan, possibly from his friend Colonel Fairfax. An experienced woodsman and militia officer by now, Washington put himself forward as the man best qualified for the mission. The governor agreed to entrust it to him.

Washington and six hired men left Williamsburg in October 1753. The party included Jacob van Braam, a translator, and Christopher Gist, a professional scout. Besides delivering the warning, Washington had been entrusted with another mission, which he kept to himself. He was a spy. Governor Dinwiddie had given him secret orders to pinpoint the French forts, make sketches of their defenses, and learn how many soldiers defended them. Lastly, Dinwiddie asked him to prepare accurate maps of the Ohio country, noting likely sites for English forts.

The party crossed the Blue Ridge and Allegheny Mountains. After traveling a month through unbroken wilderness, Washington paused at a rocky wedge of land jutting into a rushing river. He stood there with his notebook, describing "the Forks of the Ohio."[5]

What a sight! To his left flowed the Allegheny River leading northward to the French forts. To his right the Monongahela River flowed from western Virginia. They joined at his feet to form the Ohio River, which in turn flowed southwest to join the Mississippi in southern Illinois. Washington knew that the ground he stood on was the most valuable piece of real es-

Governor of Virginia Robert Dinwiddie sent George Washington to warn the French to stay out of the Ohio Valley. From an engraving based on a portrait in the National Portrait Gallery, London.

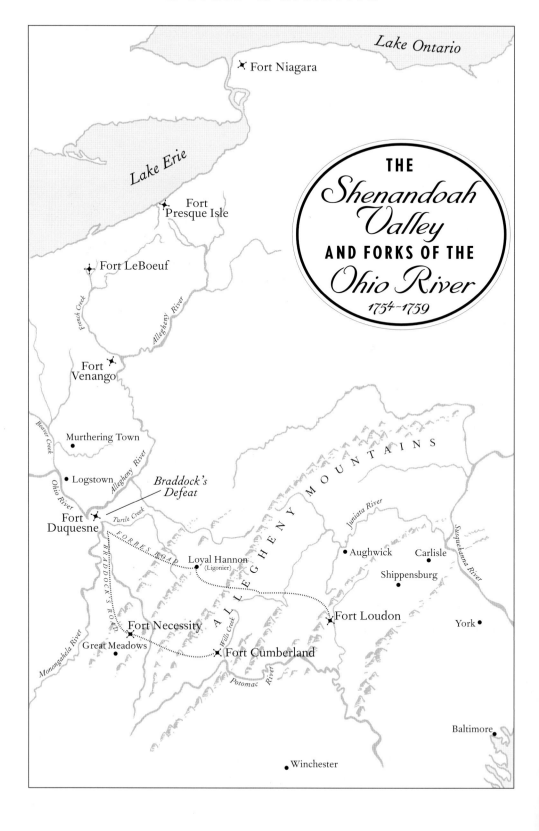

THE
Shenandoah Valley
AND FORKS OF THE
Ohio River
1754~1759

Lake Ontario

✘ Fort Niagara

Lake Erie

✘ Fort
Presque Isle

✦ Fort LeBoeuf

French Creek

Allegheny River

✘ Fort
Venango

Beaver Creek

• Murthering Town

Allegheny River

• Logstown

Ohio River

Braddock's Defeat

✘ Fort
Duquesne

Turtle Creek

FORBES ROAD

BRADDOCK'S ROAD

Loyal Hannon
(Ligonier)

ALLEGHENY MOUNTAINS

Juniata River

Susquehanna River

• Aughwick   Carlisle •

Shippensburg •

✘ Fort Loudon   York •

✘ Fort Necessity

• Great Meadows

Wills Creek

✘ Fort Cumberland

Monongahela River

Potomac River

Baltimore •

• Winchester

tate in North America. Whoever held it held the key to an inland empire stretching all the way to the Rocky Mountains. It was, he wrote, "extremely well situated for a Fort."[6]

When Washington arrived at Fort Venango early in December, he tried to hand Dinwiddie's letter to the officer in charge. The unnamed Frenchman brushed the paper aside, saying that Washington must give it to his chief at Fort Le Beouf. The officer, a jolly, outgoing fellow, invited the strangers to dinner. Before long, they were downing cups of fiery French brandy. Washington pretended to drink with the others but swallowed very little. As the brandy took effect, his hosts began to talk freely. "They told me," Washington noted in his diary, "that it was their design to take possession of the Ohio, and by God they would do it."[7]

He got a more sober reception at Fort Le Beouf. Its commander, Captain Legardeur de St. Pierre, was a veteran of the European wars. After reading the letter, St. Pierre said he also had orders. All lands drained by the Ohio River belonged to France. Any outsider caught there faced arrest—if he were lucky. If the Indians found him first, it would be too bad. That was St. Pierre's last word. There was nothing else to discuss. Washington left the following day and headed back to Virginia.

On December 24, Christmas Eve, winter arrived with a vengeance. Although Washington was used to being out in bad weather, the Virginian had never known anything like this. Temperatures plummeted. Wind-blown snow made it hard for him to see his hands in front of his face. Freezing rain coated the trees in ice, the weight causing branches to snap off with a loud *crack*. Near Murthering Town, a French outpost, an Indian leaped from behind a tree and fired his musket at close range. Luckily, the bullet missed and the attacker fled. Fearing a trap, Washington and his six companions marched all night without pausing for rest.

By morning, the men and their horses had reached the limits of their endurance. Washington sat by a campfire, his diary in his lap. "Our horses," he wrote hastily, "were so weak and feeble, and the baggage so heavy," that they could barely move.[8] Yet he could not wait for them to recover; Governor Dinwiddie needed his information that the French would fight rather than leave. There was nothing to do but leave the horses with the men while he went ahead on foot with Christopher Gist.

Each man carried a musket and knapsack with some food. Nearing the Allegheny, they expected to find a solid sheet of ice, but the river was frozen only fifty yards from either shore. In midstream it flowed swiftly, huge ice blocks tumbling in the current. There was no way to cross except by raft. Since they had "but one poor hatchet," as Washington called it, building the raft took a day's work. Finally, at sunset, they pushed off. Each had a long pole, which he sank in the river bottom to "walk" the raft forward.[9]

The rushing water tossed the flimsy craft in all directions at once. An ice block hit its side, throwing Washington into ten feet of water. "I fortunately saved myself by catching hold of one of the raft logs." With his long arms and big hands he pulled himself aboard.[10]

Yet their troubles had only begun. Unable to reach shore, they landed on a small island in midstream. There they spent the night without a fire, hungry and shivering in their wet clothes. Washington sat covered from head to toe in a sheet of ice. "The cold was so extremely severe," he recalled, "that Mr. Gist had all his fingers, and some of his toes frozen."[11] By daybreak, the river had frozen solid, allowing them to walk ashore. After

After delivering his message to the French, Washington and his guide, frontier scout Christopher Gist, had to cross the Allegheny River on a crude log raft. Engraving by Denison Kimberley, 1842, after a painting by Daniel Huntington.

further hardships, they reached Williamsburg early in January 1754.

After speaking with Dinwiddie, Washington went to Mount Vernon to recover and write a report of his adventure. The Virginia Assembly was so pleased with the report that it printed it as a small book, *The Journal of Major George Washington*, and voted its author £50. The book was reprinted in London, where readers agreed that its author had shown superb courage and intelligence. Anyone who could cover over a thousand miles of rugged country in winter was no ordinary person. Surely, he was destined to go a long way.

Meanwhile, acting on Washington's information, Dinwiddie recruited colonists to serve as soldiers in the Virginia Regiment. In the spring of 1754, he sent a work detail to build a fort at the Forks of the Ohio. Washington, whom Dinwiddie had promoted to lieutenant colonel in the Virginia Regiment, was supposed to follow with three hundred men to help complete the fort and defend it. Before setting out, he announced that, as loyal Englishmen, they must vow to defend "our Majesty's property, his dignity and land" with their lives.[12]

Moving westward, Washington reached the Great Meadows, a clearing fifty miles south of the Forks of the Ohio. As his main force made camp, scouts brought startling news. The French had captured the work detail sent by Dinwiddie, wrecked the unfinished fort, and begun a larger one of their own called Fort Duquesne.

Washington was still trying to figure out his next move when Chief Half-King of the Mingo, a tribe allied to the Iroquois, appeared with a

THE
JOURNAL
OF
MAJOR *George Washington*,

SENT BY THE

Hon. ROBERT DINWIDDIE, Efq; His Majefty's Lieutenant-Governor, and Commander in Chief of *Virginia*,

TO THE

COMMANDANT of the *French* Forces ON

O H I O.

To which are added, the
GOVERNOR's LETTER:

AND A

TRANSLATION of the *French* Officer's Anfwer.

WITH

A New MAP of the Country as far as the *MISSISSIPPI*.

WILLIAMSBURGH Printed, *LONDON*, Reprinted for *T. Jefferys*, the Corner of St. *Martin's Lane*.
MDCCLIV.
[Price One Shilling]

The title page of Washington's report of his journey to warn the French away from the Ohio country. Published as a pamphlet, it was admired in the colonies and England.

band of warriors. Half-King reported that thirty French soldiers lay hidden in a ravine nearby.

Although Washington knew France and England were still at peace, he feared the worst. Capturing the work party was hardly a friendly act. Now, if those soldiers had peaceful intentions, why should they hide? They would come to him openly, as he had come to Fort Le Beouf the year before. Their hiding proved—to the young colonel at least—that they were up to no good. Clearly, he thought, they were waiting to ambush him or to guide a larger force to his camp. He must strike first.

That night, May 27, 1754, Half-King led the Virginians through thick woods. It was slow going because they had to move quietly, so as not to alert the French. Before dawn, they encircled the camp and waited in the darkness. As the sun rose, some soldiers started to prepare breakfast; others lounged in their blankets. Then one of them saw a figure in the bushes and shouted a warning. His comrades leaped up and reached for their weapons. Someone fired a shot—whether it was a Frenchman or one of Washington's men remains a mystery to this day. Without hesitating, Washington gave the order to attack.

Ten Frenchmen, including Lieutenant Joseph Coulon de Jumonville, their leader, died in a hail of bullets. Instantly, Mingo warriors dashed in to kill and scalp the wounded. After a short fight, twenty-two soldiers surrendered. Washington sent them as prisoners to the tiny village of Winchester in the Shenandoah Valley. One Frenchman escaped into the forest.

What a day! Washington had tasted battle for the first time. He had heard his first gunshots fired in anger. He had seen his first men fall with holes in their chests and their skulls blown apart. For the first time, men had died by his command.

The experience pleased him no end. "I can assure you," he wrote his brother Jack, "I heard Bullets whistle and believe me there was something charming in the sound."[13] Only later would he realize the full meaning of that "charming" sound. Without intending to, George Washington had ignited the start of a great war. Seldom has one so young taken such a long stride onto the stage of history.

The attackers returned to the Great Meadows, where Washington and his men built Fort Necessity. The French, he knew, would want revenge and he had to be ready for them. Unfortunately, Fort Necessity's similarity to a real fort lay in name only. It was merely a trench dug in front of a stockade, or circle of logs placed upright in the ground. Half-King saw its weakness and slipped away with his warriors.

When the French survivor told his story at Fort Duquesne, the troops cried for vengeance. It so happened that Lieutenant Jumonville's elder brother, Captain Coulon de Villiers, was stationed at the fort. Nicknamed "the Great Villiers," because he had never lost a fight, he demanded the right to deal with his brother's killers in person. His commander told him to go ahead.

Villiers set out with seven hundred men. "We marched the whole day in the rain," the captain wrote in his official report. "I stopped at the place where my brother had been assassinated, and saw there the dead bodies." Victorious commanders usually buried the dead from both sides, unless they thought they had to get away fast, as Washington did. Washington had left the dead unburied, a feast for birds and bugs. Someone, undoubtedly without his permission, had driven a pole into the ground amid the corpses. A severed head gazed, open-eyed, from atop the pole.[14]

Rather than attack Fort Necessity directly, the French opened a heavy fire from behind trees and rocks. Washington remembered every detail of the fight. Years later, as president, he told the aide:

> The enemy advanced with shouts and dismal Indian yells to our entrenchments, but was opposed by so warm, spirited, and constant a fire, that to force [our position] in that way was abandoned by them. By then, from every little rising, tree, stump, stone, and bush [they] kept up a constant galling fire upon us, which was returned in the best manner we could till late in the afternoon, when there fell the most tremendous rain that can be conceived. [It] filled our trenches with water, wet . . . the ammunition . . . And left us nothing but a few . . . bayonets for defense.[15]

By nightfall, the trench was filled knee-deep with muddy water flecked with blood. Washington counted thirty dead and seventy wounded. With escape impossible, he had no choice but to ask for surrender terms.

Villiers had no choice, either. He feared that more Virginians were coming, and his ammunition was running low. So he offered to let his enemies leave with their weapons. Washington only had to give his parole—his written word of honor—that they would not return to the Ohio country for a year. He agreed. Next morning, Washington and his men began their trek southward. The date, like the event, burned itself into the colonel's mind: July the Fourth.

On returning to Mount Vernon, Washington found that Lawrence's daughter, Sarah, had died. Her mother had remarried and wanted to live on her new husband's plantation. To make that possible, Anne offered to lease Mount Vernon to her brother-in-law for 15,000 pounds of tobacco each year; tobacco was as good as money in Virginia. Washington jumped at the offer. When Anne died in 1760, Mount Vernon officially became his. It was the only place he ever called home. Although he would travel widely in the years ahead, he always yearned for the house on the bluff overlooking the Potomac. When he moved in, it was a one-and-a-half-story, eight-room farmhouse. Over the years, and at great expense, Washington turned it into a three-story mansion with twenty-one rooms and several outbuildings, including a kitchen and latrines.

In 1754, however, the young man was not ready to settle down. He still wanted that commission in the British army and to repay the French for Fort Necessity.

News of those shots fired in the backwoods reached Europe. Thanks to Washington, possession of the Ohio country had become more than a matter of land claims and beaver pelts. Once men had spilled their blood, nobody dared back down for fear of emboldening the other side. Although England and France were still officially at peace, their actions spoke of war. Each side began to outfit warships and prepare troops for service in America.

On February 20, 1755, two regiments totaling 1,500 men landed at Hampton Bay, Virginia. Their commander, General Edward Braddock, sixty years old, had been in the British army since the age of fifteen. A short, beefy fellow with a rosy red face and a booming voice, he had a reputation for raw courage, foul language, and brutal discipline. When

Washington learned of the general's arrival, he offered his services as an unpaid volunteer. A little questioning showed that this young man was not only capable but knew his way around the back country. Braddock offered him a place on his personal staff. In accepting, Washington did a brave, but also foolish, thing. By the laws of war, if the French caught him violating his parole, they could shoot him on the spot.

Washington fit in well. Although not a regular officer, everyone called him colonel, his militia rank, as a courtesy. As Braddock's aide, he joined senior officers on inspections. During these inspections, he made his first contacts with common British soldiers. He learned, as no books could have taught him, who they were and what motivated them. The knowledge would prove invaluable in a later war.

General Edward Braddock led his British regulars to defeat at the hands of the French and their Indian allies at the battle fought a few miles south of Fort Duquesne in July 1755.

Washington learned why friend and enemy feared them so. These were the redcoats, the career soldiers who formed Britain's national army. Respectable citizens called them "the filth of the nation" and "the scum of the people." Redcoats were failed men, desperate men, men with no future in civilian life. More than half were workers made jobless by downturns in the economy. The rest were "disorderly persons," a polite term for tramps, beggars, and thieves. Every regiment also had its share of "crow bait," men bound for the gallows. Hanging was not only for murderers, who never escaped execution; at least two hundred other offenses carried the death penalty in England. These ranged from rape and burglary to pickpocketing a silk handkerchief. Hanging was so common that London had a special gallows for executing ten criminals at once. When the army needed recruits, judges gave criminals an offer they dared not refuse: Enlist or hang![16]

Army life was an endless round of discomfort and drudgery. At 4:30 A.M., rain or shine, a drummer beat the *rap tap tap* of the wake-up call. Rolling out of their blankets, men rubbed their eyes and reached for their clothes. A redcoat wore just that—a scarlet coat decorated with colored piping, lace, and brass buttons. Under the coat he wore a shirt of coarse white linen with extra-long tails. Since underpants would not be invented until much later, he tucked the shirttails under his bottom. Skin-tight breeches reached from his waist to his knees, and long gaiters, each with twenty-four tiny buttons, came up over the knees from his high-heeled shoes. Wide belts crisscrossed over his chest to hold his bayonet and cartridge box. On his head he wore a tall brimless helmet of brass or canvas. In nasty weather, the lack of a brim allowed rain to run into his eyes. At other times, the sun shined in his eyes. Apart from the shirt, this uniform was made of heavy, itchy wool and worn in all seasons.

A redcoat needed two hours to dress and groom himself. After tidying his uniform with a brush, he used pipeclay to whiten his gaiters, belts, and lace. Next came his most difficult task: getting his hair just right. Every soldier wore a long pigtail and stiff curls on either side of his face. This required him to master the same devices women still use: hairpins, curlers, papers, ribbons. Men helped each other do their hair, especially before standing guard duty. Private John Shipp recalled his first experience with the army hairdo:

> A large piece of candle wax was applied, first to the sides of my head, then to the hind long hair; after this, the same kind of operation was performed with nasty stinking soap. . . . When this operation was over, I had to undergo [an operation] of a more serious nature. A large pad, or bag filled with sand, was poked into the back of my head, round which the hair was gathered tight, and the whole tied with a leather thong. When I was dressed for parade, I could scarcely get my eyelids to perform their office; the skin of my eyes and face was drawn so tight by the plug that was stuck in the back of my head, that I could not possibly shut my eyes. . . . Shortly after I was thus equipped, dinner was served; but my poor jaws refused to act on the offensive, and when I made an attempt to eat, my pad behind went up and down like a sledge-hammer.

A private might have to keep his hair bound up for days. This did not make for cleanliness. One recalled that his hair housed "an accumulated mixture of filth, dirt, and Vermin."[17]

The redcoat spent most of his day on the drill field. Since officers belonged to the upper classes, they did not train the "low rascals" they commanded in person. That task went to the sergeants, steely-eyed brutes who ruled with shouts, fists, and clubs. The redcoat was not supposed to think for himself, but to obey orders without question. Today, military drill is

British soldiers were nicknamed "redcoats," because they wore scarlet uniforms. Red allowed units to identify each other on a smoke-filled battlefield, preventing them from accidentally shooting their own men. Redcoats also wore high hats to make them look taller and fiercer.

for show, a relic of the past. Back then, every half-turn, quarter-turn, and about-face had a purpose. These movements, and not individual courage or high-tech weapons, decided the outcome of battle.

Different drills served different needs. Marching came first. Commanders liked to say "the art of war is all in the legs." Through marching, the soldier lost his individual identity and became part of a fighting team. What is more important, only by constant drill could large units deploy for battle, advance, or retreat in an orderly way.

Normally, regiments marched in columns of two or three *files,* or rows arranged one behind the other. This arrangement allowed a well-trained outfit to cover up to twenty miles a day in cool, dry weather. Once on the battlefield, however, the column made a *line of battle,* or combat formation. It did this by forming three *ranks,* or lines, one behind the other. Now the soldiers stood tightly packed, shoulder to shoulder, facing the enemy's line of battle. Each side stood on flat ground, in the open, waiting for the command to fire.

Weapons drill involved other skills. Washington knew that armies relied on the musket. The redcoat's musket, nicknamed "Brown Bess," was a smoothbore. In other words, the inner part of its barrel, or bore, was smooth, allowing it to shoot a lead ball. Brown Bess measured 4 feet 8 inches, weighed 15 pounds, and had a 21-inch bayonet at the end.

Sergeants trained their men to respond to three commands. They had to respond instantly, without thought, like machines.

Load! Each man reached into his leather cartridge box. The cartridge was a paper tube as long as a man's middle finger. Tied at the ends, it contained a one-ounce lead ball three-quarters of an inch wide. While standing—he could not lie down because the musket had to be loaded from the muzzle—the redcoat bit off an end of the cartridge. Then he sprinkled a little powder from the cartridge into the flash-pan, which had a narrow channel that led to the inside of the barrel. After that, he poured the ball and the rest of the gunpowder down the muzzle, crumpled the paper into a wad, and packed it tightly over the contents with a ramrod.

Present! Together, the men raised Brown Bess to their shoulders and drew back the hammer. The hammer held a piece of flint, a type of stone that sparks when struck with steel.

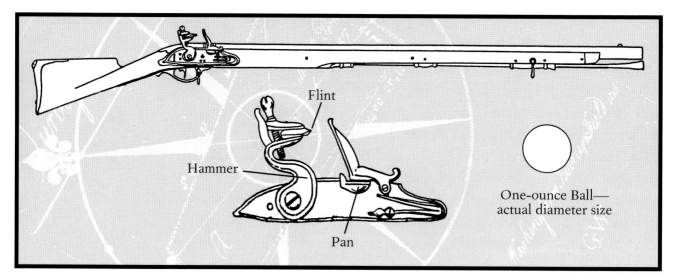

Flint

Hammer

Pan

One-ounce Ball—
actual diameter size

Firing mechanism of the British "Brown Bess" musket, along with a one-ounce lead ball drawn to actual size.

Give Fire! The soldier pulled the trigger. Brown Bess's hammer snapped forward, driven by a powerful spring. Its flint struck a small piece of steel, sending a shower of sparks into the flash-pan and igniting the main charge. The result was a loud *bang,* followed by a puff of smoke the size of a cow. After troops in the first line fired, they reloaded as their comrades in the next two lines stepped in front of them and fired in turn. By then, the first line had reloaded and was ready to step forward again. So it went: fire, reload, step forward, fire.

After a while, the "fog of battle" hung in the air, clouds of smoke that made it hard to see more than a few yards in any direction. That was the reason for the redcoat's uniform. Its designers *meant* to make the wearer obvious, not to conceal him. In the confusion of battle, each side had to know friends from enemies. Thus, brightly colored uniforms served the same purpose as those worn by modern football and hockey teams. Red also concealed bloodstains, helping to avoid panic. When someone got hit in the closely packed ranks, his blood always spattered on the men nearby.

An experienced redcoat fired once every twenty seconds. Yet his musket was so inaccurate that it lacked a rear sight, or device for guiding the eye in a straight line to the target. He never had target practice, and army rules forbade aiming, because the guns were made too poorly to allow it. To do any damage, he had to fire from close range, less than eighty yards. "You may as well fire at the moon and have the same hopes of hitting your object," a gun expert said of targets over two hundred yards away. Yet, even at close range, it took at least 260 shots to hit one enemy soldier! Thus, the line-of-battle formation: With many men firing together in the same direction, some bullets were bound to strike home.[18]

If one side began to give way, the opposing general gave the command to charge. Suddenly, fifes and drums sounded above the roar of battle. Musical instruments were as vital to warfare as weapons. Every unit had its band. Bands set the pace of the march. On the battlefield, their lively tunes raised the troops' spirits; drumrolls and bugle calls conveyed the commander's orders.

At the right signal, the battle lines swept forward with fixed bayonets attached to the ends of their weapons. Unlike modern warfare, where high-powered weapons kill most enemies from far away, in Washington's day a soldier saw his victim up close. He saw the expression on the enemy's face, felt his bayonet slicing through flesh, heard the crunch of breaking bones. Back then, military experts considered the redcoat the deadliest man on earth with the bayonet.

Men do not easily face gunfire and bayonets. Here is where discipline came in. Commanders did not see common soldiers as intelligent human beings, but as dumb brutes. Only fear, they believed, could rule the rank and file.

Disobedience brought savage punishment. Serious offenses, such as refusing to obey an order, striking an officer, and murder, meant death by firing squad. Ordinary offenses—lateness, sloppiness, stealing, gambling, drunkenness—meant the cat-o'-nine-tails, a whip of knotted cords fastened to a handle. A rule-breaker might get thirty-nine to one thousand lashes on the bare back. If he fainted during the ordeal, a bucket of salty water on the bleeding welts revived him fast enough. Some men died of shock at the whipping post. A few went insane. All survivors bore the scars for the rest of their lives.

Whipping took place before the entire regiment. Although Washington was probably in camp during punishments, we do not know if he saw them carried out. A new recruit, however, never forgot the first man he saw whipped. "Being at that time only seventeen years of age, the spectacle made a lasting impression on my mind," he recalled. "I well remember, during the infliction of his punishment, I cried like a child."[19] In any case, Washington had his first lessons in soldiering in a harsh school.

In March 1755, General Braddock met with colonial governors in Alexandria. After explaining his plans, he asked them to set up a common fund to buy needed supplies. Instead, the governors reminded him that King George II and Parliament, Great Britain's own legislature, controlled matters like war, peace, and foreign trade. Colonists controlled their own domestic affairs. Like thirteen tiny nations, each ruled itself through an elected assembly that voted taxes. Now, since the colonies belonged to Britain, the assemblies expected British taxpayers to pick up the bills.

Braddock called the Americans cheap, cowardly weaklings because they refused to pay for each other's defense. The colonists, however, saw things differently. Yes, British troops were defending them. However, Britain was also fighting to expand its own empire in North America.

Fortunately, Benjamin Franklin, postmaster general for the colonies, saved the day. He had already printed a cartoon in his *Pennsylvania Gazette* urging the colonies to unite for their common defense; it had the caption JOIN, OR DIE and showed a rattlesnake cut into parts, each representing a colony. Luckily, Franklin managed to coax enough colonial leaders to send the needed supplies. He also gave the general some advice. In moving inland, he said, the army should watch out for ambushes. Braddock smiled. His troops, he insisted, could easily handle the French. As for their Indian allies, well, "these savages may indeed be a formidable enemy to your raw American militia; but upon the King's regular & disciplined troops, sir, it is impossible they should make an impression." Franklin only shook his head and frowned.[20]

The army assembled at Fort Cumberland, Virginia, in mid-April. Besides his redcoats, Braddock had a regiment of five hundred blue-coated Virginians and a group of Indian scouts with their families. Washington had seen plenty of Indians during his surveying trips. He had gotten used to them and their ways. The redcoats, however, had never seen the likes of them before.

Redcoats stood wide-eyed as painted warriors danced around bonfires.

Shouting and waving his knife, each war-
rior went through the motions of scalping
an enemy. These dances had as much to do
with religion as war. A war dance was like a
"pep rally" before a college football game;
it got the warriors into a fighting mood.
The dance was also an appeal to the Great
Spirit to protect the warriors and give them
victory.

In this famous cartoon of 1754, Benjamin Franklin urged the colonies to unite against their common enemy, the French.

The redcoats did not see it that way. Oh,
God! If those fellows were allies, they wondered, what could they expect from enemies? The Virginians knew. In "fun," they
told spine-tingling tales of Indian cruelty. No atrocity—scalping, torture,
burning—was beyond those "red demons," they said.

Warriors *did* celebrate victory by taking enemy scalps, which also held
religious meaning for them. Native Americans believed a person's hair
contained their spirit. Taking an enemy's scalp, therefore, gave the taker
control of his spirit and added to his own spirit-power. As for torturing
captives, Indian methods were no worse than those the whites used on
criminals and slaves. Nevertheless, tales of Indian cruelty shook the redcoats' self-confidence.

On May 10, the army moved west along the trail Washington had
blazed the year before. Each redcoat carried a musket, bayonet, and cartridge box weighing a total of eighteen pounds, plus a sixty-pound backpack. The backpack contained a canteen, hatchet, shovel, blanket, three
days' rations, spare shoes and clothing, grooming supplies, sewing kit, and
leather for repairing shoes. At the outset, the fifes and drums played
snappy marching tunes. Redcoats spoke among themselves and sang of
their favorite subject:

> *Whiskey is the life of man,*
> *Whiskey! Johnnie! Whiskey!*
> *I'll drink it out of an old tin can,*
> *Whiskey for my Johnnie!*[21]

All European armies issued a whiskey ration, usually a pint a day. The alcohol warmed the soldier against the cold, dulled his aches and pains, and raised his spirits when the going got rough.

Soon the trail turned sharply upward, toward the eastern slopes of the Alleghenies. As it did, the weight of the backpacks and the sun's heat began to take their toll. The men fell silent. Their view of the world nar-

General Braddock's redcoats marched through the wilderness on their way to drive the French from Fort Duquesne. From an anonymous engraving.

rowed to the back of the man in front. Struggling under their packs, they gasped for breath, each step bringing its own special misery. Swarms of gnats buzzed around their heads, every sting painful as a hot needle. Tiny flealike creatures burrowed under their skins, causing swelling and itching. Sweat came from every pore, its sour smell hanging in the air for hours after the column passed.

Redcoats were trained to fight in open country. Now they were in forest that seemed to swallow them. "There is nothing round us but trees, swamps and thickets," a captain wrote in his diary, adding "I cannot conceive how war can be made in such country."[22]

He had reason to worry. French and Indian patrols had shadowed the column since Fort Cumberland. As it advanced, they killed anyone who lagged behind. Once the column passed three pigtailed heads stuck on poles set up beside the trail. Another time, redcoats saw bloody scalps tacked to trees. Frenchmen had peeled the bark off trees and scrawled insulting graffiti. Warriors drew pictures of captives tied to stakes to be burned alive. Redcoats let their imaginations do the rest. They were already half beaten.[23]

The column covered less than three miles a day. Forced to widen the trail for the wagons, work parties had to cut trees, dig out boulders, and bridge streams along the way. At that rate, supplies would run out before they reached Fort Duquesne. Everyone knew the problem, but nobody had a practical solution. Finally, Braddock turned to Washington. His aide knew the Ohio country better than anyone. What did he think?

Washington urged Braddock to split the army into two divisions. By using horses and light wagons to carry its supplies, the first division could advance quickly. The second division could then move at its own speed with the wagons and artillery. The general agreed. Yet he must have been desperate. In taking the advice of a military beginner, he made a basic error: He divided his force without knowing the enemy's strength or intentions. Anyway, Braddock set out on June 9 with about 1,400 men. Lieutenant Colonel Thomas Dunbar stayed behind with a reserve of about 700 men.[24]

Washington wanted to join Braddock but collapsed with a high fever and dysentery, a deadly form of diarrhea. He spent nearly a month fighting for his life, lying in a wagon back with Dunbar's division. By the time they reached the ruins of Fort Necessity, he was getting better. Although "much reduced and weak," as he put it, he left to rejoin Braddock exactly a year after his surrender to "the Great Villiers." To ease the pain in his backside, he tied cushions to his saddle.[25]

July 9, 1755. Washington found the army at a bend in the Monongahela River south of Fort Duquesne. Crossing at a shallow spot, with bands playing and flags waving, the soldiers looked magnificent. Never mind that they were terrified of an ambush and had missed breakfast! Here, the young man thought, was war in all its excitement and glory. Here was his chance to win fame and that precious commission.

Meanwhile, the French commander at Fort Duquesne sent 891 men, mostly Huron, Shawnee, and Ottawa warriors, to set an ambush by the riverbank. Although the ambush never came off, they won a victory greater than any dared to imagine.[26]

Braddock was already across and filing through the woods, Washington riding by his side, when his advance guard came to a sudden halt. Puzzled by this, he sent an officer to find out why. The officer arrived just as the French troops and their Indian allies came running down the trail.

"Fix bayonets!" redcoated sergeants bawled.

"Load!"

"Present!"

"Fire!"

Three times the British sergeants gave the order to fire. And three times a hail of lead plowed into the French and their Indian allies. The attackers wavered, stunned by the unexpected volley. Just then, Captain Dumas, their leader, dashed to the front. Motioning to the right and left, he shouted, "Follow me! Fire! Kill them!" Instantly, most Frenchmen and Indians headed for the woods on either side of the trail, while the rest raced to the top of a hill overlooking the trail. The moment they reached the trees, they vanished. Only Indian war cries and French musket flashes told that they had not gone far.

Braddock rushed to the scene with the rest of his troops. Yet more men only added to the confusion. Confined to the narrow trail, the redcoats could not form a line of battle. They just stood there, a scarlet mass huddled thirty deep in places. Blinded by their own gunsmoke, redcoats fired into the woods. But they never saw more than a few of their attackers at a time, and these only for a split second while dashing from tree to tree.

Frenchmen and Indians fired in the direction of the crowd. It was impossible not to hit someone. Musket balls shattered men's skulls, spattering their comrades with blood and brains. "Every man was alert, did all we could," an officer recalled, "but the men dropped like leaves in autumn."[27]

Many did not fall—*could* not fall. Trapped in that awful ring of fire, packed so tightly that the dead continued to stand with the living, the redcoats seemed like penned cattle awaiting the butcher.

With bullets whining past his head, Braddock plunged into the thick of the action. Yet he was helpless. A man of the Old World, he did not understand this kind of warfare. Poor, stupid-brave Braddock! He could not imagine any other way of fighting. He could only order his men to close ranks, stand up straight—and die in neat rows.

Washington had never seen redcoats in action. Now he watched, flabbergasted, scarcely believing his eyes. The redcoats, he later told Governor Dinwiddie, "were immediately struck with such a deadly Panick that nothing but confusion and disobedience of orders prevailed amongst them."[28]

This was madness! Braddock's one hope, Washington knew, lay in scattering his men among the trees. When he suggested just that, the general pointed his sword toward his chest. "I've a mind to run you through the body," Braddock shouted. "We'll sup today in Fort Duquesne or else in hell."[29]

Redcoat discipline began to crack. Rather than be mowed down in the open, a few tried to take cover. Seeing them run for the trees, Braddock spurred his horse to head them off. Dashing among them, he swung his sword from side to side. "Cowards!" he roared, as he whacked them over the head and shoulders with the flat part of the blade. To him, leaving the ranks without orders was desertion. They returned to their units.[30]

Men from the Virginia Regiment took cover anyhow. In small groups, they hid behind trees, only to pitch forward with bullets in their backs. Mistaking them for Frenchmen, redcoats kept firing even when the Virginians tried to identify themselves. Captain William Polson turned and yelled, "We are English." Afterward, a redcoat recalled that his comrades replied "they could not help it, they must obey orders, and upon one or two fires of this sort Captain Polson himself lost his life, being shot directly through the heart." Not only did redcoats shoot Virginians, they mowed down their own men if they stood in the line of fire.[31]

With his other aides killed or wounded, Braddock relied on Washington to carry orders and bring firsthand reports from various parts of the battle area. Men were dropping everywhere, but the Virginian seemed to have a charmed life. "I luckily escaped without a wound, though I had four bullets through my coat and two horses shot under me," he recalled with pride.[32]

Facing death taught Washington something about himself. He learned that he had courage under fire, the first requirement in a professional soldier. Yes, battle frightened him, as it would any sane person. However, he never let fear master him. The hotter things got, the cooler he got; soldiers said he had ice water for blood. Indians had another explanation. Years later, his friend Dr. James Craik met an old chief who had fought that day. Seeing Washington on horseback, warriors singled him out as a target. Every shot missed. Finally, the chief told them, "Fire at him no more; see ye not that the Great Spirit protects that chief. He cannot die in battle."[33]

Meanwhile, redcoats huddled together, firing wildly and dying in place. At least the dead no longer suffered. War whoops filled the air, reminding the living of the horror stories they had heard. Scalping! Torture! Burning! First by ones and twos, then by whole companies, they panicked. Washington recalled how, ignoring orders, men "broke and run as sheep before the hounds." Some officers shot men for running. Some men shot officers for trying to stop them from running.[34]

Braddock finally ordered the drummers to signal the retreat. Just then, as he was looking over his shoulder, a bullet found him. Washington saw blobs of frothy blood oozing from his mouth, a sure sign that the bullet had plowed into a lung. Overcome by pain and shame, Braddock begged for a pistol to blow out his brains.

Washington pleaded with passing redcoats to carry the general to safety. They "absolutely refused." Even when he offered money, they kept going. Frantically whipping their horses, drivers plowed wagons through the fleeing mob. Redcoats lay screaming, their legs crushed by the iron-rimmed wheels. Other drivers cut their horses' traces and rode bareback toward the Monongahela.[35]

Finally, Washington persuaded some wagon drivers to take Braddock across in a cart. Upon reaching the other bank, they turned to see warriors moving among bodies at the water's edge with raised tomahawks and knives. Returning to the abandoned wagons, the warriors looted their con-

tents and rounded up a handful of prisoners; that night, they burned twelve of them to death near Fort Duquesne.[36]

James Smith, a Pennsylvanian captured by a French patrol two days earlier, watched the terrible scene and later described it in his autobiography:

> . . . I beheld a small party coming in with about a dozen prisoners, stripped naked, with their hands tied behind their backs and their faces and part of their bodies blacked [with charcoal]; these prisoners they burned to death on the bank of the Allegheny River, opposite the fort. I stood on the fort wall until I beheld them begin to

General Braddock is shot through the lungs as his aide, George Washington (on horseback), directs his Virginia soldiers to fire against their French and Indian attackers. An 1854 copy of a painting by Junius Brutus Stearns.

burn one of these men. They had him tied to a stake, and kept touching him with firebrands [burning sticks], red-hot irons, &c., and he screamed in the most doleful manner. . . . As this scene appeared too shocking for me to behold, I retired to my lodgings both sore and sorry. The morning after the battle I saw . . . Several Indians in British officers' dress, with sash. . . . Laced hats, &c., which the British then wore.[37]

Just then, Washington was suffering his own ordeal. Before Braddock left in the cart, he sent his aide to tell Colonel Dunbar to bring up the reserves. Dizzy with fatigue, his stomach churning, Washington clung to his saddle. Screaming men, dying men, lined the trail for miles on either side. Whenever clouds hid the moon, his two guides got down on hands and knees to grope for the trail. Thirty years later, the horror of that night was still vivid. "The shocking scenes . . . the dead—the dying—the groans—lamentations—and cries along the road of the wounded for help . . . were enough to pierce a heart of [stone.]"[38] Washington made the thirty-mile trip to Dunbar's camp by early next morning. After delivering Braddock's message, he fell on a cot and slept for twenty-four hours.

Most survivors, including the general, arrived at Dunbar's camp over the next two days. In appreciation for Washington's efforts, Braddock gave him his scarlet sash as a souvenir; it can be seen today at Mount Vernon. "Who would have thought it?" Braddock moaned, tears rolling down his cheeks. "We shall better know how to deal with them another time."[39]

There would not be "another time" for Edward Braddock. He died near the ruins of Fort Necessity at 8:00 P.M. on July 13. Washington had the body wrapped in blankets and placed in a grave dug in the middle of the trail. Then he had redcoats march over the grave until no trace remained.[40]

On the day Braddock died, Colonel Dunbar decided to retreat as fast and as far as possible. Now the highest-ranking officer, he ordered 150 wagons burned. Redcoats smashed kegs of gunpowder, emptying their contents into streams. Everything else that might be of use to the enemy went into bonfires: food, clothes, shoes, harness, tools. Then Dunbar marched his troops back to Fort Cumberland. Three weeks later, he moved on to Philadelphia, declaring the fighting season over. Although it was August, the army went into winter quarters!

Braddock's defeat was like the stone tossed into a still pond. Its "ripples," or effects, spread in all directions. People measured the first effect in blood. At a cost of 60 dead and wounded, Fort Duquesne's defenders had won a stunning victory. Of the 1,400 redcoats in the first division, 977 lay dead or wounded. With casualties of 70 percent, this remains the worst military disaster in British history.[41]

The second effect involved people's attitudes. Colonists had always hated the French and the Indians. That hatred deepened. Defeat also made colonists see the redcoats differently. Once they had seen them as fearsome soldiers bound by iron discipline. Not anymore. In this, most colonists would have agreed with Washington. Although proud of his Virginians, he had only contempt for the redcoats. "The Virginian Companies," he wrote, "behaved like Men and died like Soldiers," shot in the back by "our own cowardly Dogs of Soldiers"; that is, the redcoats.[42]

Washington was the only survivor to gain from the disaster. Yet he still did not have the commission he wanted so badly.

The Native Americans saw victory as a chance—their best and possibly their last—to turn back the tide of invasion from Britain's American colonies. This was their only hope of preserving their ancient way of life, a gift sent them by the Great Spirit. If they kept up the pressure and brought the war into enemy territory, they expected to stop the invasion in its tracks, even win back lost ground.

Using Fort Duquesne as a base, Indian war parties, joined by French soldiers, crossed the Alleghenies at a dozen points. Captain Adam Stephen wrote Washington about the situation at Fort Cumberland. Raiders, he said, "go about and commit their outrages at all hours of the day, and nothing is to be seen or heard of, but desolation and murder. . . . The smoke of the burning plantations darken the day, and hide the neighboring mountains from our sight."[43]

Governor Dinwiddie offered Washington command of all forces recruited to defend the Virginia frontier. Although still not fully recovered from his illness, he agreed to serve. So began a nightmare for Washington lasting three years. At age twenty-three, he had more responsibility than most people ever have. He rose to the challenge out of a sense of duty and personal pride. Always ambitious, he simply refused to allow himself to fail. Failure would not only harm his career plans but lose the respect of his fellow Virginians.

From before dawn to long after midnight, his life was nothing but work, work, work. Making a swing through the back country, he inspected outposts, collected supplies, and rallied the militia companies in the Shenandoah Valley. Many militiamen, however, did not wish to be "rallied." Worried about their families and farms, they refused to serve for longer than a month. In reply, the Virginia Assembly offered a cash reward to those who enlisted for the entire war. More often than not, these "bounty men" were rowdies and drunks who deserted after collecting their enlistment money.

Recruits discovered that their leader, despite his youth, was no softy. Washington had learned about military discipline in Braddock's camp. Like a true British officer, he was a strict disciplinarian, threatening severe punishment for anyone who broke the rules. "Any soldier," he warned, "who is guilty of any breach of the articles [rules] of war, by swearing, getting drunk, or using an obscene language, shall be severely punished, without the benefit of [trial by] court martial." In written orders, he promised five hundred lashes for offenses like laziness. He built a gallows forty feet high to discourage deserters.[44]

These were not idle threats. After executing two deserters, he apologized to Governor Dinwiddie. "Your Honor will, I hope, excuse my hanging instead of shooting them. It conveyed much more terror to others; and it was for example sake, we did it."[45] After that, desertions dropped sharply.

Indian raids did not. During inspection trips in the Shenandoah Valley, Washington passed burned farmhouses and charred cornfields. Near Fort Cumberland, for example, he saw the mangled bodies of a scalped woman, a small boy, and a young man. Sometimes these sights were more than he could take. They made him feel so helpless—so hopeless. "But what can I do?" he wrote Governor Dinwiddie. "The supplicating tears of the women; the moving petitions from the men, melt me into such deadly sorrow, that I solemnly declare . . . I could offer myself a willing sacrifice to a butchering enemy, provided that would contribute to the people's ease."[46]

These experiences tormented him. Nevertheless, he learned how to fight Native Americans effectively. Through trial and error, he organized a defense based upon three principles: hold, hunt, hit.[47]

To hold the frontier, Washington built eighty-one small forts at key points along the eastern slopes of the Alleghenies and in the Shenandoah Valley. Each fort was manned by two dozen soldiers from the Virginia Regiment. If scouts found signs of Indians, they gave the alarm with smoke signals by day and bonfires at night. Visible for miles, these were a quick, effective means of signaling farm families, who would then rush to the nearest fort. Yet Washington believed that the best defense was "a vigorous offensive war." In this, he followed the example of the early settlers of Virginia and New England; that is, he meant to hunt and hit Native Americans where he felt safest, in their own land.[48]

Washington sent scouting parties deep into forests. After locating a camp, they led rangers to the target. Rangers were frontiersmen, recruited in western Virginia, skilled in forest fighting. Traveling lightly, they wore moccasins and camouflage clothing: buckskin jackets and breeches that blended into the forest. Rangers struck hard and vanished like ghosts, never using the same path twice. Washington had no objection if they left

After Braddock's defeat, the enemy attacked English settlements in frontier Virginia. Washington, commanding the defenses, was deeply touched by settlers' appeals to save their lives and farms. From an engraving in Washington Irving's *Life of George Washington.*

Indian scalps tacked to trees. He wanted to spread terror, to make warriors decide which they wanted most: to attack settlers or, as he put it, "leave their families exposed." In other words, he deliberately targeted women and children, something outlawed in the laws of war, even in the eighteenth century. Yet he felt the end justified the means in this case. His tactics gradually paid off, and Indians launched fewer raids. As we shall see, during the Revolution, all sides—patriots, loyalists, and redcoats—practiced the same brutality for which the colonists had denounced the Indians.[49]

Meanwhile, the forest war grew into a world war. Known in Europe as the Seven Years' War, it lasted from 1756 to 1763. That war raged not only in America, but in Europe, the West Indies, Africa, India, and on the high seas. What finally turned the tide was the rise to power of William Pitt as England's prime minister. This tough-minded politician borrowed heavily and raised taxes to pay for the war. Then he sent Britain's best generals to America with Britain's best soldiers. Their orders: take Fort Duquesne, secure the Ohio country, and conquer Canada.

In the fall of 1758, General John Forbes, a veteran of the European wars, assembled 1,500 redcoats and 2,500 colonials at Fort Cumberland. Colonel Washington commanded all the American troops. Determined to avoid Braddock's mistakes, Forbes allowed him to fight Indian-style, from behind trees.

A fort of the type Washington built when he was commander of Virginia's frontier defenses. Notice that the second floor juts out, allowing the defenders to shoot directly downward on anyone who came up to the walls.

At dusk on November 24, the army neared Braddock's old battleground. Somehow, redcoats and Virginians got confused in the half darkness. Mistaking the Virginians for the enemy, the redcoats opened fire. This time the Virginians answered in kind. Washington ran between the two units, using his sword to knock the blazing muskets aside. Although nobody got hurt, he felt the heat on his cheeks.[50]

Next morning, the army made its final approach to Fort Duquesne. As it moved through an oak forest, an explosion shook the ground and a plume of smoke rose above the treetops. The French had blown up the fort and retreated up the Allegheny River to Fort Venango. Forbes lost no time in starting work on another fort. To the sound of sawing and hammering, he wrote his report to London. The general closed by saying that he had named the place Fort Pitt in the prime minister's honor. We know it as Pittsburgh.

Rather than celebrate, Washington returned to the old battlefield. The French had left Braddock's dead where they fell. "There are men's bones lying about as thick as the leaves do on the ground," Jehu Eyre, one of Washington's officers, reported. "They are so thick that one lies on top of another for about half a mile in length, and about one hundred yards in breadth."[51] Wild animals feasted on the bones, scattering them over a wide area. The Virginians collected 450 skulls and gave them a proper burial.

Washington felt sad not only for these poor men but also for himself. He had spent the last five years in military service. What did he have to show for it? Not money. Not medals. Not an army commission. For whatever reason they had, the British military did not believe that the Virginian deserved a commission in the service of His Majesty King George II.

The war continued five more years. During that time, British armies took Quebec and Montreal, Canada's chief towns. British warships crippled France's overseas trade. King Louis XV asked for peace. In 1763, diplomats signed the Treaty of Paris. By its terms, France lost its American colonies, except some islands in the French West Indies.

George Washington played no part in these events. He had heard the whistle of too many bullets to find them charming anymore. He no longer yearned for military glory. A career as a professional soldier no longer interested him. He had grown up.

The day after Christmas, 1758, Washington rode to Williamsburg and resigned his command. When the House of Burgesses officially thanked him for his services, he rose to express his appreciation for the honor. An eyewitness recalled, "He blushed, stammered, and trembled, for a second, when the Speaker received him. 'Sit down, Mr. Washington,' said he with a smile, 'your modesty is equal to your valor, and that surpasses the power of any language that I possess.' "[52]

With that, George Washington left the room and returned to Mount Vernon to take up his new life.

3

A KIND
OF DESTINY

PHILADELPHIA, JUNE 18, 1775

My Dearest:
... It has been determined in Congress that the whole army raised for the defense of the American cause shall be put under my care, and it is necessary for me to proceed immediately to Boston to take upon me the command of it. ... But as it has been a kind of destiny that has thrown me upon this service, I shall hope that my undertaking it is designed to answer some good purpose.
—GEORGE TO MARTHA WASHINGTON

When Washington left Williamsburg on that cold December day in 1758, he hoped never to hear another shot fired in anger. Had anyone told him, then, that he would lead a rebellion against Great Britain, he would have thought them crazy. It took him seventeen years to travel the road from loyal subject to rebel general. How he came to do so is really two stories—his personal story and the story of the colonies at a vital turning point in their history. Without telling the one, we cannot understand the other.

Not only did Washington own Mount Vernon, he began to share it with a wife. Until his marriage, he had little to do with women—at least little we know of. The Fairfaxes' guests at Belvoir thought him a shy youth. Although he tried to please the young women, he was at first so awkward that they giggled behind their hands. He did show interest in an unnamed "Low Land Beauty," but nothing came of it. He also fancied Sally Cary.

Two years older than he, at eighteen she married George William Fairfax, the colonel's eldest son. Washington had a crush on her; he may even have loved her. Yet he knew they could never be anything more than friends.

Then he met Martha. Born Martha Dandridge, she had grown up on a small plantation in eastern Virginia. Just after turning seventeen, she had married Daniel Parke Custis, a rich planter twice her age. It was a happy marriage. Sadly, of the four children Martha bore, two died in infancy.

Martha Custis at the time of her marriage to George Washington. From a copy of a portrait at Mount Vernon.

Barely five feet tall and plump, Martha had small hands and feet, a hooked nose, hazel eyes, and dark brown hair. Her beauty lay not in her appearance, but in her character. She was easy to like. Nobody, it seems, had a bad word to say about her. People admired her "sweetness of manner" and "great ease and contentment." Gentle and soft-spoken, she made strangers feel at home the moment they walked through the door. A take-charge sort of person, she described herself as "an old-fashioned housekeeper, steady as a clock, busy as a bee, and cheerful as a cricket."[1]

Daniel Parke Custis died in 1757. Martha, now twenty-five and the richest widow in Virginia, was "a good catch." She inherited land and cash valued at £32,000, or $1.5 million in today's money. Like any colonist who had lost a mate, people expected her to find another quickly. She found George Washington.

When and how they met is not known. Nor do we know how he courted her. These were personal matters, and they kept them to themselves. We only know that a few weeks before joining the Forbes expedition, George visited Martha at White House Plantation, her home on the Pamunkey River near Williamsburg. She probably showed him around the mansion and introduced him to her children. Her son, John Custis, called Jacky, was three; her daughter, Martha Custis, called Patsy, was two.

Washington's arrival was more than a friendly visit. Martha had to be sure about her beau. Although physically much larger than she, and younger by eight months, these differences were not problems. Marriage itself was the problem. In certain ways, it was a bigger step in the eigh-

An engraving after a 1772 painting of George Washington by Charles Willson Peale. Now master of Mount Vernon, a proud and prosperous Washington wears the uniform of the Virginia militia. (Peale's painting appears on the jacket of this book.)

teenth century than it is today. If a bride made the wrong choice, she was out of luck, since divorce was all but impossible. Once they married, the bride practically lost control of her life. Under the laws of Virginia, a husband owned his wife's property. He might be an unfaithful brute, but she could do nothing about it—legally. Anyway, George must have made a good impression. Next morning, when he left, Martha wore an engagement ring. The wedding took place on January 6, 1759, at Martha's home. Washington was twenty-seven years old.

Their life together was no storybook romance. George once said her letters to him showed more "friendship than enamored love." They married for practical reasons. The bride gained a manager for her property, a companion, and a father for her children. The groom gained a fortune and "a quiet wife, a quiet soul," as he put it. In time, they came to love each other very much. Yet it was a "cool" love, one based on trust, kindness, honesty, and loyalty, rather than passion. They had pet names for each other. She called him "Old Man" and "Papa"; he called her "Dear Patsy." Martha usually got what she wanted in a quiet, refined way. When she wanted him to do something, and he objected, she would twist one of her giant's coat buttons and gaze up into his eyes with a smile.[2]

They had no children of their own. Smallpox may have destroyed George's ability to become a father; a serious case of measles soon after their marriage may have prevented Martha from bearing another child. Since George loved children, he treated Jacky and Patsy as his own. Patsy grew into an attractive young woman. In 1773, at the age of seventeen, she died of epilepsy, a disease of the nervous system. George mourned "the Sweet Innocent Girl" as deeply as her mother.[3]

Meanwhile, Jacky turned into a lazy, pampered young man with few interests other than riding, hunting, and gambling. A teacher described him as "surprisingly voluptuous," with a strong attraction to "the Sex"; that is,

he liked women and they liked him. Then, as if by magic, Jacky settled down. He fell head over heels for Eleanor Calvert, a descendant of Lord Baltimore, the founder of Maryland. A few months after his sister's death, they married; Jacky was eighteen, "Nelly" sixteen. Martha sent the bride this marvelous letter of welcome:

MY DEAR NELLY. God took from me a daughter when June roses were blooming. He has now given me another daughter about her age when winter winds are blowing, to warm my heart again. I am as happy as one so afflicted and so blest can be. . . .

Your affectionate Mother,
M. WASHINGTON[4]

The marriage of Martha Custis and George Washington. Marriage was a serious step for an eighteenth-century woman. In marrying, the bride turned over all her property to her husband. An 1854 lithograph after a painting by Junius Brutus Stearns.

Martha Parke "Patsy" Custis. Washington loved his wife's daughter by her first marriage. When she died of epilepsy at the age of seventeen, he was heartbroken.

Washington adopted John Parke "Jacky" Custis, Martha's son by her first marriage. An easygoing fellow, Jacky was a great disappointment to his stepfather. Rather than do any serious work, he preferred to have fun with his friends.

As for Martha's husband, the first fifteen years of marriage, 1759–74, were in many ways his golden years. During that time, he became a leader in Fairfax County, where he lived. Washington served as a justice of the peace, a guardian of the poorhouse, and a member of the House of Burgesses. On his visits to Williamsburg, he met the colony's leading lawmakers, officials, and planters. Although he helped raise money for the parish church, he was not devout. He attended services about once a month as a social duty, rather than something he enjoyed doing. Martha was the religious one. Every day, after breakfast, she went upstairs to read her Bible and pray for an hour.

Washington's day began early. Up at the crack of dawn, he quietly slipped out of bed so as not to wake his wife. Dressing quickly, he went downstairs for a light breakfast of cornmeal cakes swimming in honey and washed down with tea. With the family still asleep, he went to his study to write letters, go over the accounts, and read. His favorite reading consisted of colonial newspapers, English magazines, and books on farming. After a second breakfast with Martha and the children at 6:00 A.M., he inspected the five farms that made up the Mount Vernon plantation. On his morning rides, a guest reported, he wore "plain black clothes, a broadbrimmed white hat, and [had] an umbrella with a long staff" attached to his saddle. He used the umbrella mainly to shield himself from the summer sun.[5]

Like all plantations, Mount Vernon was a self-contained community. To make sure everything ran smoothly, Washington visited every corner of his domain once a day, rain or shine. Sometimes he dismounted and lent a hand with driving livestock, repairing a rail fence, or helping with a building project. Returning to the mansion by early afternoon, he changed clothes for dinner. Dinner was the main meal of the day. Served at two o'clock, it consisted of his favorite dishes: roast pork, leg of lamb, pigeon pie, rabbit stew, pudding, vegetables. Afterward, he sat at the table munching walnuts and drinking Madeira, a sweet red wine he bought in 150-gallon barrels. The family had a light supper at 7:00 P.M. and turned in for the night by nine.

Washington knew how to enjoy himself. Like most Virginia planters, he gambled. Unlike many of them, however, he gambled only small sums. His account books have many notations of his winnings and losses at billiards, cockfights, horse races, and cards. While staying in Williamsburg, he met other legislators at Raleigh Tavern, a favorite hangout, where they gossiped, drank, and smoked clay pipes. Washington had a keen sense of humor. No prude, he enjoyed listening to jokes about sex, and even told a few himself. Friends thought his smile "extraordinarily attractive." When

Harvesttime. The master of Mount Vernon expected his "people"—slaves—to give him a good day's work. Here we see him on his daily rounds, talking things over with a white overseer. An 1853 lithograph after a painting by Junius Brutus Stearns.

a joke really tickled him, he rocked with laughter; sometimes he "rolled on the floor and could not for a time recover himself."[6]

As he matured, Washington lost his shyness with women. He enjoyed talking to them, and looking at them, too. He admired pretty women. At gatherings, a friend recalled, "his eyes were perpetually roaming over the ladies." Some ladies, at least, welcomed the attention. Martha Dangerfield Bland wrote her sister: "He can be downright impudent sometimes—such impudence, Fanny, as you and I like!!!" Best of all, he liked dancing. George and Martha made an odd couple on the dance floor, he being so tall and she so small. For hours without a break, they did stately minuets and fast country dances like High Betty Martin and Lather-the-Strap. George also danced with any pretty woman who would dance with him—and he did it in front of his wife, who seemed not to mind at all. Why should she? Nobody ever accused him of betraying his dear Patsy.[7]

Since the South had few inns, opening one's home, even to total strangers, was a duty. Nicholas Cresswell, an English traveler, thought southerners "the most hospitable people on earth. If a stranger went amongst them, no matter of what country, if he behaved decently . . . he would be entertained with the greatest friendship."[8] In the seven years before 1775, the Washingtons had no fewer than 1,700 guests, or nearly five a week. Often, they did not know their names. Nevertheless, they fed them, gave them a bed, and entertained them for as long as they cared to stay. George prided himself on being a good host. Suffering from a severe cold, one guest awoke to find the master of Mount Vernon standing at his bedside with a bowl of hot tea.

Guests admired their host. George Washington always left a deep impression; once you saw him, you never forgot him. Standing over 6 feet 3 inches tall, weighing about 225 pounds, he must have seemed bigger than he would have appeared to us today. At a time when poor diet often stunted growth in childhood, a person his size was a rarity. Historians believed that fewer than one man in fifty who served under him during the Revolutionary War reached a height of six feet.[9]

You could tell from the way his clothes fit that Washington had a well-muscled body, a sign of immense physical strength. In addition, he had broad shoulders, a narrow waist, unusually large hands, and as he once described himself, "pretty long arms & thighs." His posture was ramrod-straight, without any hint of a slouch; had he slouched, some joked, he would have looked like an ape with the backs of his knuckles scraping along the ground.

"His head," wrote George Mercer, a Virginia friend, "is well shaped though not large, but is gracefully poised on a superb neck. [He has] a large and straight rather than a prominent nose; blue-gray penetrating eyes, which are widely separated and overhung by a heavy brow. His face is long rather than broad, with high round cheek bones. He has a clear though rather a colorless pale skin, which burns with the sun." Washington also had reddish-brown hair, a firm chin, and a wide mouth. As with many in the crowd, his face had tiny pinprick scars, reminders of the smallpox he had as a teenager. "In conversation," Mercer added, "he looks you full in the face, is deliberate, deferential and engaging. His voice is agreeable rather than strong. His demeanor [is] at all times composed and dignified."[11]

We see Washington best in a painting of 1772 by Charles Willson Peale, one of America's great portrait artists. The portrait shows a strong, confident man dressed in the blue and red uniform of the Virginia militia. A picture of health, Washington could bend a horseshoe with his bare hands, toss an iron bar farther than anyone, and crack walnuts between his thumb and forefinger. Tireless on horseback, he hunted foxes two or three times a week. For seven hours straight, he rode at breakneck speed, leaping fences and following hounds until they cornered a fox and tore it to pieces. Washington had a prize pack of hunting dogs. He bred them carefully, giving them names like Sweetlips, Truelove, Searcher, and Rover. Puppies that did not meet his high standards were drowned in a tub of water.

Washington earned a living in various ways. Part of his income came from lending money at interest and renting houses he owned in Williamsburg and Alexandria. Another part came from the sale of frontier lands. After the French and Indian War, Virginia rewarded him with a large tract of land in the Ohio Valley. Most of his income, however, came from farming. Washington loved farming. A farmer's life, he believed, was the most honorable and interesting. He also tried to make it the most profitable. His

A MAP of
the moſt INHABITED part of
VIRGINIA
containing the whole PROVINCE of
MARYLAND
with Part of
PENSILVANIA, NEW JERSEY and NORTH CAROLINA
Drawn by
Joshua Fry & Peter Jefferson
in 1751.

To the Right Honourable George Dunk Earl of Halifax First Lord Commiſsioner
and to the Reſt of the Right Honourable and Honourable Commiſsioners, for TRADE and PLANTATIONS
This Map is most humbly Inscribed to their Lordships,
By their Lordships
Most Obedient & most devoted humble Servt. Thos. Jefferys.

Virginia tobacco merchants as portrayed on a map printed in London in 1751. The large barrels at the right were called hogsheads. Each hogshead held several hundred pounds of the "bewitching weed"—tobacco.

Mount Vernon farms grew tobacco, Virginia's chief cash crop—up to 80,000 pounds of it a year.

So large an operation as Washington's needed an equally large workforce. Apart from the plantation manager, a distant cousin named Lund Washington, and the farm overseers, Mount Vernon depended on the toil and sweat of enslaved black people.

Slavery was nothing new in America. In the summer of 1619, a year before the Pilgrims sailed aboard the *Mayflower,* a Dutch sea captain sold twenty African captives at Jamestown. From then on, slavery grew along with English settlement. In 1700, some 21,000 blacks and 240,400 whites lived in the thirteen colonies. By 1750, the number had climbed to 242,000 blacks and 934,000 whites; that is, nearly one out of four Americans was a black person. Every colony had slaves, though most lived in the South. Since most whites wanted to work for themselves, and the colonies had a severe labor shortage, forced labor seemed the only way to go.

All slaves were alike in that they received no wages and had no right to a share in the profits of their labor. The law did not recognize slaves as human beings, equal to anyone in God's eyes. It defined them as chattels, articles of personal property—things. A Virginia judge explained slavery with brutal frankness. "What is the difference between a horse and a slave?" he asked. The answer: "Nothing."[12] Slaves had no more rights than horses. They did not control their lives. Free people could buy, sell, trade, mortgage, rent out, give as gifts, pay taxes, and secure loans with slaves.

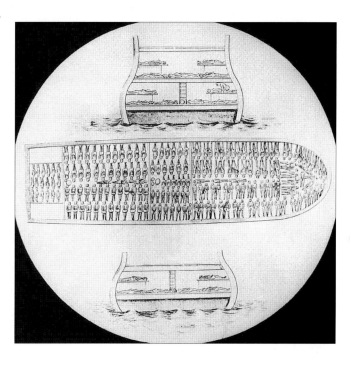

Three generations of Washingtons had prospered from slave labor before George's birth. Since his father owned fifty slaves, the growing boy saw them always. Early on, he learned to take them for granted. They did everything for him, from washing his clothes and polishing his boots, to making his bed and emptying his chamber pot. Slavery, for George, simply *was*—a reality. He accepted it as natural, just, and necessary.

So did the Christian churches. At Sunday services, George saw every adult man carrying a Bible and a gun. The Bible held God's word. The gun offered protection against a slave revolt. Twice a year, in September and March, the boy heard the minister read from the Virginia black code, the law designed to keep black people in their place. He learned, for example, that "it shall be unlawful for any Negro [to] depart from his master's ground without a pass . . . [or] to assemble at feasts or funerals." The code added that violators "will be dismembered"; that is, their arms and legs torn from their living bodies.[13]

Enslaved black people brought from Africa did most of the work in the southern colonies. Since so many died on the "middle passage" from Africa to America, slave traders crammed their ships with as many people as possible. This drawing is of a cross section of a slave ship, designed to maximize its human cargo.

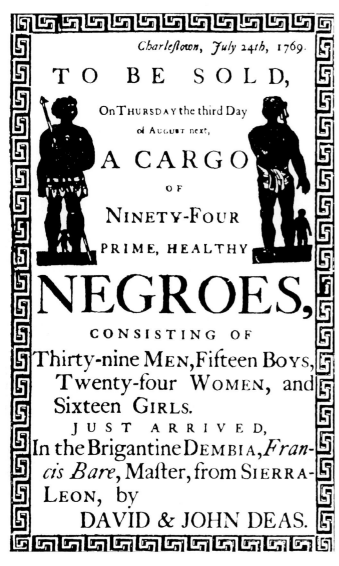

Charlestown, July 24th, 1769.

TO BE SOLD,

On THURSDAY the third Day
of AUGUST next,

A CARGO

OF

NINETY-FOUR

PRIME, HEALTHY

NEGROES,

CONSISTING OF

Thirty-nine MEN, Fifteen BOYS,
Twenty-four WOMEN, and
Sixteen GIRLS.

JUST ARRIVED,

In the Brigantine DEMBIA, *Francis Bare*, Master, from SIERRA-
LEON, by

DAVID & JOHN DEAS.

A handbill announcing the sale of slaves. As chattel— property—a slave had no more rights than a farm animal.

George inherited ten slaves from his father. After getting Mount Vernon, he steadily added to his holdings. Besides the 150 slaves Martha brought when they married, he asked West Indian dealers to buy "Negroes if choice ones can be had." Closer to home, he bid at slave auctions. For example, on July 25, 1768, he told his diary: "Went to Alexandria and bought a bricklayer from Mr. Piper and returned to dinner." Judging from his tone, he treated his human purchases as another form of shopping. An adult slave cost him an average of $3,000 in today's money. When he died in 1799, he held 317 black people in bondage.[14]

Washington called his slaves "my people," "my Negroes," "my servants," and "a certain species of property." A racist, he believed blacks naturally inferior to whites, having low intelligence and "no ambition." He agreed with Martha that "the Blacks are so bad in their nature that they have not the least gratitude for the kindness that may be showed to them." We may find this shocking. Yet we must remember that the Washingtons were people of their age, as we are of ours. Their ideas were no different from those of most Americans in the 1700s—and for a long time to come.[15]

What was it like for a black person at Mount Vernon? White people are our only source of information on this subject, so the answer must always be one-sided and thus incomplete. The blacks, who knew better than anyone, never wrote letters or left a permanent, detailed record of their experience in bondage. It seems that Washington was a typical slaveholder, no better and no worse than his neighbors. He was in business to make money. Whatever increased profits was good. Whatever reduced profits was bad. Like most slaveholders, he was as kind as he needed to be—but no more, since that would lower profits. As he put it, "Many mickles make a muckle"; that is, many small savings add up to a big saving.[16]

Mount Vernon was a typical plantation. Its slaves lived in "the quarters," rows of single-room cabins invisible from the main house. Each cabin had a dirt floor, unglazed windows, and a wooden chimney. A Polish visitor described life in Washington's slave cabins:

> We entered one of the huts of the Blacks, for one can not call them by the name of houses. They are more miserable than the most miserable cottages of our [Polish] peasants. The husband and wife sleep on a mean pallet [a straw-filled mattress], the children on the ground; a very bad fireplace, some utensils for cooking, but in the middle of this poverty some cups and a teapot. . . . A very small garden planted with vegetables was close by, with 5 or 6 hens, each one leading ten to fifteen chickens. It is the only comfort that is permitted them, for they do not keep either ducks, geese, or pigs. . . . They work all week, not having a single day for themselves except for holidays.[17]

Once a year, Washington gave his "hands" a set of clothes made of "Negro cloth," the cheapest grade of cotton or linen. Their diet consisted of cornbread, salt pork, salt fish, and vegetables. If they got sick, he had a doctor come to treat them. It was a way of protecting his property, like having a veterinarian care for sick farm animals. Nowhere in all the thousands of Washington letters I've read have I found any concern for his slaves' feelings.

Mount Vernon, like all plantations, had three classes of slaves. The slave nobility worked in the main house. House servants wore fine clothes, spoke well, and had fine manners. At Mount Vernon, eleven servants waited on the family, cooked its food, and did the chores under Martha's supervision. Artisans—carpenters, masons, blacksmiths, tailors, shoemakers, spinners, weavers, bakers, barrel makers—produced hundreds of everyday items. Most slaves, however, tended the livestock or worked in the tobacco fields. At any given time, 60 percent of these "hands" were women.

This crude drawing of a runaway slave, or one like it, was used on reward posters from colonial times until the abolition of slavery in the Civil War. Although George Washington issued posters for his runaways, none has survived to the twentieth century. Probably they had pictures like this one.

Washington expected slaves to work hard and long. The idea of wasting time gnawed at him like a toothache. He once made an overseer sign a pledge "to hurry and drive" slaves at their tasks. Another time, he demanded an overseer make sure "that my people may be at their work as soon as it is light, work till it is dark, and be diligent while they are at it . . . [and see] that every laborer (male or female) does as much in the 24 hours as their strength, without endangering their health . . . will allow of." Everyone had something to do. From the age of eleven, black children worked as adults at Mount Vernon. Younger children and the elderly pulled out weeds and did odd jobs. Women worked in the fields beside the men, plowing, weeding, and picking.[18]

Few gave their all. Experience taught Washington that "his" people resented their bondage. They yearned for freedom, yet, barring that, tried to do as little as possible. This was true not only at Mount Vernon, but on every plantation. Slaves played sick, wasted time, broke tools, and stole anything not locked up or nailed down. This made Washington furious. He threatened anyone who refused to do their duty with swift "correction," as he put it.

Even the most humane owners used force. Whipping was the most common form of punishment for soldiers and slaves, both men and women. Faced with a lazy field hand, Washington ordered his manager to "give him a good whipping."[19] This was mild compared to what awaited especially unruly or violent slaves. Washington sold them in the West Indies. That was almost a sure death sentence, since few survived the tropical climate, epidemic diseases, and brutal treatment on the sugar plantations.

Slavery allowed Washington to live in comfort, even luxury. All in all, he was a contented man.

On October 25, 1760, another man named George stepped onto the stage of history. On that day, an English prince became King George III. His Majesty, twenty-two years old, was a tall, well-built person. Portraits show him with a ruddy complexion, bulging eyes, a hawk-beak nose, and thick lips. As a youngster, he had been shy, awkward, and dull; he did not read until nearly twelve. "I despise myself as every body must," he later wrote.[20]

By his early twenties, however, he had pulled himself together. As king, he worked hard, studied official reports, and learned the art of politics. George III saw himself as a "patriot king," chosen by God to rule the British Empire with justice. Yet ruling with justice requires wisdom, a quality lacking in His Majesty. With him, things were either black or white—nothing between. "I wish nothing but good," he liked to say, "therefore every one who does not agree with me is a traitor and a scoundrel."[21] This was dangerous talk. By resenting those who thought differently, he made conflict inevitable.

Not that George III was a tyrant. Like all Englishmen, His Majesty had to obey the laws made by Parliament in London. Unfortunately, Parliament did not represent every English man, or *any* English woman. Wealthy men voted for other wealthy men in elections. And

King George III circa 1778. Although a man of modest intelligence, America's last king had a high opinion of himself. His Majesty thought anyone who disagreed with him was either a liar, a fool, or a traitor who deserved to swing at the end of a rope.

since the king was the wealthiest person in the land, he usually got his way by bribery; he called bribes "golden pills." These goodies were cash payments or government jobs with big salaries and little work. Members of Parliament and voters who took bribes called themselves the "King's friends."

Yet even the king's wealth had its limits. Although England had beaten France, victory came at a high price. To pay for the war, the government borrowed heavily at high interest rates. In 1763, the national debt stood at £137 million, worth about $30 billion today. Peace brought no prosperity, only further hardship. Trade, which had been harmed by the war and government borrowing, was slow to recover. Prices skyrocketed. Unemployment spread. Crime soared. Riots rocked the cities. In London, discharged redcoats went on a rampage; other redcoats restored order by mowing them down in droves.

Meanwhile, in America, His Majesty had plenty to worry about. France's former Indian allies, led by an Ottawa chief named Pontiac, menaced the frontier from the Great Lakes southward to Virginia. If history was any guide, France would not accept defeat. Eventually, it would start another war. To be ready, the army must station 10,000 redcoats in the colonies and send warships to guard the coast. Naturally, that coast lots of money.

Who should pay for keeping those extra troops in America? Surely not the English, King George thought. His subjects already paid taxes through the nose. The government, people said, taxed everything but the air they breathed. House owners, for example, paid a tax on every windowpane; tavern keepers paid a tax on every drink they served, and barbers for every haircut they gave. Prime Minister George Grenville decided to make the *colonists* dig into their pockets. In March 1765, he got his Stamp Act through Parliament with the king's blessing. The English had been using tax stamps for fifty years. Now the overseas English must use them, too.

The Stamp Act taxed forty-three items commonly used in the colonies. Thus, in one move, Parliament brought rich and poor colonists together. Everyone who used legal documents had to pay the tax. All wills, contracts, land deeds, and property leases needed a stamp, or no court could consider them. Printers had to put stamps on their newspapers. Marriage licenses needed stamps. So did diplomas received by college graduates and the playing cards used by sailors to pass the time aboard a ship.

Both king and prime minister knew little about America and Americans. Ignorance led them to make a serious error. Americans did not greet the Stamp Act calmly. News of it sped across the land quickly via newspapers, pamphlets, and word of mouth. Colonists had always paid *external* taxes; that is, duties on goods imported from foreign countries. The Stamp Act was different. It imposed an *internal* tax, which violated a basic principle. It was not the stamps' cost, only a few pennies each, that troubled colonists. Their own assemblies taxed them more heavily.

Their own assemblies! The colonies had always governed themselves through elected assemblies. If voters disliked a representative's actions, they turned him out in the next election. Now Parliament had bypassed the assemblies. True, it had done so in the past, but never to such an extent. How could colonists hold members of Parliament accountable at the polls? They could not, because they did not vote in English elections. Thus, the king's friends could order them around as they wished. It was taxation without representation. If Parliament got away with an internal tax, colonists feared they would lose all their rights as Englishmen.

Assemblies passed resolutions against the "cruel act." Cartoonists drew bogus stamps with skulls for the royal coat of arms. Torchlight processions wound through the streets of every city, chanting *"Liberty, Property, and No Stamps."* Local groups calling themselves Sons of Liberty warned stamp distributors to quit their jobs—or else. A favorite tactic was to hang up a dummy with the taxman's name on it. If he still refused to quit, they tore down his house. People started boycotts, vowing not to buy British goods until Parliament repealed the act; this was a serious move, since it hurt trade and raised unemployment. Prime Minister Grenville got the message. In March 1766, he asked Parliament to repeal the Stamp Act. As a show of loyalty, New Yorkers put up a huge statue of King George riding on horseback.

Although Washington resented the Stamp Act, he did not join the resistance to it. In a private letter, he called the act an "unconstitutional method of Taxation [and] a direful attack on their Liberties."[22] That was all. Nevertheless, the crisis led him to an important decision. Deep down, he felt Parliament would try to raise taxes again. He did not know when, or how, but he decided to resist—peacefully. Tobacco prices had fallen sharply, and he owed London merchants money for goods he had bought on credit. Rather than slide deeper into debt, he decided to give up the tobacco business and become self-sufficient. So, ten years before the Declaration of Independence, he declared his economic independence from Britain.

Washington planted wheat instead of tobacco. Most of his wheat sold at a good profit in Alexandria. The rest he ground into flour at his mill, then shipped to the British West Indies to buy slaves, wine, and tropical fruits. Always on the lookout for profits, he experimented with new crops like

The Stamp Act crisis. The examples at top and center are genuine British tax stamps of the sort used in the American colonies. The bottom one is an imitation created by a patriot cartoonist, warning that to buy them meant death to the cause of American liberty.

Protests against the Stamp Act became so widespread that the government in London had it repealed. When news of the action reached America, colonists held mock funerals for the hated law.

flax, oats, clover, peaches, apples, and cherries. To increase output, he tried different fertilizers—sheep dung, river sand, mud—and improved the design of his plows. He raised cows, pigs, and sheep. Slave-butchers cured the meat in his smokehouses. Slave-spinners turned wool into thread, which slave-weavers made into cloth. Slave-lumberjacks felled trees in his woods, cutting them into boards at his sawmill. Their master sold the boards or used them to enlarge his mansion. Slaves even fished the Potomac for herring and shad in a fleet of small boats.

As Washington thought, Parliament raised taxes again in the colonies. In 1767, it passed the Townshend Acts. Named for Charles Townshend, chief of the treasury, they required that colonists pay taxes on certain British goods brought into the colonies: paper, paint, glass, lead, tea. The tea tax was especially important. Tea was a popular drink, and colonists often had fifteen or sixteen cups at a sitting.

Townshend thought the colonists would not object to the taxes. After all, he said slyly, they were on imports, and therefore "external." The vast majority of colonists, rich and poor, disagreed with this measure. Since Britain was not a foreign country, they saw the duties as a trick to get around their objections to the stamp tax. Again colonists boycotted British goods. After protests at home, Parliament repealed the acts, except the duty on tea.

The Townshend duties became a turning point for Washington. Like so many others who would later become revolutionaries—John Adams, Benjamin Franklin, Thomas Jefferson—he believed in the rights of Englishmen with all his heart. Like them, too, he once thought King George and his friends meant well but made mistakes. Not anymore. Now Washington saw the "mistakes" as part of a carefully thought-out plan.

Washington gave his reasons in a bitter letter to George Mason, a friend and neighbor. He began by saying that the colonies must "maintain the liberty which we have derived from our Ancestors." Unfortunately, "our lordly Masters in Great Britain" wanted "nothing less than the deprivation of American freedom." Americans must not "hesitate a moment to use arms" to defend their freedom, if necessary. Coming from one who had wanted a British army career, this showed a total change of mind. By urging force, Washington went further than almost any other American of the day. Luckily, he did not have to turn his words into deeds—yet.[23]

Things quieted down after the repeal of the Townshend duties. On March 5, 1770, however, redcoats opened fire on a Boston mob, killing five. While off duty, British soldiers took odd jobs to supplement their meager wages. Low-paid Boston workers, like ropemakers, resented the competition. Fights broke out. When a crowd gathered to protest outside the Custom House, insults, then rocks, flew through the air. Feeling their lives threatened, the redcoats fired into the crowd.

Violent protests erupted throughout the colonies when the news came that Parliament had passed the Townshend Acts.

Paul Revere's drawing of "The Bloody Massacre" contains more propaganda than truth. The Boston Custom House is renamed "Butcher's Hall," the crowd is unarmed, and the soldiers are firing on command. None of this happened.

Although Americans now regard the victims of the "Boston Massacre" as heroes, back then many, including Washington, ignored the shootings. John Adams, a brilliant lawyer, actually took the redcoats' side. Ignoring threats to his life, he persuaded a Boston jury that the redcoats had fired in self-defense. Adams had little sympathy for the crowd, merely common workingmen. He called them a "motley rabble of saucy boys, negroes and mulattoes, Irish teagues [thugs] and outlandish jack tars [sailors]." Boston's "better"—wealthier—citizens agreed.[24]

Meanwhile, people paid the penny-a-pound tea tax or used cheaper tea smuggled from Holland. Not Washington! For Washington, the tax was a matter of principle, not cash. "What is it we are contending against?" he asked a friend. "Is it against paying the duty of three pence per pound on tea because it is burdensome? No, it is right only, we have all along disputed." The tax was wrong! It was "illegal." Yet, rather than break a bad law by drinking smuggled tea, he switched to coffee.[25]

In 1773, Frederick Lord North, King George's latest prime minister, faced a serious problem. The East India Company had a monopoly on importing tea into Britain but could not sell it in the colonies. After unloading a cargo in London, the company auctioned tea to dealers for sale directly in the colonies; customs agents collected the tax at dockside in America. Yet the drop in sales due to smuggling left the company near bankruptcy. If that were to happen, wealthy stockholders, among them the king's friends in Parliament, stood to lose a fortune.

Lord North decided to push another Tea Act through Parliament. This act allowed the East India Company to ship tea directly to American merchants, who would pay the tax and pass on the cost to their customers. His Lordship could not imagine anyone objecting. Even with the tax, the company would undersell the smugglers. By paying the tax, colonists would also be admitting Parliament's right to tax anything. A young man named Alexander Hamilton told his friends:

> Perhaps before long your tables, chairs and platters, and dishes, and knives and forks, and everything else would be taxed. Nay, I don't know but that they [the British] would find means to tax you for every child you got, and for every kiss your daughters received from their sweethearts; and God knows, that would soon ruin you.

Hamilton's friends may have laughed, but they knew the issue was dead serious.[26]

The Tea Act led directly to the American Revolution. In New York and Philadelphia, angry crowds roamed the waterfront, refusing to let the tea ships dock. The Boston Sons of Liberty went further. Sons of Liberty

Frederick Lord North served as British prime minister during the years of the American Revolution. From a caricature in the British Museum.

Sons of Liberty disguised as Mohawk Indians brew saltwater tea for cheering bystanders at the Boston Tea Party.

were mostly prosperous merchants and shopkeepers who were determined to do something about the tea tax. Something dramatic!

On December 16, 1773, disguised as Mohawk Indian warriors, they boarded three tea ships and dumped 342 chests of tea overboard, valued at £10,000, or over one million dollars in today's money. Onlookers joked that Boston had held a "tea party" and "made a teapot of the harbor." Before long, taverns across America rang with this song:

> *Rally, Mohawks! bring out your axes,*
> *And tell King George we'll pay no taxes*
> *On his foreign tea.*

His Majesty and His Lordship were not in a singing mood. Nor was the British public. News of the Boston Tea Party made them furious. As the British understood it from across the Atlantic, it was a brazen attack on law and order. If colonists wanted violence, the British were ready. Many Englishmen thought of Americans as cowardly, money-grubbing farmers and shopkeepers. Why, a thousand redcoats could easily wipe the ground with every colonist from Maine to Georgia. "We shall soon have done with these scoundrels," a nobleman boasted, "for one only dirties one's fingers by meddling with them."[27] Such people committed the first sin of politics and war. Like General Braddock, they held their opponents in contempt.

Lord North got Parliament to pass the Coercive Acts. Colonists called them the "Intolerable Acts," because they seemed so harsh and unfair. The acts suspended the Massachusetts Assembly and closed the port of Boston until its citizens paid for the tea. More. Anyone who counseled resistance to the acts was to be tried for sedition, calling for open disobedience to the law. They were not to be tried in colonial courts, which King George felt were too lenient. Instead, they were to be sent to England for trial in royal courts, where they had little chance of being acquitted. Finally, the acts put Massachusetts under military law and ordered four thousand redcoats to keep order; that is, one soldier for every adult male in town. The troops arrived on May 14, 1774, led by General "Honest Tom" Gage, fifty-five years old, a veteran of Braddock's defeat and the commander of British forces in North America.

Under Gage's iron rule, business in Boston came to a standstill. Unemployment soared, and with it hunger. Still, its people refused to pay for the tea. They had only defended their rights as Englishmen, they said. So why should they pay?

The other colonies agreed. As the months wore on, they began to make Boston's fight their own. In taverns and private homes, people gave this toast with raised wine glasses: "Damnation to General Gage, the troops under his command, and all who wish them well."[28]

If King George won in Boston, protesters reasoned, there would be no stopping him anywhere. His Majesty might have Parliament suspend the assemblies and order occupation troops in every colony. Thus, in solidarity with Boston, the other colonies sent food and money. In towns around Boston, the Sons of Liberty collected weapons—just in case. That worried General Gage. He knew Americans well; he was married to one.

A British cartoon showing patriots looking like tramps with "Death or Liberty" written on handkerchiefs worn around their heads. Many—perhaps most—English people held Americans in contempt as fighting men.

When he warned his superiors in London that colonists would fight if provoked, they paid no attention. Americans, after all, were lambs and not lions.

In the summer of 1774, Bryan Fairfax, the colonel's youngest son, urged his neighbors not even to think of using force, but to humbly beg the king to help. Yet Bryan's favorite neighbor wanted no more appeals. "Shall we . . . whine & cry for relief," he asked, "when we have already tried it in vain? I think the Parliament of Great Britain hath no more right to put their hands into my pocket, without my consent, than I have to put my hand in yours for money; and this being already urged to them in a firm, but decent manner, by all the colonies, what reason is there to expect anything from their justice?" Americans must stand up for their rights, with guns in their hands if need be.[29]

Others shared Washington's determination. When Virginia's governor, John Murray, Lord Dunmore, dismissed the House of Burgesses for calling Gage's occupation of Boston a "military invasion," its members—who were elected—refused to leave the capital. Gathering in Raleigh Tavern, they voted to call a Continental Congress to discuss united action. Leaders in every colony but Georgia agreed to meet in Philadelphia, a city that boasted wealth, beauty, a college, theater, and musical arts.

The Virginians chose Washington and six others to represent their colony. On August 30, 1774, they left from Mount Vernon. As they swung into the saddles, Martha called out, "I hope you will all stand firm—I know George will."

A black man rode with them. Billy Lee, Washington's personal servant, looked after his owner's clothes, powdered and curled his wig, and served his meals. Billy was Washington's equal on horseback. A fearless rider, he always galloped beside Washington in the foxhunts. In the years ahead, Billy would stay close to him in every battle. Washington called him "my servant" and "my fellow," never "my slave."[30] During the Revolutionary War, Billy guarded Washington's most important papers.

The Continental Congress opened in Carpenters' Hall, Philadelphia, on September 5. Independence from Britain—a country of their own— was the furthest thing from the fifty-six delegates' minds. As Washington said, "no such thing is desired by any thinking man in all North America."[31] What they wanted was the return to their rights as Englishmen— nothing more and nothing less. After denouncing the Intolerable Acts, they voted a double boycott. Not only did they ban the import of all

Second Street was Philadelphia's main shopping street when the Continental Congress first met.

British goods, they halted the export of colonial products to the mother country. Delegates hoped His Majesty would come to his senses before it was too late. Before adjourning at the end of October, they planned for a Second Continental Congress for May 1775 to discuss the colonies' next moves.

Washington returned home a revolutionary. He was ready to fight. If the boycott failed, he vowed to lead a thousand men to relieve Boston. To be ready, he drilled the Fairfax County militia, formed volunteer units, and bought them weapons with his own money. Whenever he could, he urged Virginians to tighten the boycott.

Colonists needed little urging. To enforce the boycott, the Continental Congress had created the Continental Association, a network of committees manned by Sons of Liberty. The association became an American secret police. Its committees poked into everyone's business, inspecting store shelves and forcing merchants to show their books. God help anyone caught selling British goods or drinking taxed tea! Posters like this warned violators in chilling words:

THE FEMALE COMBATANTS

OR WHO SHALL

A British cartoon depicted each side in the debate over colonial rights as a quarrelsome woman. Britannia, at the left, wears the high hairstyle popular in Europe at the time. America is depicted as a "wild" Indian with feathers in her hair.

Grant Heaven that he may never go without
The rheumatism, itch, the pox or gout.
May he be hamper'd with some ugly witch,
And dye at last in some curst foulsome ditch.
Without the benefit of psalms or hymns,
And crowds of crows devour his rotten limbs.[32]

If warnings failed, the holdout got a coat of tar and feathers. Peter Oliver, a Massachusetts judge, gave the formula:

First, strip a Person naked, then heat the Tar until it is thin, & pour it upon the naked Flesh, or rub it over with a Tar Brush. . . . After which, sprinkle decently upon the Tar, whilst it is yet warm, as many Feathers as will stick to it. Then hold a lighted Candle to the Feathers, & try to set it all on Fire; if it will burn so much the

This British cartoon is titled "The Bostonians Paying the Excise-Man, or, Tarring and Feathering." While "Mohawk" Indians dump British tea in Boston Harbor, a mob has covered a tax official with tar and feathers while forcing him to drink a pot of boiling-hot tea.

better. . . . Take also a Halter [a rope with a noose at the end], & put it round the Person's Neck, & then cart him to the Rounds [show him around town as an example to others.][33]

Such treatment could easily do permanent damage, even cause death. Just sending a ball of cold tar often persuaded holdouts to honor the boycott.

In April 1775, as Washington prepared to leave for the Second Continental Congress, he received alarming news. General Gage had wanted to avoid trouble by seizing the weapons stored at Concord seventeen miles northwest of Boston. So, on the morning of April 19, he sent 800 redcoats on a surprise raid. But it was no surprise. Alerted the night before by Paul

Shots heard round the world. Sons of Liberty shoot at British troops retreating to Boston after the fight at Concord.

Revere, a Boston silversmith, a band of minutemen, volunteers ready to fight at a minute's notice, met the column at nearby Lexington. When the minutemen refused to leave, the redcoats fired, killing eight; one redcoat received a minor flesh wound. The redcoats reached Concord, only to find hundreds of angry, gun-toting farmers waiting for them. Forced to retreat, they marched down the road in close order, while farmers fired from houses and behind stone fences. By the time they met a relief column from Boston, they had 273 dead and wounded, as compared to 95 colonists.

Lexington and Concord alarmed both sides. Some British officers saw a long, costly struggle ahead with absolutely no chance of victory. They wanted to patch up the quarrel by offering generous terms—anything to avoid another clash. General William Harvey, a crusty old soldier, said it best: "Taking America as it at present stands, it is impossible to conquer it with our British army. . . . Our army will be destroyed by damned driblets. . . . America is an ugly job . . . a damned affair indeed."[34] King George had other ideas. He saw the colonists as disobedient children in need of a sound whipping. On his orders, the army and navy drew up plans for all-out war.

In America, news of Lexington and Concord swept across the land. Volunteers from every part of New England came by the thousands, encircling Boston to make sure Gage stayed put. Village greens echoed to the sounds of fifes and drums. Militia officers bawled commands. Everyone, it seemed, wanted to take a shot at the redcoats. Even children caught the war fever. Gangs of boys "shot" redcoats with broomstick-muskets.

Patriotic women did their part, too. When the crisis first began, they supported the boycott. Calling themselves Daughters of Liberty, they stopped serving tea and using English cloth. They set up spinning schools in churches and sewed their own clothes;

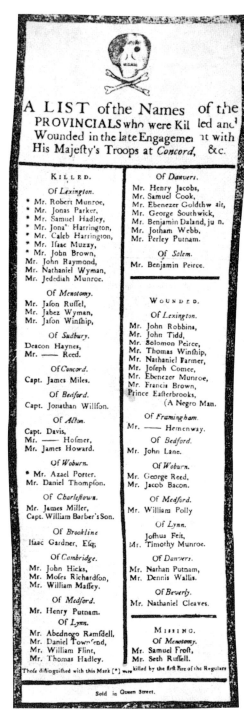

A list of colonial casualties from the fight at Concord.

Colonial women helped the patriot cause in countless ways. Here the women of Edenton, North Carolina, sign a pledge to support the tea boycott and refuse to buy English-made clothing. The dog at the lower right gives its opinion of English products.

Martha Washington worked as hard as any of her black seamstresses. When the shooting started, they sent their men to whip the British or die trying. One fellow recalled leaving home to join his company. "After I got under way," he wrote, "my wife called to me pretty loud. I stopt my hors and ask'd her what she wanted. Her answer was not to let me hear that you are shot in the back"—that is, hit while running away.[35]

War was in the air when the Second Continental Congress met on

May 10, 1775. Although many members still hoped for peace, they knew the chances for it were growing slimmer by the day. Early that morning, Ethan Allen and Benedict Arnold led a daring assault on Fort Ticonderoga at the northern end of Lake George in New York. The fort commander, roused from bed in his nightshirt, asked in whose name they seized His Majesty's property. Allen roared: "In the name of the Great Jehovah and the Continental Congress." Two weeks later, on May 25, transports dropped anchor in Boston Harbor with another 2,500 redcoats and three major generals. All veterans of the European wars, Sir William Howe, Sir Henry Clinton, and John Burgoyne were top battlefield commanders.

Members of the Second Continental Congress debated its next move. So far, the fighting had not spread beyond the Boston area. John Adams and other delegates from New England believed that the patriot cause must die if the other colonies did not join in. In other words, Adams wanted a wider, all-American war. For that to happen, the Continental Congress must create a Continental Army, a regular force drawn from every colony. A good way to start would be to "adopt" the army outside Boston and put a southerner in command. By doing that, Adams believed, the southern colonies would have to join forces with New England.

Which southerner? Adams had someone in mind. One man sat in Congress, day after day, without saying a word. Washington did not need to speak; his clothes suggested his attitude. He wore the blue and red uniform of a Virginia militia colonel, his way of saying rebellion meant war, and he meant to fight.

Adams was a little pepper pot of a man with a whiplash tongue and a razor-sharp mind. A brilliant lawyer, it was about as easy to fool him as put mittens on a grizzly bear. Adams knew the Virginian's limitations as a soldier. Washington had not fought in fifteen years and had never won a battle on an open field. Nor had he ever planned a campaign or led a large body of troops. He knew nothing of cavalry and artillery. Compared to those British major generals in Boston, he was an amateur.

The Virginian's chief qualification was his character. As a Connecticut delegate put it, Washington was "no harum-scarum, ranting, swearing fellow, but sober, steady, and calm."[36]

The Second Continental
Congress met in Philadelphia's
State House, later known as
Independence Hall.

A quiet, modest man, Washington had always shown an ability to grow and learn. Most of all, he had the soul of a civilian. Americans feared brilliant soldiers who thought too highly of themselves. Arrogant and able, such men might use the army to seize power. Not the Virginian. He saw the army as the country's servant, not its master. In short, he believed the military must take its orders from the civilian government. As it happened, Washington never questioned civilian rule, or allowed others to do so. Civilian control: that is his legacy to the American military tradition.

On June 14, Adams nominated Washington as commander in chief of the Continental Army. Washington panicked when he heard that. His face reddened and he ran out of the room. Suddenly, he realized that he was about to have more responsibility placed on his shoulders than any person in America. Awed by the task before him, he was gripped by self-doubt. Next morning, Congress elected him unanimously.

On June 16, *General* George Washington gave his acceptance speech. In it, he refused to take a salary, because he would not serve his country for personal profit. Instead, he asked only for his expenses, payable at the end of the war. After thanking Congress for the honor, he spoke from his heart, saying: "I this day declare with the utmost sincerity that I do not think myself equal to the command I am honored with."[37] By admitting

George Washington's commission as commander of all American armed forces, dated June 19, 1775.

this, he was not only being humble. He was covering himself against future charges of incompetence. After all, he had warned the Continental Congress of his limitations, a very shrewd move.

During the next week, the commander in chief made all sorts of preparations. A tailor visited his room in the City Tavern to measure him for a fine new uniform of blue and buff. Others offered skills of a different sort. In the hours after midnight, while Philadelphia slept, mysterious men appeared at his door. Washington spoke to them in whispers, then sent them away with gold coins in their purses. These men, whose names he took to the grave, were his first secret agents. In time, he became a great spymaster, the founder of American espionage.

Just before leaving for Boston on June 23, he scribbled a few lines to Martha. "My dearest," he wrote, "I retain an unalterable affection for you which neither time or distance can change."[38]

WAR AND WASHINGTON

"Huzza, huzza, huzza, huzza for War and Washington."
—PATRIOTIC SONG, 1775

As Washington rode out of Philadelphia, a messenger brought startling news from the army outside Boston. On June 17, the day after Washington's acceptance speech, General Gage hurled 2,200 redcoats against patriot positions on Charlestown Neck, a peninsula across the bay north of the city. The defenders had planned to make their stand on Bunker Hill but decided to build their forward positions on Breed's Hill nearby. Although the fighting took place on Breed's Hill, history mistakenly calls it the Battle of Bunker Hill.

Sir William Howe led the charge. Like so many Englishmen, he thought that the Yankees, as the British nicknamed New Englanders, would not fight, or if they did, that they would run away after the first shots. Instead, the Yankees waited behind breastworks, trenches with earth piled in front breast-high. The redcoats stepped through the tall grass in perfect lines of battle. As they drew near, sheets of fire poured from the Yankee line. Twice the redcoats charged, stepping over the mangled bodies of their comrades until driven back. By the third charge, most colonists had no more ammunition. The redcoats ended the battle with the bayonet. Yet it was a hollow victory. Nearly half the attackers, 1,054 men, fell dead or wounded; the Yankees lost about 400 men.

The king dismissed Gage and replaced him with Howe. Although Howe, forty-six years old, was a brave officer and a careful planner, Bunker Hill had been a transforming experience. Surrounded by the dead and dying, the grass streaking his breeches with blood, he described it as *"a moment that I never felt before."* The horror of that moment burned itself into his soul. Never again would he send masses of troops against American breastworks. This would have interesting consequences.[1]

During the last moments of the Battle of Bunker Hill, the victorious redcoats killed more Americans with their bayonets than with their bullets.

Washington reached Cambridge, Massachusetts, on July 2, 1775. The next day, he inspected the positions outside Boston. What a shock! Instead of the disciplined army he expected, he found fifteen thousand disorganized men living in wooden huts and canvas tents. For weapons,

J. Rogers.

General Sir William Howe, a brilliant officer with wide experience in the European wars, commanded His Majesty's forces in America. From an engraving in Washington Irving's *Life of George Washington.*

they had everything from muskets to blunderbusses, a type of shotgun that looked like a bell, wide in front and narrow behind. Schoolbook pictures of Continentals dressed in smart uniforms are fantasies. Very few soldiers ever had uniforms. The vast majority wore their ordinary clothes—woolen coats, homespun breeches, linen shirts, and leather vests.

Volunteers arrived daily. Warriors of the Stockbridge tribe, Christianized Indians from western Massachusetts, brought their bows and arrows. Fourteen hundred frontiersmen came from western Virginia, Maryland,

General Washington takes charge of American forces during the campaign to drive the British army out of Boston.

and Pennsylvania. These tall, lanky fellows wore buckskin hunting shirts with the motto "Liberty or Death" stitched in front—thus the nickname "shirtmen." Shirts came down to the knees and tied at the waist with a wide leather belt that held a knife and a tomahawk.

The shirtman relied on his rifle. Unlike the musket, this gun had an extra-long barrel with "riflings," spiral grooves cut inside the barrel to make the bullet spin in flight. Although slower to load than a musket, the rifle had greater range and accuracy. A rifle could easily send a bullet two hundred yards. Instead of firing a volley in the general direction of the enemy, each shirtman aimed at a particular target, chosen by himself. Only the best shots joined Washington's army. A schoolteacher watched a Virginia captain choose his company:

He took a board of a foot square and with chalk drew the shape of a moderate nose in the center and nailed it up to a tree at one hundred and fifty yards distance, and those who came nearest the mark with a single ball was to go. But by the first forty or fifty that fired, the nose was all blown out of the board, and by the time the company was up, the board shared the same fate.

Shirtmen gave their rifles pet names like Betsy and Nancy, Hot Lips and Little Darlin'. Not the redcoats. They dreaded these "cursed guns" and the men behind them, "the most fatal widow and orphan makers in the world." Shirtmen were almost impossible to control. When they got bored, they fought drunken brawls. Twice they broke open the Cambridge guardhouse to release friends jailed for fighting.[2]

Washington knew that an army must have discipline. As he put it, "an army without or-der, regularity, and discipline is no better than a commissioned mob." When the Revolu-tion began, however, volunteer units elected their officers. Being neighbors, officers and men already knew each other. That made for friendship, but not discipline. Officers felt un-comfortable ordering friends around, and they resented having to take or-ders from a social equal. Privates refused to salute, ignored commands, and insulted officers. Once a captain, a shoemaker by profession, told a private to fetch a pail of water. "Fetch it yourself Keptin," the private snarled. "I got the last pail." Another time, Washington saw a captain, a former barber, shaving a private outside his tent.[3]

Shirtmen were frontier fighters who wore deerskin hunting shirts and carried rifles. This fellow has the word *Congress* burned into his leather cap. From an old print.

Lack of cleanliness showed lack of discipline of another sort. Since most volunteers were farmers, they were used to relieving themselves in the fields while at work. Now, as soldiers, they avoided the walk to the latrines, particularly at night. Surgeons reported they "set down and ease themselves" anywhere, depositing their "excrement about the fields promiscuously." Moreover, since doing laundry was "women's work," they wore their clothes until dirt ate them away. Rather than bury their garbage, they threw it into the camp streets to rot. Disgusting smells became a normal part of life in the Continental Army.[4]

Washington cracked down—hard. In his efficient way, he began by listing each offense and its penalty. Whipping, as always in colonial America, was the punishment of choice. Although the general wanted to give offenders five hundred lashes, the Continental Congress set the limit at one hundred. Anyhow, he ordered that each morning, after roll call, officers must read their units a long list of rules. No drunkenness! No swearing! No gambling! No brawling! Each man must shave, change his clothes twice a week, and use the latrines.

General Washington, accompanied by his "man," Billy Lee, breaks up a brawl outside Boston. Etching by F. O. C. Darley.

Sometimes these orders had a touch of humor. The order of August 22 declared that, although the general expected soldiers to bathe, they must not dive off the bridge at Cambridge. He explained why. "Many men, lost to all sense of decency and modesty, are running about naked upon the bridge, whilst passengers, and even ladies of the first fashion in the neighborhood, are passing over it, as if they mean to glory in their shame."[5]

Occasionally, the general lost patience. Although usually calm, Washington had an explosive temper. If rubbed the wrong way, he would shout, flail his arms, and stamp his feet. At Cambridge, noisy soldiers gathered outside his window. Unable to concentrate, he ran out and flattened one with his fist. Another time, some shirtmen and New Englanders got into a brawl. Washington leaped onto his horse and sped toward the scene, Billy Lee leading the way. Billy dismounted to lower fence rails, but the general just sailed over his head. Plunging into the crowd, he sprang from the saddle and grabbed two brawny men by the collar. Holding them at arm's length, he lifted them off the ground and shook them so hard their teeth rattled.[6]

These outbursts rattled Washington, too. They frightened him, leaving him trembling and ashamed. It was not "proper," he thought, for one in his position to show such a lack of self-control. The general knew that, to master the army, he first had to master his own hot temper. That took a great deal of willpower, but he succeeded. In doing so, however, he overreacted by surrounding himself with an invisible wall of reserve. Stiff and formal, in public he often wore a sour expression on his face. "Oh!" said a veteran years later, "but you never got a smile out of him."[7]

Washington expected his officers to act the same way. To William Woodford, a colonel in the Continental Army, he gave this advice: "Be easy . . . in your deportment with your [junior] officers, but not too familiar, lest you subject yourself to a want of that respect which is necessary to support a proper command." His nephew, Bushrod Washington, a future justice of the U.S. Supreme Court, heard much the same. "Be courteous to all," said the older man, "but intimate with few, and let those few be well tried before you give them your confidence."[8]

Washington's public appearance of coldness stayed with him throughout the Revolution—no, for the rest of his life. Yet it served a useful purpose. By preventing others from becoming too familiar, it let them know who was in charge. Among close friends, however, he still liked to sit around the table after dinner, drinking wine and laughing at jokes.

While Washington organized his army, refugees poured into British-occupied Boston. In the weeks after Bunker Hill, patriots drove out all the royal governors and took over the colonial governments. Not everybody supported these actions. Historians believe that one in three colonists became loyalists; that is, stayed loyal to King George. Patriots called them Tories, Irish slang for bandits. Fearing these "traitors," they demanded that citizens sign loyalty oaths to the Continental Congress. Refusal brought stiff penalties. Patriots boycotted Tory shopkeepers, doctors, and lawyers. Tory teachers lost their jobs, as did ordinary workers. Each colony passed laws depriving Tories of their civil rights. These laws prevented them from voting, holding office, serving on juries, and using the courts. Tories also paid heavy fines and double taxes.

Meanwhile, outside Boston, Washington spent countless hours at his desk, writing letters and reports. Mount Vernon? How were things going there? Did Martha need anything? He flooded the Continental Congress in Philadelphia with requests for more gunpowder, more blankets, more medical supplies—more everything. When Congress failed to come through, he worked around a problem by trial and error. For example, he attacked the supply shortage by forming a "navy" of fast little ships with daredevil crews. It paid off when *Lee,* an American vessel, captured *Nancy,* a British supply ship loaded with weapons.

Yet weapons were useless without the men to use them. Most of Washington's men had enlisted for only six months. The general urged the Continental Congress to recruit soldiers to serve for the entire war and pay them accordingly. The Continental Congress, however, feared a military dictatorship and turned him down. Now, with winter coming on, shivering men counted the days left in their enlistments, most of which expired on New Year's Day, 1776. Fewer than a third reenlisted, and the army would have fallen apart had Massachusetts and New Hampshire not sent militia units to take their places.

This crisis forced Washington to take a closer look at another source of soldiers. Black minutemen had fought at Lexington and Concord. At Bunker Hill, Peter Salem and Salem Poor held the line to the end. These and other blacks in the army at Boston were not slaves but free men. Humane masters had given some their freedom. Others were born to free parents, or bought out of slavery by other free blacks. Even so, they did not have the right to vote or the guarantees of equal justice enjoyed by the poorest white person.

As a southerner, Washington feared guns in the hands of black people, slave or free. Soon after taking command, he ended black enlistments. Free blacks, however, realized that the war gave them a power they had never had before. They wanted equality. If the patriots denied it to them, they could turn to the British. Virginia's royal governor, Lord Dunmore, had already offered freedom to slaves who left rebel masters to join his "Ethiopian Regiment." Washington became furious. "If the Virginians are wise," he said, "that arch-traitor to the rights of humanity, Lord Dunmore, should be instantly crushed. . . . Otherwise, like a snowball in rolling, his army will get size. . . ."[9]

His Lordship's action brought an important change outside Boston. When free blacks demanded to enlist, Washington gave in. For the first time in his life, he followed the wishes of black people because he had no choice. About five thousand black men served under him during the war, including both freedmen and runaway slaves seeking refuge in the army. Most were wagon drivers, blacksmiths, and pioneers who repaired roads and dug trenches. There were also plenty of fighting men. At Boston, a Tory songster mocked the patriots with a crude racial slur:

> *The rebel clowns, oh! what a sight!*
> *Too awkward was their figure.*
> *'Twas yonder stood a pious white,*
> *And here and there a nigger.*[10]

Meanwhile, patriots had to decide what they were really fighting for. Was it only for the colonists' right to tax themselves and to get rid of the British occupation troops? Or was it for something far greater?

No one did more to help them find the answer than a scruffy little writer for a Philadelphia newspaper. In January 1776, Thomas Paine issued *Common Sense*. This pamphlet became an instant sensation, selling over 100,000 copies by the end of the year. Nearly every colonist either read it or knew what it was about.

Thomas Paine's pamphlet *Common Sense* was an overnight sensation in the colonies. Written in a clear, strong style, it urged Americans to fight for independence instead of knuckling down to British injustice.

Common Sense contained no original ideas—men like John Adams had made all its arguments before. What Paine did was to put into words what many ordinary people had in their minds. He spoke to them not in the language of a lawyer or a man of education, but in words they could easily understand. Not everything Paine said was true, but he made it sound true. For that reason, *Common Sense* is one of history's most effective pieces of propaganda.

In short, biting sentences, Paine condemned King George III, "the Royal Brute of Britain." This "wretch" could hear about the slaughter of innocent people in Boston and then calmly sleep "with their blood upon his soul." His Majesty *was* an arrogant, close-minded man, but no monster. A loyal husband and a loving father, he tried to do "justice" without bloodshed, unless necessary. No matter. Colonists, Paine argued, had nothing to gain, and much to lose, by staying in the British Empire. Being part of Britain cost them fortunes in lost trade with foreign countries and involved them in wars against their will. That must change! "Everything that is right or natural pleads for separation. The blood of the slain, the weeping voice of nature cries, 'TIS TIME TO PART."[11]

Common Sense made good sense to General Washington. Praising its "unanswerable reasoning," he had copies sent to every regiment outside Boston. For those soldiers who could not read, he ordered their comrades to read it to them.[12]

Washington's chief problem, however, was Boston itself. The town occupied a peninsula attached to the mainland by Boston Neck, a narrow strip of land guarded by British gun batteries. For some reason, General Howe had failed to occupy Dorchester Heights on the mainland. Cannons placed up there would make it impossible to hold Boston. Unfortunately, Washington possessed only a few light guns, and they were unable to reach the town. Or so he thought until Henry Knox reminded him that Fort Ticonderoga, which overlooked Lake Champlain in northern New York, had everything he needed.

Henry Knox, twenty-five years old, stood six feet tall in his stockings and weighed 280 pounds. He had owned a bookstore in Boston. When the redcoats first arrived in 1774, he took in a stock of military books for the officers. In his spare time, Knox read the books, especially those on artillery, a subject he loved. A friendly fellow, easy to like, he got his customers to teach him all they knew about cannons. After Lexington and Concord, Knox fled Boston with his wife, Lucy, the daughter of a wealthy Tory. Nobody held his marriage against him, for he was a wizard of artillery. Washington, who knew his reputation, recognized his unique abilities by making him the army's artillery chief.

On December 3, 1775, Knox left Fort Ticonderoga with fifty-nine cannons. Ahead lay three hundred miles of snowy trails, frozen streams, and steep hills. Knox met the chal-

General Henry Knox, formerly a Boston book dealer, was General Washington's chief of artillery.

lenge. He had each gun dismounted and tied to a sledge, a heavy-duty sled drawn by oxen. All went well until they reached the Hudson River at Albany, New York. Finding the ice too thin, Knox dug into his bag of tricks. He ordered holes cut into the ice every few yards. This allowed water to overflow and freeze hard enough to support the sledges. Within six weeks, Washington had all the guns he needed.

He asked Knox to train the six-man gun crews. A cannon worked like a

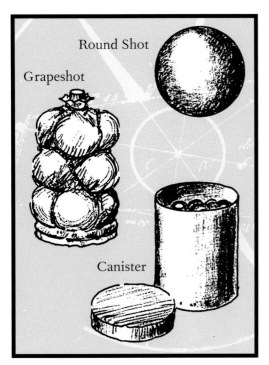

Round Shot

Grapeshot

Canister

Gunners used various types of shot in their cannons during the American Revolution. Each type had its own deadly purpose.

musket but used a larger cartridge made of cloth instead of paper. Gunners fired different "shot" for different purposes. *Round shot* was usually a twelve-pound iron ball that could travel three-quarters of a mile and smash through an earthen wall a yard thick. An exploding *shell* or *bomb* was a hollow round shot filled with gunpowder set off by a fuse. For sheer killing power, however, nothing matched *canister* and *grapeshot*, designed for use against troops in the open. Canister came in a large sheet-metal can filled with musket balls; grape was a canvas bag with lead slugs the size of golf balls. The moment a gun fired, the container burst open and sprayed its contents like shotgun pellets.

Under cover of darkness, Washington sent 5,200 men to Dorchester Heights with cannons, ammunition carts, and hundreds of large wooden barrels—his idea of portable forts. Moving quietly, the heavy wheels wrapped in rags, the men and equipment reached the heights before daybreak. While the gun crews got ready, pioneers filled the barrels with earth and placed them before each gun. If the redcoats came, they would get another Bunker Hill, topped by rolling barrels crashing into their lines of battle.

At dawn on March 5, 1776, Boston awoke to find cannons lining Dorchester Heights. "Good God!" said a stunned General Howe. "These fellows have done more work in one night than I could have made my army do in three months." The British opened fire, but they could not elevate their guns to an angle steep enough to reach the American positions. Although Washington could have blown the town to bits, he did not want to cause unnecessary civilian casualties. Instead, he held his fire, a silent signal that he would allow the British to leave peacefully. Howe understood.[13]

Redcoats began loading equipment and supplies onto their ships. Many Tories, fearing patriot revenge, joined them. There were heartbreaking scenes as relatives hugged each other for the last time, and old people left homes they would never see again. People "pigged aboard"—that is, crowded into every nook and cranny between the ships' decks. Some des-

In this painting, artist Gilbert Stuart portrays General Washington at Dorchester Heights during the last stage of the siege of Boston.

perate men, seeing the end of the world as they had known it, shot themselves. Washington had no sympathy for them. He despised Tories. When told of the suicides, he said coldly, "One or two of them have done what a great many ought to have done long ago, committed suicide. By all accounts, there never existed a more miserable set of human beings than these wretched creatures are now."[14]

On March 17, the sails of 175 ships billowed as they caught the breeze. Gracefully, like a procession of white swans, the fleet headed for Halifax, Nova Scotia, in Canada. Bostonians welcomed their liberators with shouts, laughter, and tears of joy. Washington was everyone's hero. Congress voted him a gold medal. Harvard College gave him an honorary Doctor of Laws degree. Mothers named their newborn sons after him. Ships bore his name. For countless people, he now became the living sym-

General Washington's proclamation to the people of Boston after the British army left their city.

BY HIS EXCELLENCY

George Wafhington, Efq:

Captain-General and Commander in Chief of the Forces of the *Thirteen* United Colonies.

WHEREAS the Miniferial Army have abandoned the Town of BOSTON , and the Forces of the United Colonies, under my Command, are in Poffeffion of the fame :

I HAVE therefore thought it neceffary for the Prefervation of Peace, good Order and Difcipline, to publifh the following ORDERS, that no Perfon offending therein may plead Ignorance as an Excufe for their Mifconduct.

ALL Officers and Soldiers are hereby ordered to live in the ftricteft Peace and Amity with the Inhabitants ; and no Inhabitant, or other Perfon employed in his lawful Bufinefs in the Town, is to be molefted in his Perfon or Property on any Pretence whatever.—If any Officer or Soldier fhall prefume to ftrike, imprifon, or otherwife ill-treat any of the Inhabitants, they may depend on being punifhed with the utmoft Severity.—And if any Officer or Soldier fhall receive any Infult from any of the Inhabitants, he is to feek Redrefs, in a legal Way, and no other.

ANY Non-commiffioned Officer, Soldier, or others under my Command, who fhall be guilty of robbing or plundering in the town, are to be immediately confined, and will be moft rigidly punifhed.—All Officers are therefore ordered to be very vigilant in the Difcovery of fuch offenders, and report their Names, and Crime, to the Commanding Officer in the Town, as foon as may be.

THE Inhabitants, and others, are called upon to make known to the Quarter-Mafter General, or any of his Deputies, all Stores belonging to the Miniferial Army, that may be remaining or fecreted in the Town : Any Perfon or Perfons whatever, that fhall be known to conceal any of the faid Stores, or appropriate them to his or their own Ufe, will be confidered as an Enemy of America, and treated accordingly.

THE Selectmen, and other Magiftrates of the Town, are defired to return to the Commander in Chief, the Names of all or any Perfon or Perfons they may fufpect of being employed as Spies upon the Continental Army, that they may be dealt with accordingly.

ALL Officers of the Continental Army, are enjoined to affift the Civil Magiftrates in the Execution of their Duty, and to promote Peace and good order.—They are to prevent, as much as poffible, the Soldiers from frequenting Tippling Houfes, and ftrolling from their Pofts.—Particular Notice will be taken of fuch Officers as are inattentive and remifs in their Duty ; and on the contrary, fuch only who are active and vigilant, will be entitled to future Favor and Promotion.

GIVEN under my Hand at Head-Quarters in Cambridge, this Twenty-firft Day of March, 1776.

GEORGE WASHINGTON

bol of the American cause. Newspapers started calling him "the Father of His Country."

With the departure of Howe's fleet, no redcoat remained in the thirteen colonies. For patriots, this was the best of times—the time of hope. The war was over! Britain must admit defeat! Already the Continental Congress was thinking about issuing a Declaration of Independence. During those happy days, few imagined the ordeal that lay ahead. Washington knew better.

Back in London, George III saw the loss of Boston as a setback, not a defeat. His Majesty vowed to do anything, pay any price, to crush the rebellion in the colonies. Arm the Tories and turn them loose! Send Indians to raid frontier settlements! Hang all traitors!

King George and his advisers unrolled their maps. Where should they strike? The answer leaped out at them: New York City. Militarily, this was the most valuable place in the colonies. New York lay at the mouth to the Hudson River. The side that held the city could control the river's length and thus the main link between the colonies and Canada. A major trading center with close ties to Britain, New York was also home to thousands of Tories. British forces could count on them for information, supplies, and fighting men.

His Majesty chose Sir William Howe and his elder brother, Admiral Lord Richard Howe, to lead the campaign of 1776. Known as "Black Dick," the admiral was a brilliant seaman who had often fought the French. Sailors worshiped him. "Give us Black Dick," they cried, "and we fear nothing." If anyone could defeat the rebels, it was the Howe brothers, the king thought.[15]

Even before the fall of Boston, His Majesty had begun to prepare for a full-scale war. No navy had more warships than his. Now vessels stationed as far away as Africa and India got orders to return to their home ports. Recruiters emptied the jails and offered bounties to lure men into the army. When enlistments still fell short, the king turned to Germany.

Back then, Germany was not one country, but a crazy quilt of three-hundred-odd states of various sizes. While some states were larger than Virginia, many others were smaller than a New England parish. Yet each had its own ruler, government, and army. Since the smaller states were also poor, their princes raised cash by renting soldiers to foreign countries; they called it *Blutgeld*—blood money. Like the redcoats, poor Germans "took their skin into the market" for the bounty. The majority, however, were abducted by club-swinging army patrols. Nobody was safe. Farmers in their fields, shopkeepers behind their counters, all awoke in handcuffs and with bumps on their heads. Patrols broke into homes, even took churchgoers after Sunday services. Grieving families watched them go, but no tears or wailing could bring them back. In effect, their menfolk had become soldier-slaves.

During training, they got used to wearing heavy blue or green woolen uniforms and tall leather hats that made them seem like giants. Soldiers wore thick handlebar mustaches blackened with boot polish. They grew their hair long and braided it into pigtails made so stiff with hog fat that they stuck "straight back like the handle of an iron skillet."[16] Sergeants beat them regularly to drill them into tough, obedient, soldiers skilled at killing. King George paid the equivalent of $35 a year per man. For three men wounded in action, their prince received an extra $35, the same as for a dead man; the soldier's family got nothing. In all, 29,875 Germans fought for Britain. Nearly half, 12,562 men, never returned home. Because the majority came from the state of Hesse, all the German soldiers hired during the Revolutionary War were called Hessians.

Spies sent Washington copies of Britain's treaties with the German princes. Logic told him the rest. A month after taking Boston, he sent General Charles Lee to prepare New York City's defenses. Lee was a strange man who liked dogs better than people; he said they were gentler and more loyal than human beings. Having served in the British and Polish armies, he had more battlefield experience than any other American officer.

In April 1776, New York City covered a square mile of built-up area at the southern tip of Manhattan Island, between the Hudson and East Rivers. The rest of the island was a jumble of rolling hills, tangled woods, and fields dotted with farms and orchards. Visitors found the city's inhabitants rude and crude. "There is no modesty, no attention to one another," one reported. "They are very loud, very fast, and . . . if

A portrait of a Hessian soldier with his greased pigtail. Mostly poor men abducted into the army by their rulers, the Hessians made excellent soldiers.

they ask you a question, before you can utter three words of your answer they will break out upon you again, and talk away." Another visitor found New Yorkers "so stuck up." Even so, they were fascinating people, particularly "the womenfolk, who are almost all good-looking."[17]

General Lee faced a difficult task. Deep water encircles Manhattan Island, making a fine harbor where ships can come in close and drop anchor. Thus troops could land anywhere along the shore. Nevertheless, Lee did the best he could. Every street leading from the water sprouted a barricade. Work parties placed cannons along the Hudson shore and on the bluffs overlooking the East River near Brooklyn, which then was a tiny village on Long Island. Fort Washington rose on a hill commanding the Hudson at the island's northern end; today this area is called Washington Heights. Directly across the river he built Fort Lee, now the town Fort Lee on the New Jersey side of the George Washington Bridge. These forts were simple affairs, with earthen walls eight feet high and wooden platforms for the guns.

General Charles Lee liked dogs better than people.

Washington reached New York early in June with his main army. Tories greeted the troops with jeers and balls of horse manure. The troops, aided by patriot mobs, answered in kind. Fists flew. Tar bubbled and hissed. Tories "rode the rails," an ordeal where the victim straddled a wooden rail resting on the shoulders of four men, two in front and two in back. In this painful position, patriots carried Tories to Washington's headquarters at City Hall. Judge Thomas Jones watched as the general and his aides "appeared at the windows [and] raised their hats" in approval.[18] Government officials loyal to the king had either fled or been thrown into jail by Washington's troops.

Washington soon learned of a Tory plot to kill him and blow up his

Patriots often terrorized Tories, people loyal to King George III. Here we see them riding a Tory on a rail, a painful ordeal.

gunpowder supply. The plot leaders, among them the mayor, escaped in the nick of time. Sergeant Thomas Hickey did not. On June 28, Hickey met death on a gallows set up in Bowery Lane before thousands of on-lookers. Washington intended the execution as a warning to would-be traitors. To block future attempts on his life, Congress ordered him to form the Washington Life Guard, a bodyguard made up men from all thirteen colonies. The guard's flag bore its motto: "Conquer or Die."

Next morning, at sunrise, Private Daniel McCurtin looked toward the Lower Bay from his rooftop post. He shook his head, doubting his own eyes. "I spied as I peeped out the bay something resembling a wood of pine trees trimmed. . . . In about ten minutes, the whole bay was full of shipping as ever it could be. I declare that I thought all London was afloat."[19]

Sir William Howe had arrived from Halifax with 130 ships. During the next two weeks, Black Dick brought another 295 ships. The brothers' combined fleets numbered 52 warships carrying 1,200 heavy cannons. The rest were supply vessels and transports jammed with 34,000 redcoats and Hessians. It was the largest military force ever sent from the British Isles.

The invaders camped on Staten Island to recover from their rough voyage. On July 6, sounds of cheering and gunfire reached them from New York. Before long, a spy reported that Washington's men were celebrating the Declaration of Independence, approved by the Continental Congress two days earlier.

The Declaration of Independence is more than an official announcement of the colonies' breakaway from the British Empire. Thomas Jefferson, its author, gave most of its space to explaining the colonies' grievances against the mother country. Nowadays, most Americans know little and care less about these. The part that concerns them is the second paragraph.

There Jefferson gives a ringing defense of liberty: "We hold these truths to be self-evident: That all men are created equal; that they are endowed by their Creator with certain unalienable rights; that among these are life, liberty, and the pursuit of happiness." Governments, he continues, exist only to protect those rights, which come from God and cannot be given or taken away. When a government fails in its duty, it loses its authority. The people then have the right to change it, by force if necessary, and form a new one to protect their rights.

The flag of Washington's Life Guards, a special unit sworn to protect the general with their lives. Formed after the failure of Thomas Hickey's plan to kidnap Washington, the unit's motto was "Conquer or Die."

These ideas would make the Declaration of Independence a rallying cry for people everywhere. Jefferson wanted to spread the ideas of liberty worldwide. Yet he had another, more immediate, purpose. People like him, open rebels against King George, were marked men. If Britain crushed the rebellion, they would swing from a gallows. Jefferson did not want that to happen. In addition, he knew that the colonies did not love each other, nor did the various people within each colony. Jealousy and resentment meant weakness. By appealing to "self-evident" truths, Jefferson hoped to overcome these divisions. Instead of sharing disunity, rich and poor, small farmers and large plantation owners, could share common beliefs in a common cause.

By "men," however, Jefferson meant free white men. He did not say that slaves, free blacks, and Native Americans had unalienable rights. Nor did he mention women of any color. Women were supposed to be weaker and less intelligent than men; they belonged at home with their children, not following careers or participating in government. Those left out of the Declaration of Independence would have to wait until the twentieth cen-

A New York crowd toppled King George III's statue in July 1776. Moments earlier, General Washington had officers read the Declaration of Independence to their men.

tury to begin realizing its promise of "life, liberty, and the pursuit of happiness."

Each regiment formed on its parade ground to hear an officer read it loudly and clearly, as the general ordered. The soldiers answered with shots fired into the air and shouts of "huzza," the eighteenth-century version of "hurrah" and "hurray." Dismissed, hundreds headed for Bowling Green near the Battery. There they joined patriotic civilians in front of a lead statue of King George III on horseback. They pulled the statue off its pedestal, broke it in pieces, and had the lead molded into 42,000 musket balls.

Meanwhile, redcoats and Hessians drilled constantly. Working feverishly in the blistering heat, sailors unloaded flat-bottomed landing craft from the supply ships. The summer of 1776 was the hottest ever in New York. On the night of August 21, a storm brought temporary relief.

Next morning, scores of landing craft drew away from Staten Island. Escorted by warships, they made for Gravesend Bay on the western shore of Long Island. As the soldiers splashed ashore, they were in good spirits. A British officer reported his men "as merry as in a Holiday," pausing only to pick apples from trees along the way.[20]

Washington realized that Howe meant to overrun his positions before crossing the East River to Manhattan. His army occupied two lines of breastworks. Its main line ran along Brooklyn Heights, parallel to the East River. A second line, a mile inland from Brooklyn Heights, crowned a wooded ridge called the

Barges loaded with redcoats and Hessians, supported by British warships, head for Long Island.

Heights of Guan. Although Washington had 13,000 men to Howe's 17,000, being dug in made up for the enemy's superior numbers. Still, he worried. His men had never faced a bayonet charge in line of battle. Since they had never trained with the bayonet, the thought of fighting with it

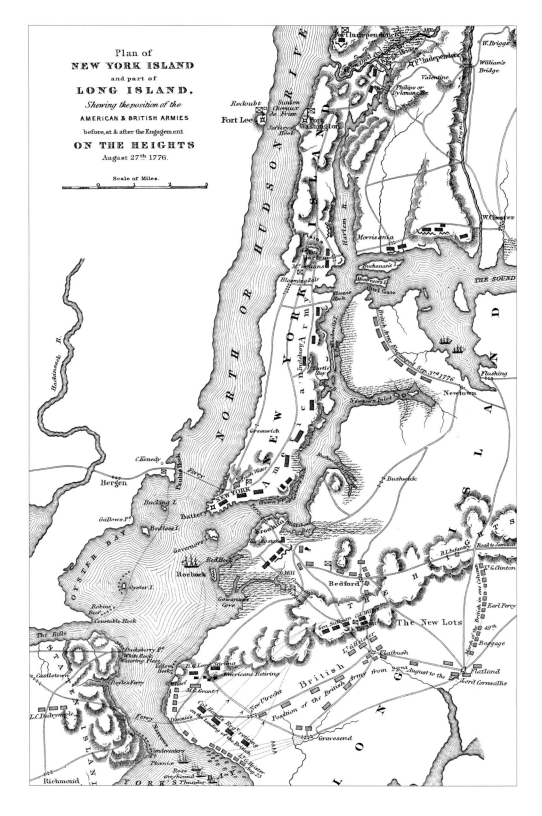

Plan of
NEW YORK ISLAND
and part of
LONG ISLAND,
Shewing the position of the
AMERICAN & BRITISH ARMIES
before, at & after the Engagement
ON THE HEIGHTS
August 27th 1776.

Scale of Miles.

terrified them. Should Howe drive them out of their trenches, Washington feared a disaster.

Howe took four days to get into striking position. His patrols constantly "felt"—tested—Washington's defenses, which made the British furious. Americans, they found, did not fight fair. Americans did not meet them in the open, face to face, like real soldiers. Instead, they sniped from behind trees, and some shot rusty nails instead of musket balls. Redcoats swore to take no prisoners and urged the Hessians to do the same. The American "fiends" tortured captives, they said. Why, they might burn Hessians alive, even eat them. Sullen Hessians sat around campfires, sharpening their bayonets.

Washington now made a serious mistake. Four narrow roads cut across the defense line that ran along the Heights of Guan. Three of the roads had strong guard units at the point where they came over the high ground. The fourth road, which came through Bedford Pass between two hills, did not. Bedford Pass lay on the American left "flank"; this is, on the Continental Army's far left side. An experienced general would have noticed the weakness there and sent reinforcements. Washington, however, still had a lot to learn about warfare. For some reason, he failed to inspect Bedford Pass. Only five cavalrymen were posted at this vital spot, and they often got drunk at night.

On the afternoon of August 26, Tory scouts sent Howe a message. Bedford Pass was poorly protected! At once, a plan formed in the British general's mind. Come evening, Sir Henry Clinton and Lord Cornwallis would leave camp with 10,000 men and fourteen cannons in a two-mile column. Guided by Tories, it must get through the pass before daybreak on August 27. As the column moved, the rest of the British army would hold the attention of the American right flank (British left) with light attacks. At Clinton's signal, both his and Howe's forces would charge at once, smashing the Americans' front and rear. This would allow Howe to accomplish two goals. First, he would smash the Continental Army. Second, he would clear Brooklyn Heights of American cannons and cross the East River to Manhattan by boat.

The plan worked like a charm. An advance party found the cavalrymen fast asleep; their knives put them to rest forever. At daybreak, redcoats and Hessians opened fire on the American right. The Americans held their ground, not realizing their true danger. Suddenly, fourteen cannons roared from behind. Clinton's signal!

Solid shot shattered trees, sending deadly splinters flying in all directions. Other cannonballs skipped and rolled along the ground for hundreds of feet, hitting anyone in their path. Canister and grapeshot whizzed through the air like swarms of angry hornets. Redcoats and Hessians came on, grim and silent, in lines of battle tipped with steel. At thirty paces, they halted, fired a volley, leveled their bayonets, and charged. In their fury, they pinned Americans to trees with their bayonets. Terrified Americans fell to their knees, begging for mercy. Few received it.

Americans had never faced disciplined troops on an open battlefield. Attacked from two directions, they simply did not know what to do.

During the Battle of Long Island in August 1776, British troops slipped behind the American lines. Pressed from the front and rear, they fled across Gowanus Creek, where many drowned.

Everything seemed strange and terrible. The noise was awful. Officers' shouted commands mingled with the screams of the wounded. Fear set men's hearts pounding, tied their guts in knots, and gave them the shakes. It made some poor fellows urinate in their pants or lose control of their bowels. Others just stood in place, frozen with fear, weeping like children. "O doleful! doleful! doleful!" Private Philip Fithian scribbled in his diary. "Blood! Carnage! Fire!"[21]

Private Joseph Plumb Martin, sixteen years old, had recently joined a Connecticut regiment. When the battle began, his unit rushed forward. Nearing the action, Martin reported, "I saw a lieutenant who appeared to have feelings not very enviable . . . for he ran around the men of his company, sniveling and blubbering. . . . A fine soldier you are, I thought; a fine officer, an exemplary man for young soldiers!"[22]

That lieutenant was the rule, not the exception. Stunned by the twin assaults, the Americans panicked. Entire regiments threw down their muskets and ran toward Brooklyn Heights. Hundreds never made it. Pursued by those awful bayonets, they plunged into the marshes bordering Gowanus Creek. Private Martin saw survivors come out "looking like water rats." Many drowned or went under riddled with musket balls.[23]

Washington sat on a gray horse, watching the disaster from Brooklyn Heights, deciding what to do. "Great God!" he cried, wringing his hands. "What must my brave boys suffer today!" Dismounting, he went among the fleeing troops to restore order.[24]

When they kept running, he lost his temper. Drawing two pistols, he ordered them to halt—or else. Private Hezekiah Munsell swore the general had murder in his eyes. Munsell heard him shout, "If I see any man turn his back today, I will shoot him through. . . . I will not ask any man to go further than I do. I will fight as long as I have a leg or an arm." Then Washington suddenly changed his tune. Something told him that two pistols would not stop this panic. He had to appeal to the soldiers' better nature—to their pride and idealism. "Quit yourselves like men, like soldiers," he shouted, "for all that is worth living for is at stake."[25] The panic subsided.

Howe, not Washington, saved the day for the Americans. Sensing victory, his men drove ahead. Although Howe wanted to destroy the Conti-

General Washington supervised the escape of the Continental Army after its defeat in the Battle of Long Island.

nental Army, too, those breastworks on Brooklyn Heights scared him. He halted the advance a few hundred yards from the breastworks. Officers protested—repeatedly. Howe gave the order—repeatedly. Dig in, set up cannons, and blast the rebels from a safe distance! True, that would take time, but it seemed better than another Bunker Hill. Washington lost nearly a thousand men killed and captured; Howe had sixty-one killed. The Englishman thought that a good day's work.

In human terms, all battles end the same way, whatever the war. Though exhausted, few in either army slept soundly that night. Those out on patrol had waking nightmares. Wherever they turned, they saw bodies and bits of bodies lying thick on the ground. "O friend," a Hessian wrote home, "that was a terrible sight when I went . . . among the dead who covered the battlefield, most of them in tatters and shot to pieces." The place reeked with the slaughterhouse smell of split-open corpses, the roast-meat smell of men burned to death in tall grass, and the musty smell of hair matted with blood. Yet the dead were lucky, if they went quickly. For the wounded, the worst torment lay ahead.[26]

Eighteenth-century soldiers had no first-aid kits or training. Those with minor wounds, known as the "walking wounded," went to a field hospital under their own power. The seriously wounded waited until the drummers came with stretchers, which might take many hours. This meant that those who might have survived if treated promptly, died of loss of blood. A field hospital was anything with a roof: tents, churches, farmhouses, barns, stables. Patients lay on the bare floors, waiting their turn on the operating tables. One surgeon described his own hospital as a "dirty, stinking place" crammed with wounded men "& many cursing & swearing."[27]

Soldiers feared surgeons more than anything. Painkillers did not exist until the 1840s. Until then, the surgeon's assistants lay the patient on a table and put a bullet between his teeth; "biting the bullet" would keep him from biting off his tongue during the operation. Then, while they held him down, the cutting and sawing began.

There was only one remedy for a serious leg or arm wound: amputation. The surgeon worked quickly, deaf to his patient's screams. An able surgeon could remove a limb in twenty minutes. He then tied the blood vessels and sewed the skin flaps around the stump. One patient in nine died of shock during surgery and of infection later. There were no antibiotics. Since nobody knew that dirt carries germs, and germs cause infection, surgeons saw no need to wash themselves or their instruments. The surgeon washed his hands after operating, not before. If he dropped an instrument, he wiped it on his leather apron and kept working; he used the same in-

The only treatment for a bullet wound in the arm or leg was to amputate the limb to prevent blood poisoning. The man shown here seems to be taking it calmly. Yet, we know, patients often died of the shock and pain.

strument on every patient. Bandages might be anything from linen bed-sheets torn into strips to old rags. Those with chest or stomach wounds had no chance of survival. Surgeons left them to die without treatment.

Luckily, another storm prevented Black Dick's fleet from sailing up the East River. Washington used the opportunity to order a fleet of small boats to cross from Manhattan. Easier to handle than heavy warships, they stood off Brooklyn Landing, a flight of stone steps leading to the riverbank. On the night of August 29–30, amid a swirling fog, they snatched the army from under the noses of enemy lookouts posted nearby. A Tory lady saw them and sent her slave to warn the British general. On the way, he met a Hessian officer who barely understood a word of English. The Hessian arrested him as a rebel spy, so word did not get through to Howe.

For two weeks, Washington rested his troops while Howe made his plans. Geography and numbers favored the invader. Washington lacked the men to defend the entire Manhattan shoreline. The Englishman, backed by the fleet, could land wherever he chose. He decided to strike twin blows from Long Island and Staten Island.

In the early hours of September 15, Private Martin stood guard at Kip's Bay on the East River, at the foot of what is today East 34th Street, a few blocks south of the United Nations. Like the other regiments there, his unit held a line of shallow ditches without breastworks. Clouds hid the moon and stars. On the half hour, sentries called to one another, "All is well." The youngster's heart skipped a beat when a voice came from the pitch-blackness of the river: "We will alter your tune before tomorrow night."[28]

Sunrise revealed five warships with masts tall as church steeples. They were so close to shore that the Americans could read the names painted on their bows. The largest ships, *Phoenix* and *Roebuck*, each carried forty guns. Like hungry sea monsters, the black guns had red circles painted around their mouths. As Private Martin stared, wide-eyed, eighty-four barges full of soldiers set out from the Long Island side of the East River. He likened their red and green uniforms to "a large clover field in full bloom."[29]

The enemy did not send bouquets of flowers. Tongues of flame lashed out from the warships' sides. "I thought my head would go with the sound," Private Martin wrote later. "I made a frog's leap for the ditch and lay as still as I possibly could." Although he tried to make himself small, he felt big as a barn door. Cannonballs plowed into the ditches, throwing earth and men into the air. Any American still able to run did just that.[30]

Washington heard the guns and hurried toward the sound. At a farm where Grand Central Terminal now stands on East 42nd Street, he found the survivors hightailing it, the enemy close behind. "Take the wall!" he shouted, pointing to a field surrounded by a low stone wall. "Take the cornfield!" Nobody obeyed. The men just whirled past him like a herd of stampeding cattle.[31]

What followed became a legend in the Continental Army. Digging his spurs into his horse's sides, Washington caught up to the fugitives in the rocky field where the New York City Public Library stands today at 42nd Street and Fifth Avenue. His face flushed with anger, he threw his hat on the ground and cursed them as cowards. "Good God," he bellowed, "are these the men with which I am to defend America?" Then he drew his pistols and pulled the triggers, but they jammed. That did it! Washington plunged into the crowd, lashing anyone, officers and soldiers alike, within reach of his riding whip. The stampede continued.[32]

Oncoming redcoats saw a lone figure on a gray horse. He did not seem to notice them. He just sat motionless, as if stunned, his chin on his chest. Bullets whined close to his head, but he ignored them. Washington's anger had spent itself, numbing him physically and emotionally. General Nathanael Greene, an aide, thought "he sought death rather than life." Another aide, whose name is lost to history, sensed his mood and rode to his side. The aide took the bridle from his hand and led him away. Washington did not seem to know what was happening or where he was going.[33]

While one group of invaders drove across Manhattan from the East River to the Hudson, others landed at the Battery—an old fort near the southern tip of Manhattan Island—and moved inland. In the confusion, they lost touch with the Americans, who only stopped running when they reached the breastworks on Harlem Heights, four miles to the north.

Washington awoke next morning, September 16, full of fight. Like their commander, the troops had also recovered; indeed, they were angry with themselves for their poor performance. They wanted revenge.

GEORGE WASHINGTON

Their chance came later that morning. An American patrol met a detachment of the 42nd Highlanders, Scottish troops wearing kilts and bearskin hats. Both sides opened fire. Washington sent in more men; more British troops came up, too. A savage fight erupted near where, today, Columbia University stands at 116th Street and Broadway. After five hours, the British decided they had enough. Although Washington called the

At the Battle of Harlem Heights, September 16, 1776, Washington's soldiers forced the enemy to retreat for the first time in open battle. Here we see them fighting the 42nd Highlanders, a crack unit from Scotland.

fight a "brisk little skirmish," he knew it was more than that. For the first time, Americans had made British regulars turn tail in open battle. His men, he realized, lacked training, not courage. Having whipped the redcoats at Harlem Heights, they might whip them anywhere.

General Howe did not enjoy New York City for long. In the early hours of September 21, a fire began in the Fighting Cocks Tavern on the site of the World Trade Center towers today. Moments later, guards on Harlem Heights gasped in wonder. Private Alexander Grayson saw a fiery glow expand until "the heavens appeared in flames." Driven by a brisk sea breeze, the flames leaped out of control. Trinity Church, the city's tallest building, stood at the head of Wall Street, a few blocks from the city slave market. Within minutes of catching fire, its wooden steeple collapsed in a cloud of hot cinders. The blaze destroyed 493 buildings, or more than one-fifth of New York.[34]

Howe's troops, sent to fight the fire, killed anyone who looked as if they might have had a hand in setting the blaze. An officer saw redcoats knock down a man caught with a torch and fling him into a burning building. Sailors caught another fellow cutting the handles off water buckets. They killed him, then hung him by the feet from a signpost. Among those arrested on suspicion of arson was a "teacher" named Nathan Hale. During questioning, he confessed that Washington had sent him on a spying mission. The rules of war left the British general no choice but to hang him. Next day, Hale spoke his last words from the gallows: "I only regret that I have but one life to lose for my country." As a prank, redcoats put a sign beside the dangling corpse. It read: GEORGE WASHINGTON.[35]

Historians do not know who set the fire, or why. Although Washington denied any responsibility, he was glad to see Tory property burn. Besides, with much of the city in ruins, the enemy would have to slow its advance—at least for a short time. As Washington watched the fire from Harlem Heights, he told aides: "Providence, or some good honest fellow, has done more for us than we were disposed to do for ourselves."[36] Within a year, the city rose from its ashes. As patriots fled Tory revenge, Tories from outside rushed to take their places. In time, New York became the capital of Tory America.

For nearly a month after the fire, Howe prepared his next move. On October 12, he sent ships up the East River into Long Island Sound. By nightfall, they had landed two regiments of redcoats in the Bronx, and more were coming. Washington knew what that meant: Howe meant to trap him on Manhattan Island. To avoid that, he left 2,800 men at Fort Washington to cover his retreat and withdrew to the mainland—to the Bronx. Howe caught up with him at White Plains on October 27. After a fierce fight, Washington escaped by crossing the Hudson River into New Jersey. Howe returned to New York and stormed Fort Washington on November 14, capturing the garrison. Two days later, Lord Cornwallis ferried troops across the Hudson to surprise Fort Lee. The defenders fled with only minutes to spare, leaving tons of precious equipment. Washington could only continue his retreat.

. . .

Artist Thomas Davies painted this watercolor of British troops climbing the Palisades to capture the American outpost at Fort Lee, New Jersey.

The British now held Manhattan Island and a large part of the countryside to its north and east. They held Staten Island and Long Island, including Brooklyn.

And the rebels—what of them? Nothing seemed to be going right for Washington and his men. Pouring rain turned New Jersey's roads into swamps. From sunrise until well past midnight, bone-weary men slogged through cold, slippery mud that sucked the shoes off their feet. When they finally lay down, it was on the bare ground. Always hungry, they ate anything. Private Martin once marched a whole day on a handful of walnuts, six turnips, and a swig of whiskey; another time, a sheep's head "was all the provisions I had for two or three days."[37]

As rebel resistance crumbled, each day hundreds of civilians rushed to British army units to swear allegiance to King George. Tories took revenge on their patriot neighbors with tar, feathers, and clubs. Redcoats and Hessians had their own brand of revenge. These poor men, particularly the Hessians, had never seen such prosperity as in New Jersey. Eager for their "share," they stole whatever they could carry and ruined the rest. Although Cornwallis forbade looting, he did little to prevent it. He hoped it would provoke Washington into turning and fighting a major battle. Then he would crush the Continental army, ending the war by Christmas.

Washington refused to take the bait. He had grown a lot, both as a man and a soldier, in the last eighteen months. Defeat had taught him to change his strategy and tactics. Strategy is a commander's total plan, tactics the way he fights each battle. Washington built his strategy around one word: survival. The British, he believed, could capture every town and still lose the war. The war was not about towns and territory, but people. While its army survived, the Revolution lived. "Our side of the war should be defensive," he wrote the Continental Congress. The Americans should "avoid a general action," an all-out battle, and "protract the war"; that is, drag it out until the enemy grew weary. Washington's tactics followed from his strategy. He meant to dodge and weave, striking only if he had the upper hand.[38]

Yet a protracted war seemed unlikely when Washington reached Tren-

When British forces invaded New Jersey, they drove people out of their homes and stole whatever they could carry.

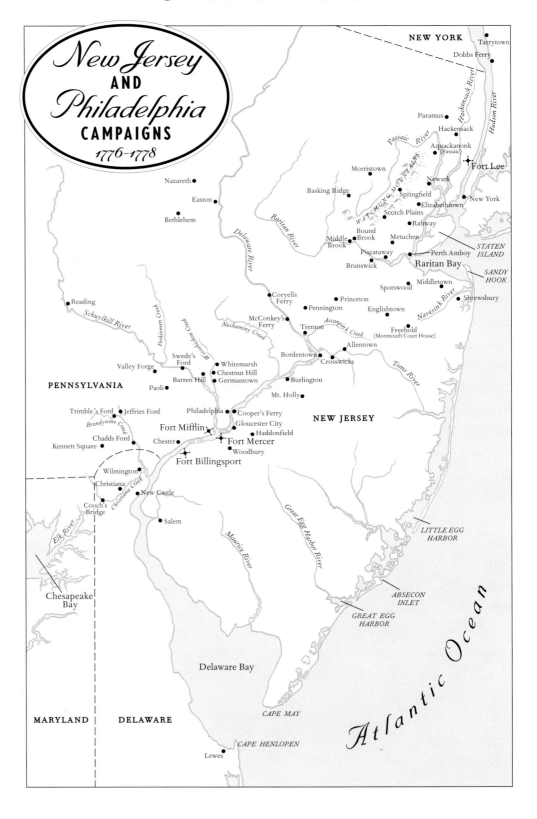

New Jersey AND Philadelphia CAMPAIGNS 1776–1778

NEW YORK

Tarrytown

Dobbs Ferry

Paramus

Hackensack

Aquackanonk (Passaic)

Morristown

Fort Lee

Newark

Basking Ridge

Springfield

Elizabethtown

New York

Scotch Plains

STATEN ISLAND

Nazareth

Rahway

Easton

Bound Brook

Metuchen

Middle Brook

Bethlehem

Piscataway

Perth Amboy

SANDY HOOK

Brunswick

Raritan Bay

Spotswood

Middletown

Reading

Coryell's Ferry

Princeton

Englishtown

Shrewsbury

Pennington

McConkey's Ferry

Trenton

Freehold (Monmouth Court House)

Swede's Ford

Whitemarsh

Bordentown

Allentown

Valley Forge

Chestnut Hill

Crosswicks

PENNSYLVANIA

Barren Hill

Germantown

Paoli

Burlington

Mt. Holly

Trimble's Ford

Jeffries Ford

Philadelphia

Cooper's Ferry

NEW JERSEY

Fort Mifflin

Gloucester City

Chadds Ford

Chester

Haddonfield

Fort Mercer

Kennett Square

Woodbury

Fort Billingsport

Wilmington

Christiana

New Castle

Cooch's Bridge

Salem

LITTLE EGG HARBOR

Chesapeake Bay

ABSECON INLET

GREAT EGG HARBOR

MARYLAND

DELAWARE

Delaware Bay

CAPE MAY

Atlantic Ocean

CAPE HENLOPEN

Lewes

Hackensack River

Hudson River

Passaic River

WATCHUNG MOUNTAINS

Raritan River

Delaware River

Navesink River

Toms River

Schuylkill River

Perkiomen Creek

Wissahickon Creek

Neshaminy Creek

Assanpink Creek

Brandywine Creek

Christiana Creek

Elk River

Maurice River

Great Egg Harbor River

ton, a village on the east bank of the Delaware River. On the night of December 7, he crossed his troops into Pennsylvania in open boats gathered from the river towns. Bonfires guided the rowers to the landing sites. Once ashore, shadowy figures shuffled past the leaping fires for a moment, then vanished into the darkness. Washington watched the scene on horseback. Clearly his army, now numbering only 3,500, was steadily dwindling. Men were defecting every day, or dropping out from hunger, sickness, and exhaustion. "I think the game is pretty near up," he wrote his brother Jack.[39]

General Howe thought so, too. With the rebels facing ruin, he saw no reason for a winter campaign. Let the cold do the fighting for him! Come spring, he would easily roll over any survivors. Besides, he wanted to enjoy the Christmas season and reorganize his army in New York. So, a few days after Washington reached Pennsylvania, Howe ordered Cornwallis to set up a chain of outposts across New Jersey and return to New York with his troops. The Englishman had ignored an ancient rule of war: Know your enemy. He did not know the man who had risen from a sickbed twenty-one years earlier to fight beside Edward Braddock. By halting the chase, Howe gave Washington the opening he needed. Washington could now launch a surprise attack that he hoped would revive the patriot cause.

One of Washington's best spies, John Honeyman, had recently sold some cattle in Trenton, the main Hessian outpost on the Delaware River. Honeyman brought amazing news. The Hessians planned to celebrate Christmas in style, with parties and whiskey—lots of whiskey! Their commander, Colonel Johann Rall, had no fear of a surprise attack. If anything, Rall welcomed the chance for action. "Let them come!" he blustered. "We'll [go] at them with the bayonet!"[40]

Washington decided to strike Trenton on Christmas night, December 25–26, while the Hessians slept off their hangovers. Attacking was a big gamble, he knew, but worth taking anyhow. Success would breathe life into the Revolution. Failure would only hasten the inevitable end. Others might beg King George's pardon. Not him. Passing his hand over his throat, he said: "My neck does not feel as though it was made for a halter [noose.]" If necessary, he promised to lead those who would go with him into the wild country west of the Allegheny Mountains and fight to the last man.[41]

At sundown on Christmas Day, Washington marched 2,400 men to McKonkey's Ferry on the Pennsylvania side of the Delaware River, where boats waited for them. Washington knew what the next couple of hours meant for his country; he chose "Liberty or Death" as the password.

Freezing rain cloaked the trees, turning leafless branches into skeletons glistening in the pale moonlight. As it began to snow, the temperature fell, and passing soldiers noticed that Washington's nose had turned a bright cherry red. They grumbled, as soldiers always do at such times. But it was good-natured grumbling. Although miserable and homesick, they knew what they were fighting for. Colonel John Fitzgerald, a member of Washington's staff, captured the moment in his diary:

> *Christmas.* 6 P.M.—It is fearfully cold and raw and a snowstorm setting in. The wind is northeast and beats in the faces of the men. It will be a terrible night for the soldiers who have no shoes. Some of them have tied old rags around their feet; others are barefoot, but I have not heard a man complain. They are ready to suffer any hardship and die rather than give up their liberty.[42]

At 11:00 P.M., the rowers shoved off. Washington had been in a similar situation before, on a raft crossing the Allegheny River. The wind howled. Windblown snowflakes stung men's faces. Blocks of ice ground against the boats' sides. Boats nearly tipped over in the swift current. Henry Knox rode in his chief's boat. The big man sat to one side in the rear, throwing it off balance. Washington turned and shouted: "Shift your tail, Knox, and trim the boat." The rowers smiled grimly.[43]

By 3:00 A.M., December 26, everyone was ashore. The weather had not improved, but Washington meant to fight no matter what happened. He divided the army into two columns and set off for Trenton ten miles to the north. At 8:00 A.M. sharp, his soldiers struck from two directions at once. The attack took the Hessians by total surprise. Sentries ran from their posts shouting, *"Der Feind! Der Feind! Heraus! Heraus!"*—"The Enemy! The Enemy! Turn out! Turn out!"[44]

Their comrades, many with thumping headaches, awoke to the sound of gunfire. Although some recovered and put up a brave fight, it was too little too late. Before long, they had to call it quits. Twenty-two Hessians lay dead, including Colonel Rall, and 948 surrendered; 2 Americans died. Washington was thrilled. "This is a glorious day for our country," he told an aide, grinning from ear to ear.[45]

Trenton was both a military and a psychological victory. Washington advertised the victories in a way that spoke louder than any words. First, he returned the Hessian loot—all twenty-one wagon loads of it—to the local farmers and townspeople. This earned their trust by proving he could defend them. Next, he marched his prisoners through Philadelphia.

In a desperate effort to save the American cause, on Christmas night, 1776, George Washington led his army across the Delaware River to attack a Hessian force at Trenton, New Jersey. This famous painting, by German artist Emanuel Leutze, was done in the 1850s, long after the event.

George Washington leads his troops into action against the Hessians at Trenton. As always, the general was always in the thick of the fight, where the danger was greatest. An engraving based on a painting by Edward L. Henry.

Angry people lined the city's streets. "When we came directly in front of them, they looked sharply at us," a Hessian officer wrote. "The old women howled dreadfully and wanted to throttle us all because we had come to America to rob them of their freedom."[46] Prisoners had no idea that Washington had ordered their guards to keep them safe. Nevertheless, he put them through this abuse to make a vital point. By seeing the dreaded Hessians not as supermen, but merely as men, people would fear them less. Although shaken, the Hessians also learned something. Americans were not savages, but people fighting for dearly held beliefs. Nor did they eat a single prisoner.

Washington wanted to attack other outposts in New Jersey before winter arrived in full force. That, too, was a gamble. With enlistments due to expire at midnight, December 31, he had to persuade the troops to sign up again. If he failed, he would lose his army without the enemy having fired a shot.

Washington ordered the troops to line up by regiments. He faced them on horseback, his jaw set as if frozen in place. He spoke formally, without emotion, of the victory at Trenton, saying he hoped they would reenlist for another crack at the enemy. When he finished, drumrolls invited them to step forward to sign the enlistment papers.

The troops stood at attention, staring straight ahead. Enlistments could not end soon enough to suit these men! Despite Trenton, they had a bellyful of war. Sure, they were fighting for liberty. But they had already done their share—*more* than their share. Now let others do theirs!

Their chief, we recall, had surrounded himself with an invisible wall. Yet he could not always stay behind the wall. Sometimes he lost his temper and burst through it. At other times, he opened the front gate to reveal his humanity. This, too, increased his authority. An appeal on a personal level carried more weight, since it came so rarely and so unexpectedly. That is what happened now.

The general wheeled his horse about and rode along the line, looking each man in the eyes as he passed. Finally, he stopped and spoke again. "My brave fellows," he said, his voice trembling, "you have done all I asked you to do and more than could be reasonably expected. But your country is at stake, your wives, your houses, and all that you hold dear. You have worn yourselves out with fatigues and hardships, but we know not how to spare you."[47]

Those words from Washington's heart went to the hearts of those ragged scarecrows. He had swallowed his pride to beg them to serve as a personal favor to himself and for the sake of their country. How could they refuse? "I will remain if you will," one soldier told another. "We cannot go home under such circumstances," others chimed in. Moments later, they broke ranks and rushed to sign the enlistment papers.[48]

Washington recrossed the Delaware, only to have Lord Cornwallis corner him at Assunpink Creek east of Trenton late in the afternoon of January 2, 1777. Since it was almost dark, and His Lordship wanted to rest his troops, he postponed the attack. "I'll bag the old fox in the morning," he said.[49]

The old fox—Washington—refused to be bagged. Next morning, no sound came from the American lines. Inching forward, a British patrol found only smoldering campfires. Under cover of darkness, Washington had led his army out of the trap by a back road. It was a hard march for the infantry. Hungry and cold, their heads bowed into the biting wind, they trudged ahead. One soldier recalled how, after a short rest stop, "one, two, or three men in each platoon would stand . . . fast asleep; a platoon next in the rear, advancing on them, they, in walking or attempting to move, would strike a [stump] and fall."[50]

The retreat across New Jersey as imagined by artist Howard Pyle.

Cornwallis learned Washington's destination when a messenger brought bad news from Princeton, ten miles to the north. Two fresh British regiments had just joined their comrades at Princeton when Wash-

ington spurred his horse forward to lead the charge in person. Turning in the saddle, he cried: "Parade with me, my brave fellows!"[51]

Moments later, the redcoats fired a volley at close range, shrouding Washington in gun smoke. Horrified, one of his staff officers, a colonel, covered his eyes to avoid seeing his chief shot dead. He need not have worried. A wind gust parted the smoke, and there was the general full of life. Washington stood in the stirrups for all to see and shouted, "It is a fine day for a fox chase, my boys!"

So it was. They chased the redcoated "foxes" into Princeton and out the other end of town. The town had a supply dump heaped with barrels of flour and piles of tents, blankets, and shoes. When the guns fell silent, 273 redcoats and 40 Continentals lay dead.[52]

The Continentals were as proud of themselves as of their commander. When things looked bad, he always came through, inspiring his men by

After evading a trap, George Washington took the enemy by surprise outside the college town of Princeton, New Jersey, on January 3, 1777.

Charles Peale Polk's portrait of General Washington at the Battle of Princeton, January 3, 1777.

example. "O, my Susan," a private wrote his wife. "It was a glorious day, and I would not have been absent from it for all the money I ever expect to be worth. . . . I shall never forget what I felt at Princeton on [the general's] account, when I saw him brave all the dangers of the field and his important life hanging as it were by a single hair with a thousand deaths flying around him. Believe me, I thought not of myself."[53]

General Howe ordered Lord Cornwallis to abandon all his outposts in New Jersey except Perth Amboy and New Brunswick. With nearly the whole state again in patriot hands, Washington took his army into winter quarters near Morristown.

Both sides understood the meaning of Trenton and Princeton. The news stunned the British. Now they understood: This was going to be a long, nasty war with an uncertain outcome. Reports of Washington's victories in colonial newspapers electrified patriots, reviving their hopes for winning independence. Had Washington failed during those nine days (December 26–January 3), the Revolution would have failed, and with it the chance of creating an independent United States.

Washington's men understood that better than anyone. As they warmed themselves at campfires, they sang a song that captured their spirit and hopes. It echoed their chief's rallying cry at Princeton:

> *Come on, my brave fellows, a fig for our lives*
> *We'll fight for our country, our children and wives.*
> *Determin'd we are to live happy and free;*
> *Then join, honest fellows, in chorus with me.*
> *We'll drink our own liquor, our brandy from peaches,*
> *A fig for the English, they may kiss all our breeches.*
> *Those blood-sucking, beer-drinking puppies retreat;*
> *But our peach-brandy fellows can never be beat.*[54]

POUNDS OF
SORROW

When troubles fall within your dish,
And things don't tally with your wish:
It's just as well to laugh as cry —
To sing and joke, as moan and sigh: —
For a pound of sorrow never yet
Cancel'd a single ounce of debt.
—A POPULAR SONG OF 1777

On the last day of 1776, the Continental Congress agreed to Washington's request for a regular army. To encourage enlistments, it offered a bounty of twenty dollars and one hundred acres of land to those who enlisted for the rest of the war. The new Continentals were young, ranging in age from their midteens to their midtwenties. The majority were landless, unskilled, and poor. They became soldiers not only out of patriotism, but because they saw the army as a chance to rise in the world. Still others resembled the redcoats in that they were criminals forced into military service. New England towns even sent orphans to save the cost of their upkeep in the local poorhouse. Boys between the ages of nine and twelve often became drummers.

As recruits reached Morristown, smallpox swept the camp. Normally, surgeons fought the disease by taking pus from a victim's sores and inoculating, or introducing, it into a healthy person through a cut made in the skin. This caused a mild attack that gave immunity by triggering the body's capacity to produce antibodies against the disease. One problem: many people saw forced inoculation as a form of tyranny, like taxation without representation. Washington refused to take "no" for an answer. His handling of the epidemic made him an early hero of American public health. Beginning in January 1777, he ordered inoculation for everyone who, unlike himself, had not had smallpox the "natural way." This was history's first mass inoculation, and it worked better than anyone expected. Thanks to his quick action, the epidemic ended. Eventually, inoculation erased this killer from the Continental Army.

The army was still in no shape to resist an all-out attack. Yet General Howe held back, partly because his opponent turned out to be quite a slippery character. In business and private life, Washington was a model of honesty. In war, however, he believed the truth so precious that it must be protected—by lies and trickery if need be. He became a master at "disinformation," leaking false information to deceive the enemy. At Morristown, for example, he refused to arrest a British spy, but let him leave with fake reports enlarging Washington's troop strength. These convinced Howe not to attack until his own reinforcements could arrive in the spring.

Howe also had a personal reason for holding back that winter. Although he had a lovely wife, she was in England. Mrs. Elizabeth Loring, however, was in New York. The lonely general took a liking to her and she to him. Her husband Joshua, a Tory businessman, ignored their "friendship" for the sake of profitable army contracts. All New York gossiped about the affair, which made British officers furious. Suspecting that Washington was weaker than he seemed, they urged Howe to make an immediate attack on Morristown. When Howe refused, they recited a wicked little poem behind his back:

> *Awake, arouse, Sir Billy,*
> *There's forage on the plain.*
> *Ah, leave your little filly,*
> *And open the campaign.*
> *Heed not a woman's prattle*
> *Which tickles in the ear,*

But give the word for battle
And grasp the warlike spear.[1]

Sir Billy preferred his little filly to the warlike spear. By enjoying winter in New York, he missed a chance to damage, perhaps crush, the Continental Army.

Meanwhile, in France, King Louis XVI and his advisers closely watched events in America. These men had long memories. They had not forgotten, or forgiven, their country's humiliating defeat in the Seven Years' War. To them, the Revolution offered a chance to get back at Britain. Still, another war would cost much blood and gold. Before France made that investment, they wanted the rebels to prove they could survive. The Declaration of Independence was a good start, as were Trenton and Princeton. Yet the French needed more proof. Until it came, they would play it safe by secretly sending aid.

The French formed a company to trade with the French colonies in the West Indies. It was a fake. Instead of delivering fine wines and foods to the islands, company ships cruised about, waiting for a chance to run the British naval blockade. In March 1777, the first ships reached ports in New Hampshire with tents, clothing, cannons, muskets, and tons of the finest gunpowder in the world. They also brought European officers.

The majority were Frenchmen who had come for various reasons. A few were military experts ordered by their superiors to "volunteer" for the Continental Army. These included a team of engineers sent to teach Washington's men how to build permanent ports and floating bridges across streams. Others came because they saw the chance of a lifetime in America. When not fighting their own wars, European armies allowed junior officers to serve in other nations' wars. This allowed them to gain experience and win higher rank, which they later took back to their own army. Finally, there were the idealists, noblemen who believed the rebels were fighting for rights they hoped to see the French people enjoy someday.

One nobleman stood in a class by himself. At nineteen years old, this tall, thin, redhead had a big nose and a tongue-twister name. Marie Joseph Paul Yves Roch Gilbert du Motier, Marquis de Lafayette, belonged to one of France's wealthiest and most powerful families. "The Boy," as older men called him, had recently taken a four-teen-year-old bride, who was pregnant with their child. Her husband, however, found the idea of fatherhood not nearly as exciting as serving the cause of liberty. "The moment I heard of America, I loved her," he said. "The moment I knew she was fighting for freedom, I burned with a desire to bleed for her." That did not sit well with his family. To keep him at home, they asked the king to jail him until he came to his senses. Lafayette eluded the police, rented a ship, and sailed for America with some friends.[2]

The Continental Congress liked The Boy's spirit, especially since he offered to pay his own expenses. Equally important, it valued his connections in French high society. Some-day, it hoped, those connections would help draw France into the war. Although Lafayette spoke only a few words of English at this time, and had never seen a battle, he was sent to Morristown with the rank of honorary major general. Let Washington figure out what to do with him!

At the age of nineteen, the Marquis de Lafayette joined Washington's army, eager to "bleed" for the cause of American liberty. From an engraving in Washington Irving's *Life of George Washington*.

Both men would remember their first meeting for the rest of their lives. Immediately they felt a strong personal bond. For Washington, the charming youngster became the son he had always wanted. Lafayette saw in the older man a substitute for the father who had died fighting the British when Lafayette was two years old. He called Washington "my spiritual father," and himself his "adopted son." Washington helped turn The Boy into a man, as his brother Lawrence had once helped him. Under Washington's guidance, Lafayette discovered qualities in himself that he hardly imagined. A born leader, he soon proved his worth on the battlefield.[3]

Meanwhile, in London, King George's advisers were planning more battles. Their idea was to come down on the rebels like the jaws of a grizzly bear. The upper jaw, with 12,000 "teeth" under Major General John Burgoyne, would descend from Canada by way of Lake Champlain and the Hudson Valley. Simultaneously, the lower jaw, Sir William Howe's army, would move up the Hudson River from New York City. The jaws would close at Albany, then chew eastward into New England, biting the rebel states in half.

It was a fine plan, and might have worked, had its authors remembered a simple detail. By some oversight, nobody ordered Howe to cooperate with Burgoyne. Of course, the commander of British forces in North America knew about the plan. Yet, without written orders, Howe felt free to choose his own target: Philadelphia. If he succeeded, he might then move up the Hudson—or just stay with Mrs. Loring.

News of Burgoyne's capture of Fort Ticonderoga on June 15 hit Washington hard. Confused, he could not decide whether to block Burgoyne's advance from Canada or stay at Morristown. His spies in New York City reported feverish British activity along the waterfront. Admiral Howe had gathered a fleet of 267 ships, which his brother, General Howe, was loading with 15,000 redcoats and Hessians. The fleet sailed on July 23, bearing southward toward Chesapeake Bay—then vanished. Washington had questions but no answers. Would it head for the Delaware River and Philadelphia? Would it double back and go elsewhere? Where? Albany? Virginia? Only the Howe brothers knew its destination, and they kept it to themselves.

Mother Nature cares nothing about military plans. She made the voyage south, a total of 350 miles, last a month instead of the usual week. Once at sea, the fleet met strong headwinds. The ships' constant dipping and rolling made their passengers seasick. Then the wind died down, letting the ships drift for days without seeing a whitecap or a wave. Temperatures rose to a hundred degrees above-decks, and hotter in the dark holds, where soldiers lay on straw mats, puking over themselves. The whole world, it seemed, stank of melting tar, rotting food, and vomit. Aboard the horse transports, hundreds of animals went mad in the suffocating heat and had to be shot. Again the wind picked up, bringing thunderstorms and lightning that split ships' masts. Finally, the battered fleet entered Chesapeake Bay. On August 25, it anchored off Head of Elk, Maryland. Philadelphia lay fifty miles overland, to the north.

By then, lookouts ashore saw the fleet and marked its course. Washington quit worrying and sprang into action. While his major deputies, Generals Horatio Gates and Benedict Arnold, challenged Burgoyne in New York, he would try to halt Howe's advance.

With Lafayette riding at his side, Washington let 11,500 men through Philadelphia. To give the illusion of strength, he had them parade twelve abreast in a single column. John Adams was not impressed. "Our soldiers have not quite the air of soldiers," he wrote his wife, Abigail. "They don't step exactly in time. They don't hold up their heads quite erect nor turn out their toes exactly as they ought." But their muskets glistened in the bright sunlight.[4]

Few Philadelphians saw Washington's other army. Before breaking camp at Morristown, he ordered "the multitude of women, especially those who are pregnant and have children," to go around the city so as not to offend respectable citizens. Women and children always accompanied his army, as they did with the British and Hessian forces. They marched on foot or drove farm wagons, their personal property; Washington did not allow them to ride in army wagons. These women followed their soldier husbands and lovers; some came to sell whiskey and other things.

Other women were called "Women of the Army." They had enlisted to nurse the wounded or help with the cannons, a vital job. After each shot, a crew member used a "sponge"—a damp mop made of sheep wool—to douse smoking bits of gunpowder clinging to the inside of the barrel. If a fresh cartridge went into a poorly cleaned barrel, the gun exploded, killing its crew and anyone standing nearby. Women often handled the sponges. If necessary, they also loaded and fired the guns.[5]

Washington marched to Brandywine Creek, a stream that joins the Delaware River twenty-five miles southwest of Philadelphia. Back then, the creek flowed between high banks with shallow crossing places, or "fords." The general placed his men along the creek for several miles to the right and left of Chadds Ford, the best crossing, and waited. Thinking the enemy would try to cross there, he planned to allow them to advance, then blast them in midstream. By then, the British cannons could not give the foot soldiers any support, for fear of hitting them.

General Howe did not take the bait. One look told him that the setup was ideal for a replay of the Battle of Long Island. His plan called for Hessian infantry assaults and artillery bombardments to keep Washington's attention fixed at Chadds Ford. Meanwhile, Lord Cornwallis would cross three or four miles upstream, beyond the American outposts, slip behind their right flank, and attack from the rear.

At 4:00 A.M., September 11, Cornwallis set out with the bulk of the army. An hour later, as the sky brightened in the east, the Hessians opened fire. Washington, as usual, ignored his personal safety. Bullets whizzed overhead, but he rode forward with an aide to get a better look. Ahead lay the ford with a clump of trees nearby.

British Major Patrick Ferguson lay hidden in the trees with his men. Suddenly, he saw two rebel officers approach on horseback. As they drew near, he called to the first man, a big fellow on a big horse, to halt. The officer stopped, glanced at the redcoat, and kept going. "I could have lodged half-a-dozen balls in or about him before he was out of my reach," the major wrote. "But it was not pleasant to fire at the back of an unoffending individual, who was acquitting himself very coolly of his duty, so I let him alone." Next day, a prisoner told him that he had saved George Washington. Ferguson had no regrets. He still thought it shameful to shoot anyone, even the enemy leader, in the back.[6]

Washington knew nothing of his close call, nor of Cornwallis's undetected move upstream. Only the rumble of distant cannon alerted Washington to the danger. Stunned that the enemy had outwitted him again, he ordered part of his force at Chadds Ford to support the troops on the right flank.

His order came too late and asked too much. "Changing front," as soldiers called it, was a difficult maneuver. It required troops to leave their positions, fall back a short distance, form a column, and then march quickly in another direction. Redcoats and Hessians could change front easily. The Continental Army had never learned how.

The Americans retreated to avoid the closing trap. Yet it was no panic retreat, like Long Island, thanks to the relief force Washington sent from his position at Chadds Ford. Despite their lack of training, the newcomers saved the day by keeping the retreat route open. An eyewitness saw them standing "almost Muzzle to Muzzle" with the charging enemy, trading shot for shot. Even so, they took a fearful pounding. Washington lost about 1,200 men killed, wounded, and taken prisoner; Howe had 583 dead and wounded. The Englishman captured so many wounded Americans that he wrote Washington to send surgeons to treat them. Howe expected

the survivors to be downhearted, but they were not. Why should they be? They had fought bravely and had nothing to be ashamed of. Soldiers called to each other in the darkness, "All right, boys, we'll do better another time."[7]

Brandywine was Lafayette's first battle, and he fought it like a veteran. Amid all the excitement, he did not notice that a bullet had taken a chunk

Washington's troops check the British advance at the Battle of the Brandywine. Etching by F. C. Yohn.

out of his leg. Only afterward, when a soldier saw Lafayette's boot over-flowing with blood, did he go to a surgeon. Washington found him with a bloodstained bandage around his leg. Only a scratch, The Boy said, smiling. Nothing to worry about! The general wore his sourest expression. While turning to leave, he snapped an order to the surgeon: "Treat him as if he were my son, for I love him as if he were." Meanwhile, other surgeons cut away, and the shrieks of the wounded continued far into the night.[8]

For the next two weeks, the armies played a deadly game of tag around Philadelphia. Howe tried to lure Washington into a decisive battle. Washington, refusing to be lured into anything, always managed to avoid the trap. Yet it was not just a matter of running or hiding. Washington had not forgotten his idea of protracted warfare. To keep the enemy off balance, he sent small units to strike isolated outposts. Meanwhile, the Continental Congress decided it was too dangerous to remain in Philadelphia. It fled

Take no prisoners! A scene from the Paoli Massacre.

south to York, a town near the Maryland border; a third of the population also left.

Howe's forces terrorized the countryside around Philadelphia. Before dawn on September 21, redcoats surprised a detachment of Continentals at Paoli Tavern near the city. History knows the incident as the Paoli Massacre, because they bayoneted unarmed men begging to surrender. Four days later, the British took Philadelphia without firing a shot. Tories celebrated with torchlight parades and burned likenesses of Washington.

What had Howe really gained? Not much. The Englishman thought of Philadelphia in European terms. A European capital was the center of national government and authority. If the capital fell, the rulers gave up, since they had lost the ability to govern their country. The United States, however, had no central government.

Having learned to distrust a powerful central government in London, state legislatures did not wish to give power to the same kind of government closer to home. To make sure the Continental Congress did not become a tyranny, the states deliberately kept it weak. The Continental Congress could do only three things. First, it conducted diplomatic relations with foreign countries, particularly France, hoping to draw it into the war against Britain. Second, whenever state governments refused to raise taxes to pay for the war, it issued nearly worthless paper money. Finally, it appointed officers in the Continental Army. Apart from these activities, it could make no laws anybody had to obey.

Benjamin Franklin, America's chief diplomat in Paris, understood why Europeans might mistake the powers of the Continental Congress. One night, a guest at a dinner party announced that Howe had taken Philadelphia. Franklin's faced flushed. "I beg your pardon, Sir," he snapped. "Philadelphia has taken Howe." Holding Philadelphia gave the Englishman no real advantage. The city was merely a British island in an American sea. Howe did not have enough men to occupy and hold the surrounding countryside. The British controlled the land they stood on—not an inch more. By seizing Philadelphia, Howe left Washington free to move about as he pleased.[9]

On October 4, Washington struck Germantown, a British outpost seven miles from Philadelphia. He nearly won that battle; he planned it

Washington might have won the Battle of Germantown, October 4, 1777, had he not followed Henry Knox's advice to capture the house of Judge Benjamin Chew before advancing farther. The British had turned the house, a building with thick stone walls, into a fortress.

carefully and surprised the enemy. Unfortunately, American units got confused when a thick fog set in. They fired on each other, forcing a hasty retreat. Yet Germantown proved the Americans could still strike hard. Howe decided to pull in his outposts and fortify his prize. Washington camped nearby, at Whitemarsh, to block any further advances before winter. Meanwhile, he waited for news from the other fighting front.

On October 18, Washington's guns fired a victory salute. "Let every face brighten and every heart expand," ran his order of the day.[10] An express rider had just brought word of Burgoyne's surrender of his entire army at Saratoga, New York. Although Major General Horatio Gates, the American commander, claimed the victory, Benedict Arnold, his aide, deserved the credit. In two battles near Saratoga, Arnold halted the invaders, trapping them in the wilderness. The battles of Saratoga and Germantown made a deep impression in France. Since the Americans were clearly surviving, King Louis stepped closer to supporting them openly.

By mid-December 1777, Washington decided Howe would stay put for a while in Philadelphia; now it was safe to take the army into winter quarters. He led it westward from Whitemarsh, through driving rain and sleet, toward a place that would become famous in American history. The temperature plummeted. To save their feet from frostbite, some officers poured whiskey into their shoes. Most common soldiers, who had torn shoes, or no shoes at all, would rather have poured it into themselves.

Temperatures continued to drop, freezing the trampled mud into sharp-edged ridges that slashed men's feet. Lafayette sat on horseback at the roadside, watching the columns limp past. "Their feet and legs froze until they became black," he wrote, "and it was often necessary to amputate them." His companion, stone-faced and grim, also watched. Now and then, troops heard the big Virginian mutter, "Poor fellows! Poor fellows!"[11]

The army crossed the Schuylkill River on a bridge of wagons set end to end and joined by wooden planks. On December 18, Washington halted eighteen miles northwest of Philadelphia.

LE GENERAL GATES de l'Armée Américaine, qui fit capituler le General Burgoine au Camp de Saharatoga le 16 8bre 1777. CHEF

General Horatio Gates, a veteran of the British army, joined the Americans and won a great victory at Saratoga.

Before him lay the village of Valley Forge and the ruins of an iron forge recently destroyed by British cavalry. The campsite lay beyond, on a wooded slope about two miles long, exposed to fierce winds. Washington had chosen this place because it was easy to defend and close enough to keep an eye on Howe in Philadelphia. Other than its location, Valley Forge had nothing to offer.

Washington began by building nearly a thousand log cabins. To speed construction, he offered a prize of twelve dollars to the first unit in each regiment that built the best shelter. Soldiers worked day and night, often in pouring rain and knee-deep mud. Yet even that did not dampen some men's sense of humor. When two men passed each other, the first would say: "Good morning, Brother Soldier, how are you?" His comrade replied: "All wet, thank'e; hope you are so."[12]

Before long, rows of cabins lined newly formed streets and avenues.

Troops trying to keep warm by a campfire at Valley Forge.

Nearly every cabin was 16 feet long by 14 feet wide, with walls 6 feet 6 inches high. Each had a roof of straw and earth, and an earthen floor. It also had a chimney and fireplace of wood lined with clay, and windows covered by sheets of paper dipped in melted hog fat. The paper kept out the wind (sort of), while allowing some light to enter.

Soldiers compared their cabins to a cold corner of hell. Since they had only damp wood to burn, the fireplaces smoked terribly. Dressed in crumbling rags, they huddled indoors, shivering as tears rolled down their cheeks. Some men, virtually naked, had to borrow a comrade's rags before going out on guard duty. Always hungry, they often did not see a scrap of meat for days. At such times, they lived on "fire-cake," a paste of flour, salt, and water baked on a flat stone set near a fire. Even so, at least one private found something to laugh about. When a colonel passed, he noticed the private had put a kettle over a log fire. "What have you in that kettle?"

he asked. "A stone, Colonel, for they say there is some strength in stones, if you can get it out."[13]

Still, there was precious little to joke about during those early days. Dr. Albigence Waldo, twenty-eight years old, had left home to join a Connecticut regiment. The doctor kept a diary during his stay at Valley Forge. Although it is sad reading, it is our best description of life in the cabins by one who lived there.

> I am Sick—discontented—and out of humour. Poor food—hard lodging—Cold Weather—fatigue—Nasty Cloaths—nasty Cookery—Vomit half my time—smoak'd out of my senses—the Devil's in't—can't Endure it—Why are we sent here to starve and Freeze—What sweet Felicities have I left at home; A charming Wife—pretty Children—Good Beds—good food—good Cookery—all agreeable—all harmonious. Here all Confusion—smoke & Cold—hunger & filthyness—A pox on my bad luck. There comes a bowl of beef soup—full of burnt leaves and dirt. . . . There comes a Soldier, his bare feet are seen thro' his worn out Shoes, his legs nearly naked from the tatter'd remains of an only pair of stockings, his Breeches not sufficient to cover his nakedness, his Shirt hanging in Strings, his hair dishevell'd, his face meagre; his whole appearance pictures a person forsaken & discouraged. He comes, and crys with an air of wretchedness & despair, I am Sick, my feet lame, my legs are sore—my Cloaths are worn out, my Constitution is broken, my former Activity is exhausted by fatigue, hunger & Cold, I fail fast.[14]

Many failed for good. Of the 10,000 men Washington had brought to Valley Forge, no fewer than 2,500 died of disease. Weakened by hunger and cold, they fell victim to pneumonia, typhus fever, and "the itch"—that is, scabies, a disease carried by mites, tiny insectlike creatures that burrow into the skin. Highly contagious, scabies covered men's bodies with sores that drove them wild. Lacking medicines, they tried to help themselves in any way they could. Private Martin and his friends used an old folk remedy. One freezing night, they lay outside naked before a roaring bonfire, drinking hot whiskey and plastering their bodies with a mixture of hog grease and sulfur. That was a drastic treatment, "but we killed the itch and were satisfied, for it had almost killed us."[15]

Their sufferings tormented their chief. Almost daily, he wrote the Continental Congress and state legislatures to describe living conditions at Valley Forge and ask for help. Many politicians wanted to win independence—but as cheaply as possible. They cared little about the army, saying the general had nothing else to do with his time than nag them with "whining complaints." The Pennsylvania assembly even scolded him for going into winter quarters when he should be fighting Howe.

Washington seethed with anger at such cruel stupidity. Two days before Christmas, he lashed out at those who imagined his soldiers dumb sticks and stones, insensitive to pain.

> I can assure these Gentlemen that it is a much easier and less distressing thing to draw remonstrances [protests] in a comfortable room by a good fireside than to occupy a cold, bleak hill, and sleep under frost and snow, without clothes or blankets. However, although they seem to have little feeling for the naked and distressed Soldiers, I feel super-abundantly for them, and, from my Soul, I pity those miseries, which it is neither in my power to relieve or prevent.[16]

Some congressmen wondered whether Washington should remain in command. Members of his military "family," as he called his staff, thought there was a cabal, or plot, to dump him. They called it the Conway Cabal, after Thomas Conway, an aide to General Horatio Gates. Conway was an Irish-born French officer serving with the Americans. One night, a friend of his had too much to drink. As the alcohol took effect, it muddled his brain and loosened his tongue. He blurted out that Conway had written Gates, saying "Heaven" had chosen him to save the country, and that Gates agreed.

Lafayette learned of the incident and warned his friend. Washington promptly wrote letters to Gates and Conway, accusing them of disloyalty. After saying they meant no harm, they begged his forgiveness. Dissatisfied with the apology, General John Cadwalader of Pennsylvania challenged Conway to a duel. A dead shot, he put a bullet through his opponent's face. Conway survived and returned to France.[17]

News of the cabal sent shouts of "Washington or no army" echoing across Valley Forge. That was a huge personal triumph for Washington. Despite his failures, the common soldiers never lost faith in him. They understood that the solemn, weary man was doing his best for them. Most patriots agreed. Military talent, though important, was only part of what they expected in a leader. Character and devotion to the cause were of equal, if not greater, importance. It was not Washington's military expertise, but the integrity of the man himself who inspired confidence. After the Conway affair, no politician or army officer dared challenge his authority. For his part, Washington never abused their trust, or used it for anything but the good of the country. Never once did he criticize the right of civilians—the Continental Congress—to give him orders, however mistaken they might be.[18]

Yet the suffering at Valley Forge was needless. Pennsylvania was a prosperous state, and its farmers had enjoyed a good harvest in 1777. Unfortunately, farmers and tradespeople kept their goods off the market to drive prices up. Yet high prices did not guarantee high quality. Often the army received spoiled meat, wormy flour, and watered-down whiskey. Some Americans even traded with the enemy in Philadelphia. These were not Tories, but greedy folks out to profit at the army's expense. To supply his own troops, and to keep supplies from Washington's, Howe paid in gold instead of paper money. To destroy the value of money printed by Congress, he flooded the country with counterfeit thirty-dollar bills, further raising prices.

Washington did not take that lying down. In January 1778, he made Nathanael Greene his chief quartermaster, or supply officer. "Brother Nat," as he called him, was a thirty-five-year-old Rhode Islander who had learned the art of war from books. He learned well, rising from private to general in less than two years. At first, he objected to the quartermaster's post, saying he was a fighter, not a grocer. After his boss insisted, gently but firmly, Greene changed his mind.

Brother Nat did whatever it took to get results. Those known to have kept goods from the market had them confiscated, paid stiff fines, and spent a week thinking about their sins in a frigid guardhouse. Any man caught trading with the enemy got 250 lashes "on his bare back, well laid on." Rank carried no privileges, as one thieving officer discovered. Greene sentenced him "to have his sword broke over his head on the parade ground." Finally, he told search parties to "forage the country naked"; that is, take whatever the troops needed and pay with paper money. It worked! By late February, wagons were rolling into camp every day filled with supplies.[19] Although the local population resented these tactics, it learned a valuable lesson: Desperate men with guns in their hands will do anything to eat.

While his men built the cabins, Washington lived in his private tent, equipped with a folding bed, a chest for his clothes, and trunks for his personal belongings: tableware, dishes, glasses. Afterward, he moved into a cozy stone cottage near camp, the home of Mrs. Deborah Hewes. He awoke early, ate a light breakfast, and then spent hours at his paperwork. This included reports to the Continental Congress, letters to state officials asking for help, and letters to Martha. Unlike future wartime leaders— Abraham Lincoln in the Civil War, Franklin D. Roosevelt in World

George Washington visiting a log hut at Valley Forge. The figure on the left is Baron von Steuben.

War II—the constant stress did not affect his health. Sometimes he lost a night's sleep or lost his temper with an aide. Even so, he coped pretty well. The secret lay in Washington's physical activity; he was always doing something to stay in shape and burn off tension.

Washington set out on horseback every morning with Billy Lee, whatever the weather, galloping across fields and jumping fences. At other times, he passed the time with staff members. A French officer reported that he "sometimes throws and catches a ball for whole hours with his aides." Other visitors saw him shot-putting with his aides, tossing an iron weight farther than men half his age.[20]

Yet nothing could replace his "Dear Patsy." Martha used to say she heard the last shots of one year's campaign and the first shots of the next year's. That was no exaggeration. Starting in Boston in 1775, she arrived in camp every winter like clockwork. She hated war, the bloodshed, the misery. "I shudder every time I hear the sound of a gun," she admitted, "but I endeavor to keep my fears to myself as well as I can." Martha came because the "Old Man" needed her. Like him, she was a very private person. She never spoke about what passed between them. Still, we can imagine him pouring out his frustrations and sorrows to her.[21]

Martha reached Valley Forge in February 1778, just as the starving time ended. Soldiers always welcomed "Lady Washington," as they called her. Years later, aged veterans remembered her as "a short, thick woman; very pleasant and kind." Wherever she went, it seemed, she brought brightness and a warm feeling.[22]

Martha got other officers' wives to join her in doing good works. In a red, speckled apron, she sat with her circle of ladies, knitting woolen scarves and rolling bandages. Alexander Miller, a drummer, once heard her ask the Old Man where he had gone that morning. "To look at my boys," he answered, meaning the troops during drill. "Well," said she, "I will go to see *my* children." With that, she went to a nearby hospital cabin. Lady Washington often visited hospital cabins with a servant and a basketful of small gifts. Veterans always remembered her "motherly care." Sometimes her kind words and tender touch eased a dying man's last moments.[23]

Soon after Martha arrived, a stranger strolled into headquarters trailed by a sleek greyhound. A chunky, red-faced man, he wore a splendid blue uniform ablaze with medals and ribbons. He spoke only German and French, and had a long name: Friedrich Wilhelm August Heinrich Ferdinand, Baron von Steuben. The baron, forty-eight years old, introduced himself as a former lieutenant general in the army of Frederick the Great, the warrior-king of Prussia, Germany's most powerful state.

The truth, however, was not that simple. Steuben was neither a nobleman nor a general. He *had* been a soldier since the age of sixteen. During the Seven Years' War between 1756 and 1763, he had served as a captain on Frederick the Great's staff but had held no command for fourteen years. When Benjamin Franklin met him in Paris, he was looking for a job—any job. Franklin sent him to Washington with a letter of introduction. Washington knew the truth, too, but kept it to himself. For this man of lies was a genius at training soldiers.

Just then, Washington desperately needed such a man. Experience had taught him that his opponents won battles not because they led the best troops, but because their troops had the right training. Every soldier fears death; that is natural. Yet, with proper training, he can overcome his fear—can act *as if*

Baron von Steuben, a veteran of the European wars, turned the Continental Army into a professional fighting force at Valley Forge. From an engraving in Washington Irving's *Life of George Washington.*

he has no fear. Here is where Steuben came in. "The business," he explained, "is to give our troops a relish for their trade, to make them feel a confidence in their own skill." That meant teaching skills they had never learned, or learned well enough. If Washington hoped to win, his men could not hide behind breastworks and pray for the enemy to come to them. They had to fight in the open, European style.[24]

The baron turned Valley Forge into America's first military academy. A natural teacher, he began on a personal level. Since he hated to eat alone,

he said, he invited young officers to meals of stringy beef and musty potatoes. One catch: everyone who entered his cabin had to wear torn clothes.
That way, everyone would be equal. After eating, Steuben taught his
guests to drink "salamanders," glasses of whiskey set on fire and swallowed with the flames. Although not very nutritious, salamanders took the
edge off the cold.[25]

Gradually, their host turned the conversation to serious matters.
Steuben believed that an officer had to earn the right to lead. To do that,
he must "gain the love of his men." For Steuben, love meant respect. An
officer won respect by giving it. Steuben expected officers to treat their
soldiers as human beings. That meant learning their names, tending to
their needs, and speaking to them politely. Unlike fellow officers, including Washington, he did not believe in physical punishment. He never ordered a man whipped.[26]

Steuben taught by example. He began by forming a model company
from the army's hundred best and brightest veterans. Each night, he wrote
out the next day's lesson in French. An aide translated it into English and
had scribes make copies for selected officers. Washington expected them to
watch the baron teach the lesson, then follow it with their own units. In
this way, drillmaster Steuben became the trainer of drillmasters.

Until he took charge, Americans followed British methods. Officers in
both armies saw drill as a chore best left to sergeants. Not the baron! He
appeared on the drill field promptly at 6:00 A.M. in full uniform, medals
and all. For the next twelve hours, he put the model company through its
paces in person. That impressed the onlookers more than anything he said.
For if a Prussian lieutenant general was not too proud to drill common
soldiers, it was not "beneath the dignity" of an American lieutenant or
captain.

Steuben had never seen such shabby-looking men as those at Valley
Forge. Yet he also saw beyond outward appearances into their very souls.
And what he saw there was marvelous. No European army would have
held together after what they had been through. No professionals had
their grit in the face of hardship. None matched their belief in their cause
and faith in their commander. Standing before him was, quite simply, the
finest raw material for an army anywhere on earth. These were not auto-

matons, mindless fighting machines, but free men with minds of their own. As he explained to an old comrade, in Europe "You say to your soldier, 'Do this, and he doeth it.' But [here] I am obliged to say, 'This is the reason why you ought to do that,' and then he does it."[27]

Training them was not easy, especially since Steuben did not speak their language. If a lesson went well, he beamed with happiness. *"Sehr gut!"* he said. *"Wunderbar!"* ("Very Good! Wonderful!") If it went badly, he loosed a deluge of German and French curse words. Finally, after several minutes of nonstop cursing, he would turn to Captain Benjamin Walker, his translator, and growl: "My dear Walker . . . come and swear for me in English.

Baron von Steuben turned the snowy fields of Valley Forge into open-air classrooms. Here George Washington watches an exercise, while an officer explains it to Martha and another lady.

These fools won't do what I bid them." The soldiers stood at attention, silently, struggling to keep a straight face. But they learned. At the end of a week's course, Steuben sent the class back to their units to help with drill, and another class took its place.[28]

We recall that Washington's men often panicked when fighting in the open or if taken by surprise. Steuben's training changed all that. He began with "the position of the soldier"—basic movements like right turn, left turn, about-face. Next, he taught more complicated maneuvers. Soldiers learned to march in columns, form a proper line of battle, fire, reload, and advance together at a steady pace. The baron let no day pass without bayonet drill. As men became proficient, their pride soared. Yes, they were still ragged. Yet, for the first time, Washington had an army he could depend on.

Steuben completed his work toward the end of April. That by itself made Washington happy. Early in May, he became overjoyed. He learned that Benjamin Franklin had negotiated a treaty with the French. According to the treaty's terms, France recognized the independence of the United States and pledged to fight if necessary. This was just diplomatic sweet talk. Without saying it in so many words, France had declared war on Britain. All the bad feelings left over from the French and Indian War evaporated as if by magic. Spain joined the allies a year later.

Washington asked the drillmaster to arrange a celebration. Steuben used the occasion to show the results of his hard work. On May 7, the army formed two double lines, one behind the other. At 9:00 A.M. sharp, Washington and his generals rode along the lines. As they passed each unit, the men snapped to attention, their muskets held in the "salute" position, bayonets glinting in the sunlight.

After the review, Washington led the generals to a position in front of the first line, facing the army. The moment they halted, a single cannon shot signaled the *feu de joie*, French for "the joyful fire."

Thirteen cannons, one for each state, fired in quick succession. After the thirteenth shot, the muskets took up the "tune" with blank cartridges. Firing began at the right of the first line, then back along the second line, from left and to right.

Another cannon shot. Instantly, thousands cheered "Long live the King of France!"

The soldiers reloaded and gave two more joyful fires. One fire ended with a cheer of "Long live the friendly European Powers," the other with "Long live the American States."

The celebration ended with an officer's banquet given by the commander in chief. Common soldiers got an extra ration of "fat meat, strong wine and other liquors." Washington left the officers' banquet at five o'clock. As he rode off with his staff, everyone shouted "Long live George Washington!" Turning in the saddle, he waved his hand and cheered them, too.

Sir William Howe was taking it easy until fresh orders came from London. Benjamin Franklin had been right: Philadelphia had captured the British general. He spent his days reading reports at headquarters and his nights drinking and gambling. Mrs. Loring's arrival from New York lent further spice to his life, making Tory tongues wag in disapproval. A popular song sneered at his loose ways and self-indulgence:

> *Sir William, he, snug as a flea,*
> *Lay all this time a-snoring;*
> *Nor dreamed of harm, as he lay warm,*
> *In bed with Mrs. Loring.*[29]

The army took its cue from its chief. For officers, life in Philadelphia became a round of dances, card games, and affairs with local women. Common soldiers carried on in much the same way but added looting to their activities. Soldiers stole everything from the shirts off men's backs to children's toys. Nobody, Tory or patriot, felt safe. Soldiers even stabled horses in fine houses and swept the manure into the basements through holes cut in the floors, where it piled up and decayed. The return of warm weather brought swarms of flies; travelers said they could smell the city clear to Germantown. Philadelphia, a Hessian lieutenant wrote, was like the Biblical cities of Sodom and Gomorrah "in respect to all the vices."[30]

A packet of letters arrived in Philadelphia soon after Washington celebrated the French alliance. One letter relieved Howe of command, ordering him home without delay. Mrs. Loring returned to her husband, and her lover started packing. Another letter turned over his command to Sir Henry Clinton, fifty-two years old, a shy bachelor but a brave soldier. Clinton's promotion came with bad news. British spies had learned that a French fleet under Charles Hector Théodat, Count d'Estaing, was already at sea, and heading for America. Since most of the army's supplies came by sea, the French could easily block the Delaware River, trapping the British in Philadelphia. Clinton and his men must hurry back to New York City.

Meanwhile, officers threw a going-away party for Howe. May 18 was a day of fireworks displays, boat races, band concerts, and balls. Tory women in dresses of scarlet and gold stood on platforms decked with silk banners. Gallant officers, imitating knights of old, pranced before them on horseback. Then, to the sound of trumpets, the Knights of the Burning Mountain fought a mock battle with the Knights of the Blended Rose. Not everyone cheered. Killjoys stood on the sidelines, shaking their heads in disgust. "Why, child," one told a boy who asked the difference between the opponents, "the Knights of the Burning Mountain are Tom Fools, and the Knights of the Blended Rose are damned fools. I know of no other difference between 'em. What will Washington think of all this?"[31]

Not very much. His spies were busy in Philadelphia. They reported that Clinton planned to cross the Delaware River in June. From there, he would move eastward past Monmouth Court House, New Jersey, to Sandy Hook on the coast.

S.ᴿ HENRY CLINTON.

Waiting ships would then carry his army the short distance to New York City.

Sir Henry Clinton replaced Sir William Howe as commander of British forces during the American Revolution.

Washington unfolded his map. Yes, Clinton's escape route was a narrow road across flat, open country. A large army on the move, especially one with heavy equipment, had to travel slowly. Washington planned to send a detachment under General Charles Lee to attack its rear guard. Then, while it struggled to break free, Washington would come up with the main force and attack its right and left flanks. This was his chance for a knockout blow, a thing all generals dream about and few get.

On June 17, Clinton crossed the Delaware over a floating bridge. Besides his army, he had a wagon train that stretched for twelve miles. Perhaps 1,500 Tory refugees plodded beside the wagons. Like the patriots who fled when Howe took Philadelphia, they did not want to be there before the Continental Congress arrived. Apart from the clothes on their backs, and the few things they carried, they had left all their possessions behind.

Next day, Washington led the army out of Valley Forge to the music of fifes and drums. He, Lafayette, Greene, and Steuben sat by the roadside on horseback, watching the soldiers stream past. When the soldiers saw the four generals, they burst into cheers. Some sang a new song to the tune of "Yankee Doodle":

> Come, join hand in hand,
> Brave Americans all.
> And rouse your whole band
> At Liberty's call.[32]

Others sang earthier tunes, such as "Nothing Like Whiskey." By nightfall, a cavalry escort led Benedict Arnold's coach into Philadelphia. His left leg, injured at Saratoga, hurt terribly, and he found it difficult to walk. As a reward for his victory, Washington made him the city's military governor.

A heat wave held New Jersey in its grip, with temperatures of 105 degrees in the shade. Everyone suffered, but not equally. Dressed in their ragged clothes and wide-brimmed hats, the Americans carried only their weapons and light packs. Enemy troops sweltered under fifty-pound packs in woolen uniforms and brimless hats. Many dropped by the roadside, victims of sunstroke. A terrified Hessian described how friends thrashed about, delirious, while "blood gushes from the mouth and nostrils." Giving them water from a spring or well usually killed them. Nothing was deadlier to a soldier overheated with marching or fighting than cold water. His insides suddenly chilled, his body temperature dropped, and he began to fight for breath; most died within four or five minutes of drinking. American doctors thought "cold water disease" deadlier than smallpox.[33]

Pennsylvania and New Jersey militiamen operating in small units slowed the retreating column by burning bridges and felling trees across the road. When Clinton's soldiers reached a farmhouse, they found the well ropes cut and the buckets gone; some wells had been filled with earth. The British soldiers, for their part, shot cattle and took the choice steaks from the hindquarters, leaving the rest to rot. Since it was the height of the cherry season, they did not bother climbing the trees to get the fruit; they cut them down. "Such conduct," Private Martin noted, "did not give the Americans any more agreeable feelings toward them than they entertained before."[34]

Washington's scouts found the column just east of Monmouth Court House on the morning of June 28. As planned, General Charles Lee went ahead with a strike force to halt the retreat until Washington arrived with the army. Clinton understood what was happening; he would have done the same. His only hope of escape was to turn and drive Lee away before Washington got there.

Clinton counterattacked, and Lee panicked. Although an able soldier, something snapped in him that day. Instead of hanging on, as agreed, he ordered a retreat. Although Lafayette offered to lead a charge, Lee would not hear of it. "Sir," he stammered, "you do not know British soldiers. We cannot stand against them."[35]

The retreat continued. Yet Lee's men were more angry than frightened. They knew they were better than their commander thought; Steuben had proven it to them. They were not beaten. All they needed was a leader to tell them what to do.

As Washington and his staff rode through Englishtown a half mile to the west, they met a boy fifer. Washington asked him how much farther it was to the advance troops. "They are coming this way, your honor," the youngster replied, "and the British right after them." "Impossible!" cried Washington, shocked at the news. Yet he had to find out for himself. So he galloped ahead and, sure enough, met Lee's retreating troops.[36]

Moments later, Lee himself appeared. Those who saw Washington confront Lee never forgot the scene. It is said that Washington never cursed. If so, he broke the rule at Monmouth. Private Martin heard him shout "Damn him!" as Lee appeared. General Charles Scott, who had known

Washington confronts Charles Lee at the Battle of Monmouth. But for Lee's incompetence, Washington might have destroyed the British army, winning the war in one decisive battle. Engraving of a painting by F. O. C. Darley.

Washington since Braddock's defeat, said he swore "till the leaves shook on the trees, charming, delightful. Never have I enjoyed such swearing, before or since. Sir, on that . . . day he swore like an angel from Heaven." Washington took away Lee's command and sent him to the rear in disgrace.[37] Then Washington's quick thinking saved the day.

The moment he finished with Lee, he ordered the baron to halt the retreat. Luckily, by then, Steuben spoke some English. His favorite word, apparently, was "damn."

All those hours of drill at Valley Forge paid off. Nobody could mistake the Prussian's harsh accents rising above the sounds of battle. Halt! About-face! Form ranks! Forward! Expertise and discipline conquered fear. Men wheeled about, forming lines of battle as they had done on the parade ground.

Washington led the attack in person. He rode along the lines, giving encouragement by word and example. Musket balls whined. Grapeshot whizzed. Shells exploded. The commander in chief never flinched; never, it seems, even noticed his danger. Wherever he appeared, cheers rose from the ranks. "Never," wrote Lafayette, "was General Washington greater than in this action."[38]

Sir Henry Clinton was at his best, too. Without hesitating, he kept feeding more troops into the battle. Yet, hard as he tried, he could not break Washington's lines. For the first time in the war, Americans held firm under fire and faced redcoats as equals with the bayonet.

Both sides gave their all despite the cruel heat. Private Martin's regiment took a position in a plowed field. "The mouth of a heated oven," he wrote, "seemed to me to be but a trifle hotter than this plowed field; it was almost impossible to breathe." Squads of redcoats and Hessians toppled over with sunstroke. Clinton himself said he was "near going raving mad with heat." Washington did not complain. Virginians knew about hot weather; besides, he was too busy to notice the sweat pouring down his

Cheering soldiers present George Washington with a British flag captured at the Battle of Monmouth. On the right, a surgeon treats a wounded American officer.

back and staining his uniform. When his horse dropped dead from sunstroke, he shouted for Billy Lee to bring another.[39] Seven hundred black soldiers fought under Washington that day. So did at least one white woman. Mary Ludwig Hayes—Molly for short—worked as a cannon sponger. Since she moistened the mop with water from a tin pitcher, soldiers called her Molly Pitcher. During the battle, she joined her husband's gun crew. When the loader was killed, she did his job as well. Then, while she was reaching for a cartridge, a cannonball came too close for comfort. Private Martin saw it all:

> . . . A cannon shot from the enemy passed directly between her legs without doing any other damage than carrying away all the lower part of her petticoat. Looking at it with apparent unconcern, she observed that it was lucky it did not pass a little higher, for in that case it might have carried away something else, and continued her occupation.[40]

Mary Ludwig Hayes, otherwise known as Molly Pitcher, loaded and fired a cannon after its crew had been killed at the Battle of Monmouth.

By late afternoon, the battle sputtered to a close as both sides waited for darkness. The heat still clung to the fields of Monmouth. Washington made his final inspection and wandered into an apple orchard. Amid the lengthening shadows, he stepped into puddles of blood. Everywhere he saw clumps of exhausted men, wounded men, dying men, dead men. After a while, he found Lafayette sleeping under a tree. The general lay down beside his young friend. In an instant, he was fast asleep.

Sir Henry Clinton forced himself to stay awake. He allowed his troops to rest for an hour or two, then, under a full moon, headed for Sandy Hook and the waiting ships. Next day, before going aboard, he ordered his men to slit their horses' throats, to keep them out of enemy hands.

The Battle of Monmouth Court House claimed the lives of 250 redcoats and Hessians; the Americans had 72 killed. Critics noted that Washington had not won the battle. His plan had failed, and the enemy had escaped.

Technically, the critics were right. Washington, however, was thrilled, as were his soldiers. They realized that they had won a tremendous moral victory at Monmouth. General "Mad" Anthony Wayne, a brilliant field officer, put it this way: "The heavenly sweet pretty redcoats, the accomplished gentlemen of the Guards and Grenadiers, have humbled themselves on the plains of Monmouth." Americans had proven themselves equal to Europe's finest soldiers. Had it not been for Charles Lee, Washington might have won the war that day. Because of Lee, it would drag on for another five years.[41]

GREAT WASHINGTON'S ADVANCE

I saw the plundering British bands
Invade the fair Virginian lands.
I saw great Washington advance
With Americans and troops from France;
I saw the haughty Britons yield
And stack their muskets on the field.
—PATRIOTIC SONG, 1781

Count d'Estaing anchored off Sandy Hook on July 11, 1778, just twelve days after Sir Henry Clinton's escape to New York City. Washington, though disappointed, took the news of the escape calmly. With seventeen big warships, the French outnumbered the British fleet. Now, if d'Estaing attacked from the water, and if Washington landed troops at the northern end of Manhattan Island, Clinton would be trapped.

Washington crossed the Hudson and camped on the old White Plains battlefield. The place held horrible reminders of the past, and it gave his men the creeps. Bits of bloodstained clothing, rusty muskets, and broken equipment littered the ground. Rain and wild animals had uncovered hundreds of shallow graves. That troubled Private Martin. "The skulls and other bones and hair were scattered about the place," he wrote. "Here were Hessian skulls as thick as a bombshell. Poor fellows! They had, perhaps, as near and dear friends to lament their sad destiny as the Americans who lay buried near them. But they should have kept at home; we should then never have gone after them to kill them in their own country."[1]

A message from d'Estaing ended any hope of a combined operation. The admiral informed Washington that the British had placed ships and gun batteries on either side of the channel between Staten Island and Brooklyn. Rather than brave the deadly crossfire, the admiral decided to sail north and seize Newport, Rhode Island, a seaport held by a small British garrison. Storms upset that plan, too, and d'Estaing's fleet sailed instead for the French West Indies, having accomplished nothing.

Washington now turned to another problem. British agents had armed the Iroquois nation, six powerful tribes living in the Finger Lakes region of central New York. Fearing the Americans would take their lands if Britain lost the war, the Iroquois sent war parties to strike frontier settlements. They attacked Cherry Valley in New York, Minisink in New Jersey, and the Wyoming Valley of northern Pennsylvania. Sometimes British officers disguised as Indians led the raiders.

Vowing to halt the raids, Washington sent General John Sullivan, a

Tories and their Indian allies attacked settlers in Pennsylvania's Wyoming Valley, leaving hundreds dead. Etching based on a painting by Alonzo Chappel in the collections of the Chicago Historical Society.

On Washington's orders, John Sullivan led a punishing campaign against the Iroquois, Britain's Indian allies, in northern and western New York State.

New Hampshire veteran, against the Iroquois with 4,600 of his best troops. Sullivan's orders left no room for leniency. Washington wrote that Indians understood just one thing: force. "A disposition to peace in these people can only be ascribed to a [fear] of danger and would last no longer than till it was over and an opportunity offered to resume their hostility with safety and success. This makes it necessary that we should endeavor to punish them severely for what has past, and by an example of rigor intimidate them in future."[2]

Sullivan obeyed orders. He was ruthless. That summer of 1779 he destroyed forty Iroquois villages, burned cornfields, and cut down orchards. The Indians fled to Fort Niagara on Lake Ontario, where the British had to feed them for the rest of the war. Although the raids continued, they were fewer and less severe than before. The Iroquois knew who had sent Sullivan on his rampage. For years afterward, they had a name for Washington: The Town Destroyer. At the mention of his name, an old chief said, "Our women . . . turn pale and our children cling to the necks of their mothers."[3]

Washington knew that punishing the Iroquois was a necessary task, although it could not defeat their British allies. Unable to attack New York City without a fleet to aid him, he decided to sit tight and bide his time.

Time passed slowly. Mount Vernon never left his mind. At odd moments, he went over every inch of it in his imagination. In a homesick letter to Lund Washington, his cousin and plantation manager, he asks:

> How many Lambs have you had this spring? How many Colts are you like to have? . . . Have you any prospect of getting Paint or Oyl? Are you going to repair the Pavement of the Piazza? . . . Have you made any attempts to reclaim more Land for meadow, etc.,

etc.? An account of these things would be satisfactory to me and amusing in the recital, as I have these kind of improvements very much to heart. As soon as you can conveniently do it after receipt of this letter, give me a list of the numbers and kind of Mares I possess [and] the number of Colts. . . . Mrs. Washington . . . has taken a fancy to a Horse belonging to Mr. James Cleveland. . . . If you can get him . . . I will be very well pleased with your doing it.[4]

Yet the master of Mount Vernon could not escape the war for very long. He had a dilemma. Unless the French sent another fleet, he knew he could never take New York. Nor could he strike elsewhere. New York was the center of British power in North America, and thus his main objective. Apart from it, he had no other target worth hitting. Clinton had a similar problem. Where should he go next? New Jersey? Pennsylvania? He had been there before. All those hard-fought battles, all those costly "victories," had not ended the war. Whatever he did, Washington came back fighting.

King George worried about the future, too. With the war going nowhere, his people had begun to ask whether it was worth the cost. In Parliament, even bribery failed to silence criticism of the "unjust war." Unemployment and hunger, caused by the loss of American trade, brought riots. In London, rioting by desperate workers grew so bad that the authorities called out the redcoats. The Boston Massacre was kid stuff compared to the butchery in the capital of the British Empire. When the smoke cleared after a severe riot, over five hundred bodies lay in the streets of London.

Yet His Majesty refused to quit. Instead of heeding public opinion, he ordered his advisers to come up with a victory plan. Again they unrolled their maps. Again they pointed to this place and that place. Finally, they decided to open a new front in the South.

Although a thinly settled region with few large towns, the South was vital to the patriot cause. The Continental Congress paid for war supplies imported from France and Holland with southern tobacco and rice. Southern horses drew Washington's artillery and wagons. Choking off these supplies would also choke the Revolution, they believed. Better yet, many

Tories lived in the South. Given proper leadership, they would become a potent military force.

The plan called for a small British army to gain a foothold on southern soil. After seizing a base on the coast of Georgia, the southernmost state, it would drive inland. Once the army secured an area, it would help local Tories take over the civil government and organize a militia to keep the rebels down. This would allow the army to continue northward through the Carolinas and Virginia, following the same methods each time. Having secured the South, planners expected the middle and northern states to fall like ripe fruit from a tree.

The campaign began well. On December 29, 1778, Archibald Campbell, Clinton's aide, took Savannah and quickly restored royal government in large areas of Georgia. With Georgia secure, Clinton struck the hardest blow in person. His target: Charleston, South Carolina, the South's largest city and its best seaport. On May 12, 1780, he captured the city and its 5,500 defenders after a six-week siege.

Clinton returned to New York, leaving Lord Cornwallis to finish the job in the South. We have met His Lordship before and must now get to know him better. The man Americans called "Corn Wallace" was a short, stocky person of forty-three. A soldier's soldier, brave and smart, he had led troops in every major battle since Long Island. He held a deep personal grudge against the rebels. Before he sailed for America in 1775, Lady Cornwallis begged him to ask the king to keep him in England. A frail person, she could not bear to have an ocean between her and her beloved husband. The general, however, thought it dishonorable to stay behind while brother officers risked their lives. Relatives blamed her death in 1778 on a "broken heart" caused by loneliness. Cornwallis blamed the rebels and vowed to get even.[5]

After the fall of Charleston, the Continental Congress gave Horatio Gates command of the southern army. Washington, who had distrusted "the hero of Saratoga" since the Conway Cabal, thought him a fool and a sneak. Although he preferred Nathanael Greene for the job, Congress ignored his advice. Washington took that as an insult but did not protest publicly. He believed so strongly in civilian control that he never questioned the right of Congress to give the army orders, even bad orders.

Lord Charles Cornwallis led British forces during the struggle for Virginia and the Carolinas. After surrendering to George Washington at Yorktown, he became governor general of India. From a painting by Sir W. Beechley.

Gates gathered troops, mainly raw militiamen, and plunged blindly ahead. On August 16, 1780, he ran into Cornwallis near Camden, South Carolina. The redcoats killed and wounded over a thousand Americans, mostly due to Gates's poor leadership. At the height of the action, he galloped to safety sixty miles away, leaving his men on their own.

Cornwallis seemed unbeatable after Camden. South Carolina families who refused to swear loyalty to King George crammed their belongings into wagons and fled with their slaves. And that gave new life to an old question.

What to do about the South's slaves? Both sides had always known that the region's economy would collapse without slave labor. For that reason, in the fall of 1775 Lord Dunmore had freed all Virginia slaves of rebel masters and had enlisted runaways in his Ethiopian Regiment. His action backfired in two ways. First, we recall, it forced Washington to allow blacks to join his army at Boston. Second, it scared many whites into siding with the rebels. Militia bullets defeated the Ethiopian Regiment at Great Bridge, Virginia, on December 9. Soon afterward, an outbreak of smallpox all but destroyed the Ethiopian Regiment, ending British hopes of a black army in Virginia.

Four years later, in 1780, Sir Henry Clinton picked up where Lord Dunmore left off. During his stay in Charleston, he promised freedom to slaves of rebel masters who joined the king's forces. Between three and five thousand black men took the offer. The British army, however, never used them fully. Owing to racial prejudice, very few, if any, blacks saw action. Instead, the British put them to work doing camp chores, driving wagons, and building gun batteries. Some became spies, reporting rebel troop movements. At Savannah, a runaway named Quamino Dolly led redcoats through a swamp to the rear of the rebel positions, avoiding a bloody frontal assault.[6]

Washington could spare few men for duty in the South. Blacks, however, formed a vast reserve of likely soldiers. Should Congress recruit them to fight? His secretary, Colonel Alexander Hamilton, thought it should "give them their freedom with their swords." Washington disagreed. Southern whites, he believed, would never allow slaves to fight.[7]

He was right. When a committee of the Continental Congress voted to recruit slaves, owners in Georgia and South Carolina said they would rather live under King George than tolerate such an "outrage to decency." In other words, they preferred to see their land ravaged by the British than defended by black people. Blacks served anyhow. Virginia and Maryland allowed freedmen to enlist; certain regiments recruited fugitive slaves with no questions asked. All southern states rented or bought slaves for war-related work. Yet that could not give the patriots victory in the long, drawn-out war. Nothing but a divine miracle—or the French—could do that.

Lafayette had gone home in 1779 to see his son for the first time and work for the American cause in France. Now a popular hero, he used his influence to win the king's promise of more aid. In April 1780, he brought Washington the good news. For Washington, however, seeing was believing; he refused to raise his hopes until the French actually arrived. Sure enough, a naval force took Newport in July, two months after the fall of Charleston. Five thousand French soldiers were ashore and ready for action!

On September 21, at Hartford, Connecticut, Washington had a two-day meeting with the French commander. Jean Baptiste Donatien de Vimeur, Count de Rochambeau, was a lean, wiry man of fifty-five. Although he had elegant manners and spoke softly, his eyes told that he expected to get his way. Fighting was his heritage; his family had served in France's wars for seven centuries. Soldiers called him Papa Rochambeau because he inspired their love and confidence. Americans, unable to pronounce his name, called him "Rush on Boys."

With Lafayette acting as interpreter, Washington outlined a plan to attack New York City by land and sea. Rochambeau agreed that capturing it would surely end the war. He would be glad to help, he said, adding: "The commands of the King, my master, place me under the orders of Your Excellency." Yet there was a catch. His master wanted the French army and navy to act together. Unfortunately, Rochambeau said, he needed more ships for such a dangerous operation. Until another, larger, fleet arrived, he would have to stay at Newport. The meeting ended with polite handshakes and a toast to future victories.[8]

The Count de Rochambeau, commander of the French army sent to fight beside the Americans, came from a line of soldiers that had served their country since the Crusades. From an engraving in Washington Irving's *Life of George Washington.*

Although Washington felt frustrated, nothing had prepared him for what happened next. On September 25, two days after leaving Rochambeau, he learned of a stunning betrayal.

Had Benedict Arnold not turned traitor, today Americans would honor him as a hero of the Revolution for his actions at Saratoga in 1777. But Arnold was a bitter man who felt that the Continental Congress did not appreciate his talent or reward him as he deserved. Soon after becoming military governor of Philadelphia, he married the beautiful Peggy Shippen, daughter of a family that included patriots and Tories. During the British occupation, she had become friendly with Major John André, a talented artist and poet. André also headed Sir Henry Clinton's spy service.

Urged by his wife, Arnold asked Washington to put him in charge of West Point, the fortress overlooking the Hudson River north of New York City. Called "the key to America," it guarded a huge chain that army engineers had stretched from shore to shore to prevent British ships from sailing upstream. The chain was 1,097 feet long. It had iron links, weighing one hundred pounds each, attached to logs anchored a few feet below the water's surface. Anyway, Washington gave Arnold the post.

Benedict Arnold was hated almost as much by the British, whom he served, as the Americans, whom he betrayed. From an engraving in Washington Irving's *Life of George Washington.*

What Washington did not know was that Arnold was secretly writing to André in New York. He eventually agreed, for a price, to weaken West Point's defenses, allowing the British to seize it in a raid. To sweeten the deal, Arnold also promised to deliver the commander in chief to them, if possible.

On September 25, three militiamen stopped André near Tarrytown, just north of the British lines. Growing suspicious, they searched him and found drawings of West Point hidden in his boot. Under questioning, he admitted he was returning from a meeting with Benedict Arnold. Since

André wore civilian clothes and not his uniform, Washington had him tried as a spy, a hanging offense under the laws of war. A jury of officers, Lafayette among them, found him guilty and sentenced him to death.

In return, Clinton made hostages of twenty leading New Yorkers. If the American commander hoped to save their lives, Sir Henry warned, he had better give up André in exchange. Washington did not scare easily; threats only made him stubborn. Angrily, he wrote that if Clinton hung innocent people, he would hang twenty captured British officers. However, he would gladly trade André for Arnold, who had escaped to New York. Clinton refused. Although Washington pitied André, even sent him the last meal from his table, he said he must die as a warning to others. An aide recalled that his hand shook as he signed André's death warrant on October 2.

Andre's execution sent the British army into mourning. Clinton was

Links of the great chain stretched across the Hudson River at West Point and a few of the mortars used in its defense. From Benson Lossing's *Pictorial Field Book of the Revolution.*

Major John André was searched and arrested by an American patrol while trying to return to the British base at New York City.

Self-portrait of Major John André made shortly before his execution as a spy.

stunned. "The horrid deed is done," he wrote in a private letter. "Washington has committed premeditated murder. . . . Washington has become a murderer." The British general forgot that Nathan Hale had died for the same offense. No matter. Redcoats wearing black armbands roamed the streets of New York shouting, "André! André! Vengeance with the bayonet to the Sons of Rebellion."[9]

Although Arnold's plan to betray West Point failed, he still did plenty of damage. As a reward for his treachery, Clinton gave him £6,300 in cash—a huge sum—and the rank of brigadier general in the British army; he returned the favor by giving the names of nearly every spy Washington had in New York. His treason also left Washington personally crushed. Lafayette recalled his friend's shock and sadness. "Arnold has betrayed me," he groaned. "Who can I trust now?" Then he burst into tears.[10]

The tears dried quickly, leaving a terrible thirst for vengeance. Washington felt a hatred for Arnold such as he never felt for any human being. He had approved many death sentences; he once signed the death warrant for a man who forged army discharges. Arnold, however, was the only man he ever truly *wanted* to kill. He gave his own money and approved a plan to kidnap the traitor and bring him to trial. "My aim," he said, "is to make an example of him." Luckily for Arnold, American agents never got close enough to grab him.[11]

Unluckily for patriots, everything seemed to be going wrong. Besides defeats in the South and Arnold's treason, Washington's men were furious over their lack of wages and supplies. Since the states refused to tax themselves to support the war, the Continental Congress kept printing paper money. By mid-1780, a thousand paper dollars equaled one dollar in "hard money," that is, gold or silver. Prices soared. Butter cost $12 a pound, tea $90 a pound, and stockings $300 a pair. Washington complained that "a wagon-load of money will scarcely purchase a wagon-load of provisions." As at Valley Forge, merchants sold the army spoiled food and poorly made clothing; cobblers used odd scraps of leather to make shoes that quickly fell apart.[12]

Tearful soldiers came to Washington with letters telling of desperate wives begging neighbors for food to feed their children. Washington told the Continental Congress that his soldiers felt neglected, cheated, and abused by the people they were risking their lives to defend. Some of his men hated civilians more than the enemy. "I hate my countrymen," Colonel Ebenezer Huntington, a combat veteran, wrote his brother back

An American cartoon showing Benedict Arnold as a two-faced traitor and a servant of the devil.

home in Connecticut. "I wish I could say I was not born in America. I once gloried in it, but am now ashamed of it. . . . My cowardly country-men . . . flinch at the very time when their exertions are wanted and hold their purse strings as though they would damn the world rather than part with a dollar for the Army."[13]

The problem came to a head in 1780. During the first six months of that year, regiments from Connecticut, Massachusetts, and New York grew restless. Finally, they refused to follow orders until the Continental Congress met their demands for back pay and new clothes. Congress put them off with promises, but nothing changed—nor could it without money. As he had done during the dark days at Valley Forge, Washington badgered members of Congress and state officials to help his men before things got out of hand. Unfortunately, those who held the purse strings drew them tighter.

In January 1781, Pennsylvania and New Jersey regiments mutinied, killing two officers. Although Washington sympathized with the soldiers' aims, he could not tolerate disobedience and murder in the ranks. So he sent trusted troops from West Point to put down the uprising. Washington gave a harsh order to their commander, General Robert Howe (not a relative of the British general). Howe was "to compel the mutineers to unconditional surrender and execute a few of the most active and incendiary leaders."[14]

After surprising the mutineers in their sleep, Howe had two ringleaders tied to a rail fence and shot by a firing squad at close range. As their friends watched in terror, bullets blew their heads to bits, splattering the fence with blood and brains. Without that drastic action, Washington might have lost his entire army. Just then, however, he needed every man he could get.

Congress dismissed Horatio Gates after the Battle of Camden and gave Nathanael Greene the southern command. Although Washington had few men to spare, he sent him some topnotch aides, all fellow Virginians. Daniel Morgan, at six feet and two hundred pounds, was Brother Nat's second in command and a daring frontier fighter. Morgan had hated the British since the French and Indian War, when they whipped him for talking back to an officer. Greene's cavalry chiefs were William Washington, the general's cousin, and "Light-Horse Harry" Lee, a master at hit-and-run raids.

Greene reached South Carolina in December 1780, only to find the situation worse than he expected. Cornwallis usually sent British cavalry and mounted Tories to clear the way for his army. By doing so, he ignited a merciless civil war. Redcoats arrested rebel sympathizers and looted plantation houses. Tories went wild. All the abuses they had suffered at patriot hands exploded into violence. South Carolina's Tories routinely tortured wounded patriots before killing them; some raped and murdered their womenfolk.

Patriots were no better. There are eyewitness reports of them forcing hog manure down Tories' throats and slowly strangling them with thin wire. Private William Gipson, furious at Tories for whipping his widowed mother, orga-

General Nathanael Greene, one of Washington's most trusted officers, led the campaign against the British in the Carolinas and Georgia.

nized a manhunt. When his unit caught the guilty man, they "spicketed" him; that is, set one of his feet on a nail driven into a board and spun him around until the nail came through. "The Whigs [patriots] seem determined to [exterminate] the Tories, and the Tories the Whigs," Greene wrote Washington. "If a stop cannot be put to these massacres, the country will be depopulated in a few months more, as neither Whig nor Tory can live." We do not know how Washington felt about the atrocities; his letters are silent about them.[15]

Brother Nat's forces were too weak to challenge Cornwallis to a full-scale battle. Instead, he decided to fight a kind of war the British did not understand. Like Washington, he believed the weaker side might lose every battle and still win the war. The trick was to wage a "war of maneuver," in which he would avoid battle except on his own terms. By drawing the invader into the interior, far from his supply base on the coast, he would let hunger and long marches wear down his army. Then, at the right moment, he would strike hard.

Greene split his force in two. While he headed for North Carolina,

Daniel Morgan was a veteran frontier fighter who crushed a strong British force at Hannah's Cowpens, South Carolina, on January 17, 1781.

Morgan struck enemy outposts in South Carolina. Cornwallis took the bait, splitting his own force to meet the twin threats.

On January 17, 1781, Morgan let Banastre Tarleton, the British cavalry chief, find him at Hannah's Cowpens, South Carolina. Morgan's men held their fire until the last moment, slaughtered the charging redcoats, and then joined Greene in North Carolina. Together, they fought Cornwallis to a draw at Guilford Courthouse on March 15. Greene kept moving. He marched his entire force into South Carolina, only to have the British beat him at Hobkirk's Hill on April 25. Yet he was satisfied, for he always hurt the enemy at little cost to his own army. As he told a friend, "We fight, get beat, rise, and fight again."[16]

Cornwallis retreated to Wilmington on the North Carolina coast to meet a fleet of supply ships from New York. During his stay there, he decided to invade Virginia. It was a desperate move, he knew, for it meant turning his back on his conquests in the lower South. That would leave Greene free to retake Georgia and South Carolina, except Savannah and Charleston, which were held by strong garrisons. Nevertheless, Cornwallis believed the invasion was worth a try. Greene's army, he knew, could not exist without men and supplies from the Old Dominion; nor could Washington's army outside New York. So, late in May 1781, he marched north to join Benedict Arnold.

Arnold had landed in Virginia with 1,600 redcoats five months earlier. Moving along the James River, he burned Richmond, the state capital, then swept through the countryside to destroy rebel supply dumps. Washington sent Lafayette with 1,200 men and orders to kill the traitor on sight. "If he should fall into your hands, you will execute him in the most summary way"—without a trial. But that was not to be.

Cornwallis took over Arnold's troops, and Arnold returned to New York. Although Arnold was a very good soldier, His Lordship considered him a very bad man. Like most British officers, he would have been glad to take West Point without a fight. Yet they had no use for the dishonorable traitor who would have sold it to them. America's greatest traitor survived the war and died in 1801, in London, after losing most of his traitor's pay to bad business deals.[17]

His Lordship waged a brutal campaign of looting, burning, and killing.

One of his ships even anchored in the Potomac at Mount Vernon. Its captain turned his guns toward the big house and demanded food. Lund Washington sent the food. When eighteen slaves ran away, Lund did nothing to prevent their leaving with the British. Lund's actions angered his

Nicknamed "the Butcher" by patriots, Colonel Banastre Tarleton led daring cavalry raids deep behind American lines in the Carolinas. This painting, by Sir Joshua Reynolds, was done in 1782 and hangs in the National Portrait Gallery, London.

employer. Washington sent a stinging letter, saying: "It would have been a less painful circumstance to me, to have heard, that in consequence of your non-compliance with their request, they had burnt my House and laid the Plantation in ruins," even taken "all my Negroes."[18]

Lafayette asked for more men. Washington sent eight hundred Pennsylvania troops. Like the British, Hessians, and French, these northerners were ignorant of southern ways, particularly slavery. Although slavery was legal in the North at this time, it was not nearly as common there as in the South. A farmer or frontiersman might go his entire life without seeing a black person, slave or free.

Soldiers' letters and diaries give a chilling picture of southern slavery. They had never seen anything so degrading. "No white man ever labors, but all the work is done by black slaves," observed Count Axel Ferson, a Swedish volunteer. Others noted slave children of mixed race, the offspring of black women raped by white masters. Lieutenant William Feltman of Pennsylvania had the surprise of his life when his regiment passed some plantations near Richmond. In his diary, he told of fair-skinned white women greeting the column:

June 22, 1781—They sometimes come to the road side in order to take a view of us as we pass by, but a person can hardly discern any part of them but the nose and eyes, as they have themselves muffled up with linens, &c., in order to prevent the sun from burning their faces (I mean the female sex). At the same time they will have a number of blacks standing around them, all naked, nothing to hide their nakedness. You can easily distinguish their sex; I mean the blacks, for reasons already mentioned. They will also have their attendants dressed in the same uniform. They will also attend their table in this manner.[19]

The cruelties of patriots and Tories toward each other paled before the horrors of slavery. Lieutenant Feltman saw all that remained of a black man punished for a crime. His killers had stuck his severed head on a tree branch beside the road and tied his right hand to another branch. Hector St. John de Crèvecœur, a French settler, found an iron cage hanging high in a tree. Inside it he saw a black man with his hands tied, his eyes pecked out by crows, and his body covered by flies feeding on his open wounds. The man said his master had put him up there, to die slowly, for striking an overseer. He begged Crèvecœur to end his misery with a bullet, but the Frenchman had no ammunition and hurried away. Sights like these sowed the seeds of abolitionism, the effort to abolish slavery in the new nation.[20]

Lafayette's forces were still not strong enough to halt the British rampage. Nevertheless, he kept snapping at the enemy, ambushing patrols and burning supply wagons. The tactic worked. Frustrated by endless marches, his men exhausted by the stifling heat, Cornwallis returned to the coast. On August 1, 1781, he occupied a sleepy tobacco port of three hundred houses near the tip of the Virginia Peninsula. Formed by the York River on the south and the James River on the north, the peninsula juts into Chesapeake Bay. The town lay on the bank of the York River—thus the name Yorktown. Without realizing it, His Lordship had walked into a trap. It was not a trap Washington planned, but it would do nevertheless.

Three months earlier, on May 19, 1781, Washington had had a second meeting with Count de Rochambeau. The Frenchman brought wonderful news. Another fleet, commandered by François Joseph Paul, Count de Grasse, had already put to sea. De Grasse, fifty-nine years old, had been in the navy since the age of twelve. A living legend in the fleet, he stood six feet two inches, but his sailors said he was "six feet six on days of battle." Now he meant to stand ever taller. He commanded thirty-eight vessels, including the *Ville de Paris (City of Paris)*, the largest warship in the world. His ships also carried 3,500 troops and dozens of field guns. De Grasse would arrive sometime in August to cooperate with the allied armies.[21]

Washington still had his heart set on taking New York City. Not Rochambeau, who argued that its defenses were stronger than ever. Nothing could change Washington's mind. Rochambeau finally gave a written promise to join forces for a combined attack when the fleet arrived. Yet he still felt that destroying the enemy in Virginia would destroy Britain's will to continue the war. To avoid a quarrel, Rochambeau decided to go behind Washington's back. He sent a coded message to de Grasse's stop in the French West Indies. It advised the admiral to set a course for Virginia but keep it to himself until the last moment.[22]

Late in June, the French army left Newport, bound for the Hudson and from there to Washington's camp at Dobbs Ferry. This was the soldiers' first experience with the interior of America, and it shook them up. In certain ways, even the "settled" areas of New England and New York were still wilderness. Forest fires started by lightning burned until they ran out of fuel or reached a natural barrier, like a river. The Americans' attitude toward the fires amazed the French more than the fires themselves. An officer wrote that the fires "caused no excitement at all among the nearby Americans, whose country is full of forests. Sometimes they even congratulate themselves on having a big conflagration, as it saves them the trouble of cutting down the trees to clear the land."[23]

On July 6, the French reached Washington's camp at Dobbs Ferry on the Hudson, fifteen miles north of Manhattan. That meeting was an eye-opener for everyone.

Americans still had prejudices left over from the French and Indian War. They pictured their allies as perfumed dandies with big noses, who spent hours "frizzling their hair and painting their faces." The French *did* enjoy dazzling colors. Infantrymen wore white linen uniforms with different color lapels and collars—scarlet, yellow, green, pink, violet—for each regiment. Cavalrymen had skintight red breeches, light blue coats, and rode black horses with tiger-skin saddle cloths. Each night, bands played lively tunes as men paired off to dance in the light of roaring bonfires. Americans hung back at first, not sure what to make of men dancing together. They soon got into the swing. Frenchmen and Americans, officers and soldiers, danced together in "a feast of Equality."[24]

It was not all fancy clothing and fun, however. Rochambeau led the cream of the French army. Flags advertised each regiment's deeds and fighting spirit with a list, embroidered in gold thread, of its battles and its motto. The flag of the Soissonais Regiment, for example, quoted a sergeant's dying words: "What does it matter? We have won the battle." Soldiers lived up to their regimental traditions. Their drills impressed even Baron von Steuben, and they handled their weapons expertly. Not a few had scars on their faces, souvenirs of bayonet charges.[25]

The newcomers had expected to find fiery patriots eager for a fight. At first glance, however, Washington's men resembled scarecrows more than soldiers. Such lean, hungry-looking fellows! Their hair hung down around their ears like dirty string mops. Flies hovered around their unwashed bodies. "These brave fellows made one's heart ache," wrote Baron Ludwig von Closen, a German serving with the French. "It is almost unbelievable! For the most part they are almost without clothes. They only had trousers and a little coat, or jacket, of linen. The greater number wore no socks."[26]

Continentals slept four to a tent on branches covered with thin blankets that had never met warm water and soap. Despite their shabbiness, however, they swaggered like men who knew their business. Black soldiers swaggered with the rest. Visitors praised the Rhode Island Regiment, a mostly black unit. One found it "the most neatly dressed, the best under arms, and the most precise in its movements."[27]

French soldiers with big noses, as seen by a soldier in Washington's army.

Everyone admired the American commander. Officers filled letters and diary pages with word portraits of him. These keen observers studied *le grand Washington*, "the great Washington," from every angle. His appearance and manner fascinated Count Axel Fersen. "He looks like a hero; he is very cold and says little, but he is frank and polite." In addition, Fersen noted that Washington always wore a stern expression, which "renders his face more interesting."[28]

Still other visitors focused on the general's character. The Count de Ségur wrote a friend in Paris that Washington "inspired rather than commanded respect, and in the eyes of all the men around him, one could read their real affection and whole-hearted confidence in a chief upon whom they seemed to rely entirely for their security." If America ever won independence, the count added, it would be due chiefly to his courage, decency, and good sense.[29]

Washington's effect on ordinary people amazed the French. Abbé Claude Robin, an army chaplain, noted the difference between him and a European ruler. In Europe, people greeted kings at elaborately staged spectacles, with low bows and high-sounding praise. Americans really loved Washington—and freely showed it. Whenever he appeared, their greetings came from the heart. "They consider him in the light of a beneficent God, dispensing peace and happiness around him. Old men, women and children press around him when he passes along, and think themselves happy, once in their lives, to have seen him. They follow him through the towns with torches, and celebrate his arrival with public illuminations. The Americans, that cool and sedate people . . . are roused, animated and inflamed at the very mention of his name."[30]

From Dobbs Ferry, the allies probed New York's defenses for a month, actions that convinced Rochambeau of the impossibility of taking the city. His showdown with Washington came on August 14, less than two weeks after Cornwallis reached Yorktown. Rochambeau reminded Washington that only de Grasse commanded the fleet. The admiral would work with the soldiers, but not obey their orders. Rochambeau lied and said he had just learned the fleet was bound for Chesapeake Bay. If the armies arrived by early September, de Grasse might cut off Yorktown from the sea and support a land attack. If they did not come in time, he would return to the Caribbean. Washington must decide. He could march to Virginia and go for a knockout blow, or mark time outside New York.

Washington took the news hard. He controlled himself until the Frenchman left, then exploded in a blind fury. An aide found him striding back and forth, shouting in "resentment, indignation and despair." Yet the storm passed as quickly as it came. He returned to headquarters to plan the Yorktown campaign.[31]

The allies had to carry out an incredibly difficult operation. To succeed, they must juggle distant land and sea forces that did not know the other's whereabouts. Each force had to arrive at the right place, at the right time, and gain overwhelming superiority before the enemy reacted. Unfortunately, the fleet depended on things beyond human control: wind, weather, currents, tides. Yet Washington *could* do something about the movements of the land force.

He knew the army must clear the New York area before the enemy realized its destination. If Clinton learned the truth in time, he might reinforce Cornwallis by sea or cross the Hudson to attack the lumbering columns. If he believed Washington meant to attack New York via Staten Island, he would sit tight, safe behind his defenses. In short, Washington had to persuade Clinton that he meant to attack him and not Cornwallis.

Washington, a master at leaking false information, now outdid himself. He began by swearing his aides to total secrecy. "If we do not deceive our own men," he explained, "we will never deceive the enemy." Nevertheless, only he and Rochambeau knew the entire truth, and they kept it to themselves.[32]

Washington's cover plan had many parts, like a jigsaw puzzle. Each part had a place in the total scheme. The commander in chief, for example, knew that Clinton had spies in the allied camps; he even knew the identity of most. Rather than arrest them, he used them to feed their boss false information. He also had American agents spread rumors meant for the ears of enemy spies. Elsewhere, engineers burned barricades and filled holes in the roads leading to New York, as if preparing for an attack. Bakers built huge bread ovens at Chatham, New Jersey, four miles inland from Staten Island. Washington enjoyed the farce, writing long letters meant for messengers to "lose" when chased by British cavalry patrols. In one letter, he asked an unnamed spy to "inquire minutely" into British gun positions in New York. Clinton also "captured" notes of a meeting where the allied leaders agreed to go to Virginia if the attack on New York failed!

After leaving a small force to cover New York, Washington crossed the Hudson on August 20–21; Rochambeau followed four days later. The allied columns turned south, moving through clouds of dust raised by tramping feet and iron-rimmed wheels. Passing Staten Island on their left, they continued southward. At that point, Washington ordered the troops to toss their packs into the wagons and increase the pace. Now the soldiers realized! They were going to Virginia! Meanwhile, Clinton waited for an attack that did not come. When spies spotted the allies near Philadelphia, Clinton realized it would never come—at New York.

The allied armies marched through Philadelphia on September 1. Citizens swarmed around Washington, happy for a chance to touch his boots or pat his horse. The unsmiling general answered their cheers by tipping his hat. Still, he could not hide his emotions entirely. A French officer,

Count Mathieu Dumas, saw tears glisten in the corners of his eyes. Turning to Dumas, he said: "We may be beaten by the English; that is the chance of war. But here is the army that they will never conquer.[33]

Everything depended on the French fleet arriving on schedule. Where was de Grasse? Washington often asked the question but got no answers. Nobody knew. It seemed as if de Grasse had vanished amid Atlantic fogs. Finally, on September 5, a rider brought a message from the admiral. Great news! His warships stood at the entrance to Chesapeake Bay. Washington galloped away to tell Rochambeau. When he found the French general, he hugged him so tightly that aides swore they heard his bones crackle.

On that very day, de Grasse won a battle off the Virginia coast. When Clinton had realized his mistake, he ordered Admiral Thomas Graves, Black Dick Howe's replacement, to sea with nineteen ships. Although de Grasse failed to sink any British ships, his guns damaged two so badly that their crews abandoned them and set them on fire. De Grasse lost no time in putting his troops ashore to join Lafayette at Williamsburg, twelve miles from Yorktown, trapping Cornwallis by land and sea.

The French soon realized how deeply patriots and Tories hated each other. An officer reported that his patrol saw the most horrible sight imaginable. Upon entering a deserted plantation house, they found a pregnant woman "murdered in her bed through several bayonet stabs." Written above the bed canopy, in blood, were the words: "Thou shalt never give birth to a rebel." In another room, they found five human heads neatly arranged on the shelf of a cupboard.[34] The French never caught the killers, so we cannot know their exact reasons for committing such a crime. Yet it seems pretty certain that hatred between patriot and Tory went so deep that by 1781 some were willing to kill unborn babies.

Meanwhile, the allied armies increased their pace, often marching twenty miles a day. On September 7, they reached Head of Elk, Maryland. There they met scores of small boats Washington had ordered to take the artillery across Chesapeake Bay. The overloaded boats plowed through the choppy water, scaring the wits out of their passengers. Even so, Dr. James Thacher would not have traded the experience for the world. As his boat neared the Virginia shore, "We enjoyed a distant view of the grand

French fleet, riding at anchor at the mouth of the Chesapeake. . . . This was the most noble and majestic spectacle I ever witnessed, and we viewed it with inexpressible pleasure."[35]

Washington grew restless. After leaving orders for the army to follow overland, he cried, "Billy, hand me my horse!" Together, the general, Billy Lee, and an aide left the troop columns in their dust. Washington saw no need for bodyguards; he knew this countryside like the back of his hand and trusted its people. Besides, no cavalry escort could have kept the pace he set.

The three men raced the wind, halting only to water their horses and gobble a few hard biscuits. They covered the sixty miles to Baltimore, Maryland, in a day and were off before dawn next morning, September 10. Only another sixty-five miles to go!

They galloped along familiar lanes, across familiar bridges, past familiar plantation houses. Farmers recognized the big man in blue and buff and doffed their hats; women curtsied. Suddenly, there it was: the pebbly driveway and the house on the hill overlooking the Potomac. After an absence of six years and four months, George Washington stood at the front door of Mount Vernon.

Martha greeted him. So did four grandchildren, three girls and a boy he had never seen. Their father, Jacky Custis, had not changed a bit. Now twenty-eight years old, he had not spent a day in the army, but stayed home, living a life of leisure. To amuse his drinking buddies, he taught daughter Elizabeth to sing dirty songs. Yet it must have hurt Jacky to think that other men his age had won respect during the war. So, when Washington left again, he went along as part of Washington's military family. Jacky went not to fight, but to see the end of the war.[36]

Within the week, the allied armies joined Lafayette's force at Williamsburg. The marquis lay in bed, feverish with malaria. When the drums sounded assembly, he rushed to greet his hero. Thousands watched in shocked amusement as he ran toward Washington, his arms flung wide open. Without slowing down, he "caught the General around his body, hugged him as close as it was possible, and absolutely kissed him from ear to ear once or twice." A few days later, Washington visited Admiral de Grasse to discuss his plans. As he clambered aboard the *Ville de*

Paris, de Grasse kissed him on both cheeks and cried, *"Mon cher petit Général!,"* "My dear little general!" The little general's aides roared with laughter.[37]

The allied armies left Williamsburg at dawn on September 28. It was a clear, hot day, with small, puffy clouds hanging motionless in the sky. The sweating men trudged through ankle-deep sand. Yet their spirits had never been higher. They had the enemy where they wanted him—trapped by land and sea. Victory was in the air; they could smell it, taste it, feel it in their bones.

Joseph Plumb Martin, a sergeant at last, described the day in his humorous way: "We prepared to move down to pay our old acquaintance, the British, at Yorktown, a visit. I doubt not but that their wish was not to have so many of us come at once. . . . They thought, 'The fewer the better cheer.' We thought, 'The more the merrier.' We had come a long way to see them and were unwilling to be put off with excuses." Reinforcements, including militia units from all over the South, gave Washington a total strength of about 21,000 men. Cornwallis had around 7,500 men.[38]

His Lordship prepared to resist with his usual skill and energy. While sailors unloaded cannons from their ships, he put runaway slaves to work on his defenses. This was hot, heavy work that exhausted most soldiers quickly. Most blacks were used to hard labor outdoors; others keeled over from sunstroke. They toiled day and night, by the light of torches and lanterns. When they finished, Cornwallis did a shameful thing. To save food, he ordered redcoats to "turn out every nonessential mouth." Guards drove away some 4,000 black people with their bayonets. Fearing capture by their former masters, they fled in terror.[39]

Sergeant Martin saw them trapped between the lines. He wrote bitterly: "During the siege, we saw in the woods herds of Negroes . . . scattered about in every direction, dead and dying, with pieces of ears of burnt Indian corn in their hands and mouths, even of those who were dead." Some had smallpox. Throughout his Virginia campaign, Cornwallis used smallpox sufferers as weapons of germ warfare. He deliberately left them by roadsides and at likely campsites to spread the infection to the allies. Fortunately, Washington had been inoculating his troops since 1777. We do not know if he saw any smallpox victims, or, if he did, what he thought of such a human tragedy. The French had a few smallpox cases, but surgeons isolated them to prevent an epidemic.[40]

Yorktown's defenses consisted of several redoubts, small forts with cannons, anchoring a line of deep trenches with high breastworks. Each trench had scores of "blinds," or barrels of sand, for men to hide behind when shells landed nearby. A tangle of felled trees, their sharpened branches pointing outward, lay in front of the breastworks, like coils of barbed wire. In some places, hundreds of logs pierced with rows of sharpened stakes blocked the approaches.

Washington decided that only a full-scale siege would force Cornwallis to surrender. Fortunately, he had a team of French engineers to plan the operation. Rochambeau himself was a master of siegecraft, the art of taking fortresses. During the European wars, he had conducted twenty successful sieges.

A siege required the attackers to dig a line of trenches facing the fortress, then bring their cannons as close to it as possible. That is harder than it sounds. Since the defenders also had cannons, they dared not work in the open. Starting at the main trench line, which lay beyond the range of the enemy's guns, engineers dug "saps," or zigzag trenches, toward the fortress at night. When the saps got out far enough, they dug to the right and left, forming a new trench parallel to the main line. Gunners then brought up cannons to bombard the enemy at closer range. The engineers, meanwhile, dug more saps. Gradually, the trench lines tightened until cannons fired day and night, blasting the defenders' positions at close range. Finally, the infantry charged with the bayonet.

British gunners kept up a steady fire, trying to stop the digging. Washington rode everywhere, encouraging his men to dig faster. As usual, he ignored his personal safety. He had a job to do, and he would do it whatever the danger. Once a shell landed near him and an army chaplain, showering them with earth. The chaplain held out his hat to Washington and stammered, "See here, general." A smile crossed the general's face. "Mr. Evans," he said, "you had better carry that home and show it to your wife and children."[41]

Washington expected a civilian to show fear his first time under fire. Yet he would not tolerate it by a veteran, let alone an officer. While riding with his staff in daylight, he paused to scan Cornwallis's positions with a spyglass. British gunners found their range and started to bang away. Soon the "incoming" came too close for comfort. That rattled Colonel David Cobb of Massachusetts.

"Sir," said Cobb, "you are too much exposed here. Had you not better step a little back?"

Washington would do no such thing. "Colonel Cobb," he snapped, "if you are afraid, you have the liberty to step back."[42]

Nobody dared head for cover after that remark. The little group stayed in the open, anxiously watching cannonballs plow the ground and shells explode overhead, until Washington folded his spyglass. Common soldiers repeated this story. Soldiers were forever dodging shells, and it was good to know that the general took his chances along with them.

Everything was ready on October 9. At exactly 5:00 P.M., Washington fired the first cannon shot in the siege of Yorktown. Seconds later, every allied gun fired with a deafening roar. That was just the beginning. As the trench lines advanced, gunners brought more cannons into action. Finally, over one hundred heavy guns pounded Yorktown without letup.

The British guns gradually fell silent, leaving Yorktown defenseless. The ground shook, as in an earthquake. Buildings collapsed with a gut-wrenching crash, burying soldiers in their rubble. Fires raged out of control. Streams of fiery cinders shot skyward, while clouds of smoke hung over the doomed town. Dr. James Thacher described the terror, and beauty, of the scene:

> Being in the trenches every other night and day, I have a fine opportunity of witnessing the sublime and stupendous scene which is constantly exhibiting. The bombshells from the besiegers and the besieged are incessantly crossing each others' path in the air. They are clearly visible in the form of a black ball in the day, but in the night, they appear like a fiery meteor with a blazing tail, most beautifully brilliant. . . . It is astonishing with what accuracy an experienced gunner will make his calculations, that a shell shall fall within a few feet of a given point, and burst at the precise time, though at a great distance. . . . I have more than once witnessed fragments of

the mangled bodies and limbs of the British soldiers thrown into the air by the bursting of our shells. . . . The whole peninsula trembles under the incessant thunderings of our infernal machines. . . .[43]

It was more than human nature could bear. At 9:00 A.M. on October 17, the eighth day of the bombardment, a boy drummer mounted the British breastworks. At first, the allied guns drowned out his quick *rap-tap-tap*, the traditional signal for a parley. Gradually, the gunners noticed him and ceased fire. *Rap-tap-tap. Rap-tap-tap.* "I thought I had never heard a drum equal to it—the most delightful music to us all," said Lieutenant Ebenezer Denny. A British officer waving a white handkerchief then came forward with a message for Washington from Cornwallis. His Lordship wished to surrender.[44]

Next morning, before dawn, a strange sound came from the British lines. It seemed harsh at first. Yet, as the allied troops listened more closely, they found it pleasant, even mournful. In a show of respect for fellow soldiers, Scottish bagpipers were serenading them with Highland tunes. When the Scots finished, a French band gave its musical reply. So it went: serenade, reply, serenade.

Slowly, the rising sun revealed a fantastic scene. The opposing armies stood atop their breastworks, without weapons, finally able to show themselves without fear. The music stopped. Lieutenant Denny recalled that "a solemn stillness prevailed" as thousands of soldiers just stood there, staring at the battlefield and at each other. Before long, American and British officers met between the lines to work out the surrender details.[45]

October 19, 1781. The allied armies lined the Yorktown-Williamsburg road for over a mile, the Americans on one side and the French on the other. At 3:00 P.M. sharp, the British and Hessians marched out of the ruined town by regiments. As they did, French warships anchored offshore, their guns ready for action should anything go wrong.

Cornwallis's troops carried their unloaded muskets without bayonets, signs of surrender. They had their flags furled and cased, with black ribbons dangling from the fifes and drums, also signs of defeat. Regimental bands played a nonsense tune called "The World Turned Upside Down":

If ponies rode men and if grass ate cows,
And cats should be chased into holes by the mouse.
If summer were spring and the other way round,
Then all the world would be upside down.[46]

John Trumbull painted this famous picture of the British surrender at Yorktown.

Those words had special meaning today. For the defenders of Yorktown, the world *had* turned upside down. They had just lost a war, and everyone knew it. An officer, a red-faced fellow splendid in scarlet and gold, led the column on foot. Rather than suffer the "disgrace" of surrender, Lord Cornwallis had sent Brigadier General Charles O'Hara in his place. O'Hara, forty-two years old, a soldier since the age of twelve, had tears rolling down his cheeks.

The redcoats kept their heads turned toward the French, desperately trying to blot out the Americans standing across the road. Lafayette took this as an insult to his ragged troops. He snapped an order, and instantly an American band exploded with "Yankee Doodle." "Then," Lafayette wrote a friend, "they did look at us, my dear sir, but they were not very well pleased."[47]

O'Hara was even less pleased when he offered his sword, representing the whole army's surrender, to Rochambeau. A French staff officer shook his head and pointed across the road, saying "We are subordinate to the Americans. General Washington will give you orders."[48]

Washington refused the sword, but ordered O'Hara to a field ringed by French cavalry. American officers showed the prisoners where to stack their weapons. The Hessians looked relieved, glad to escape with their skins intact. The redcoats were grim and sullen; an American said they seemed "much in liquor"—drunk. "The British officers in general behaved like little boys who had been whipped in school. Some bit their lips, some pouted, others cried," an American recalled.[49]

Washington treated his prisoners according to the laws of war. Officers went free after signing their parole, promises not to fight in America on pain of death if recaptured. Common soldiers would stay in prison camps until diplomats signed a peace treaty. Others, however, paid a heavier price for the British defeat. Patrols scoured Yorktown for Continental Army deserters; firing squads executed at least a dozen men. Washington gave plantation owners permission to hire soldiers to hunt down runaway slaves in the woods. Sergeant Martin earned $1,200 in paper money catching slaves and spent it all on a quart of whiskey.[50] (That seems like a lot of money, even today, but by that time paper money was almost worthless.)

Without realizing it, the commander in chief had fought his last military campaign. Yet, ahead lay more struggles and even greater risks.

THE THING
IS DONE

The Lord above, in tender love,
Hath sav'd us from our foes;
Through Washington the thing is done,
The war is at a close.

America has won the day,
Through Washington our chief;
Come let's rejoice with heart and voice,
And bid adieu to grief.

— "THANKSGIVING HYMN," 1781

An express rider reached Philadelphia with news of Yorktown after midnight on October 24, 1781. A city watchman, an old German, heard it first. After taking the rider to the house of Thomas McKean, the president of Congress, he walked through the darkened streets with his bell and lantern, calling in a thick accent, "Basht dree o'glock, und Gorn-wal-lis isht da-ken."[1]

The news spread quickly. Across America, patriots celebrated with bonfires, bands, and toasts to George Washington, "our savior and our hero." Washington, however, did not enjoy his victory very long. On the same day that Cornwallis surrendered, the general learned that Jacky Custis had come down with a "fever"; he died two weeks later. Mount

Vernon went into mourning. Martha had lost her last child, the only family member to die during the war.

Jacky's widow followed Virginia custom. She soon remarried and brought her two eldest daughters to her new husband's plantation. Washington adopted the two youngest children. Eleanor Parke Custis— "Nelly"—grew into a beautiful woman who won the hearts of all she met. George Washington Parke Custis—"Wash"—took after Jacky. Following a lifestyle of ease and fun, he passed the time by painting heroic pictures of his stepfather and wrote a book describing him as almost Godlike. Gossips said he had several children by his slave women.

On November 25, 1781, news of the surrender reached London. When Lord North heard it, he threw up his arms as if shot in the chest. "Oh God! Oh God!" he cried. "It is over! It is all over!"[2] Then he ran around the room, repeating the words in a daze.

Lord North's master declared it was not over. King George still had his army, his navy, and his belief that whatever he wanted was right. So he intended to continue the war. Parliament, however, decided to call it quits. When His Majesty heard that, he threatened to abdicate—give up the throne and become a private citizen. After thinking the matter over more carefully, he reversed himself and agreed to stay on for the good of the country, he claimed.

His Majesty accepted Lord North's resignation and chose a new prime minister, Lord Rockingham, to make peace. Sir Guy Carleton, governor of Canada, replaced Sir Henry Clinton as chief of British forces in North America. In March 1782, Congress sent Benjamin Franklin, John Adams, John Jay, and Henry Laurens, a former president of Congress, to negotiate a peace treaty in Paris.

Meanwhile, the Continental Army marched back to its encampments outside New York. Washington had no idea that he would spend nearly two more years struggling with familiar problems that kept growing worse. The reason, as before, was that the United States had no government with power over all the states.

A year earlier, in March 1781, the states had adopted the Articles of Confederation. The articles gave Congress authority over military and foreign affairs, but no power over individual citizens or the separate states.

Congress could only raise money by asking the states to tax themselves. Yet, when it asked for a tax to support the army, the states refused. As a result, rumors began to spread among the troops. Congress, they said, meant to dismiss them after the peace treaty without their back pay or any of the benefits it had promised when they enlisted.

That was too much for Colonel Lewis Nicola of Pennsylvania. In May 1782, he wrote Washington about the need for a strong government with him as king. Washington agreed with the part about a strong government; he had always wanted that. The part about becoming king, however, made him furious; he answered Nicola with a stinging rebuke. Americans did not need another King George! He advised the colonel to "banish these thoughts from your mind," and never breathe them to another living soul. Deeply humiliated, Nicola sent three apologies in as many days.[3]

Meanwhile, the diplomats haggled in Paris. On November 30, 1782, they approved the first draft of a peace treaty. The Treaty of Paris would end the war, guarantee American independence, and set the boundaries of the new nation. These would reach from the Atlantic coast to the Mississippi River, and from the Great Lakes and Maine to Spanish Florida. Although further discussions lay ahead, British forces left Charleston early in December; the French army sailed for home after Christmas. Washington and Lafayette parted with hugs and tears.

The draft treaty would bring the final crisis of the Revolution. When Washington's army returned to the North after Yorktown, it camped at Newburgh, New York, north of West Point. It was not a happy encampment. The soldiers were desperate for money, not having been paid for months. They were bitter, angry, and resentful. While they had been fighting for America's independence, others had stayed home and made money, often at their expense. That was wrong! If things did not improve soon, there was no telling what these veterans might do.

The Continental Congress could not, and the states would not, help. With the war effectively over, state legislators believed the army had lost its main reason for existing. Whether British redcoats or American Continentals, legislators distrusted regular soldiers—particularly those recruited from the lower classes of society. Rather than tax their people for the army's upkeep, legislators wanted to disband it as soon, and as cheaply, as possible.

Washington saw trouble ahead. He kept warning Congressmen and state legislators that they must do something for his soldiers:

> I cannot help fearing the result . . . when I see such a number of men . . . about to be turned into the world, soured by penury and what they call the ingratitude of the public, involved in debts without one farthing of money to carry them home, after having spent the flower of their days . . . in establishing the freedom and independence of the country. . . . The patience and long sufferance of this army are almost exhausted. . . .[4]

When conditions did not improve, the soldiers at Newburgh took matters into their own hands. In March 1783, officers circulated an unsigned letter called the Newburgh Address which demanded back pay for the army, aid for disabled veterans, and pensions for the families of dead soldiers. These demands had sharp teeth. If negotiations for the final peace treaty broke down, officers threatened to take their men to the frontier, leaving the country unprotected. If peace came after all, they would use force to get justice. Baron von Steuben had taught them well. They had the skill, and the will, to destroy any who stood in their way.

Washington thought the Newburgh Address more dangerous than the loss of any battle. He understood the justice of their demands, but if the officers carried out their threats, America would slide into anarchy, the total absence of law and order. Fearing a bloodbath, he called a meeting in the Temple, a large wooden building used as a church and dance hall.

On March 15, hundreds of officers filed into the Temple and sat down in silence. That was a bad sign, for officers always chatted and compared notes when they got together. The only sound was the metallic rattle of their swords as they moved about. Washington stood on a platform, looking down at a sea of grim faces. From their expressions, hard as stone, he knew they were in no mood to be put off.

Washington began by reading a prepared speech. The army, he said firmly, was the nation's servant and not its master. It existed to serve the people—nothing more and nothing less. Although he supported the officers' demands, using force to win them "has something so shocking in it that humanity revolts at the idea." Whom, and what, did they think they would leave unprotected? "Our wives? Our children? Our farms?"[5]

Nobody moved or changed expression. Washington sensed he was losing his audience. Not knowing what else to say, he unfolded a letter from a member of Congress promising to find some money somehow.

After reading the first paragraph, he paused and took out a pair of spectacles. Although he had used reading glasses for years, only his aides ever saw him wearing them at headquarters. "Gentlemen," he said, "you will permit me to put on my spectacles, for I have not only grown gray but almost blind in the service of my country."[6]

There was something so simple, so *human*, in his manner. It was like that time, after the victory at Trenton, when he asked soldiers to reenlist as a favor to him personally. Now memories like this came flooding back. Everyone had a story about the chief's decency. He had never let them down, never lied to them, never did less than his best for them. His appeal, an officer wrote, "forced its way into the heart." Hard expressions softened as the audience blinked back tears. Overcome by emotion, they voted to reject all threats and asked Washington to redouble his efforts for them.[7]

This was his finest hour. Yet few Americans realize what he really did during that historic meeting in the Temple. Washington had already led the army to victory. Now he saved the country after the guns fell silent. Most revolutions do not end with kindness and forgiveness. After defeating a common enemy, rebels feud among themselves, the winners setting up a dictatorship. Surely, the general's action avoided these tragedies. Washington's action at Newburgh was one of his chief contributions to the cause of American liberty. By his words and example he firmly established the principle that the military is under the civilian authorities.

Diplomats signed the final version of the peace treaty on September 3, 1783. By its terms, the British had to remove all their remaining troops, particularly from New York. That raised a serious problem for thousands of people. The city, we recall, had filled with Tories driven from their homes elsewhere. When an official read the treaty from the steps of City

Hall, the crowd booed and cursed King George "for having deserted them." The treaty merely bound Congress to "earnestly recommend" that states protect Tories and return their property.[8]

This would not happen. Too much blood and misery lay between patriot and Tory. The winners did not ignore those wrongs any more than the losers would have done in their place. Americans might forgive a foreign enemy, never a traitor. Nowadays we condemn "ethnic cleansing," driving an entire group from its homeland. After winning independence, one of the new nation's first acts was a "cleansing" of vast proportions. Patriots set out to rid America of Tories. Those "rotten, two-faced Benedict Arnolds" had chosen the wrong side and must pay the price. All "enemies of the liberties of America" had to go. An anonymous poet put it in one brief, cruel verse:

Tories, with their brats and wives,
Should fly to save their wretched lives.[9]

Tories desperately wanted to leave before Washington entered New York. The British offered to take them away free of charge and repay a small fraction of the value of the property they left behind. Convoys of ships sailed with about 25,000 people. These joined an additional 60,000 to 70,000 who had fled during the war. Seen another way, the Revolution created 30 refugees per 1,000 people; this is a horrendous number even by twentieth-century standards. Tory regiments like the British Legion, Queen's Rangers, and Loyal Americans left New York as complete fighting units. Most Tories, however, left in family groups with barely the clothes on their backs. The majority went to Canada, others to Britain or its West Indian colonies. The majority remained Americans, if not American citizens, to the end of their days. They missed their old homes and a way of life they could never recapture. Nowhere in his letters did Washington show any pity for these outcasts.

The Continental Army entered New York City after a seven-year absence. On the morning of December 4, nine days after the army's return, the last British transports lay in the outer harbor. At noon, Washington joined his officers at Fraunces Tavern on Pearl Street. It was a meeting he both welcomed and dreaded. With the war over at last, he must say good-bye to those he had grown to love, and who loved him.

Waiters had set a long table with a cold meal and bottles of red wine. Colonel Benjamin Tallmadge, of Washington's staff, described the event in his diary. The general arrived with his jaw set, wearing his most severe expression. Tallmadge, however, had learned to see beyond his chief's outward expressions. Obviously, he thought, an "emotion too strong to be concealed" held Washington in its grip. At his signal, they sat and began their last meal together. They ate silently, mechanically, barely tasting the food.[10]

Time dragged. Finally, the meal over, Washington filled his wineglass and wished them long life and prosperity. "With a heart full of love and gratitude, I now take leave of you," he said in a quivering voice. "I cannot

General Washington enters New York City after the British evacuation in 1783.

Washington's tearful farewell to his officers at New York's Fraunces Tavern. An engraving based on a painting by Alonzo Chappel.

come to each of you, but shall feel obliged if each of you will come and take my hand."[11]

Henry Knox went first. Weeping openly, he took his chief's hand. That did it! The invisible wall cracked wide open. Washington hugged the artilleryman, burst into tears, and kissed him on the cheek. Then each officer in turn came for a handshake and a kiss. "Such a scene of sorrow and weeping I had never before witnessed, and I hope I may never be called upon to witness again," Tallmadge wrote. "Not a word was uttered to break the solemn silence . . . or to interrupt the tenderness of the . . . scene."[12]

Regaining his poise, Washington left for the boat ride across the Hudson and his last official duty. As the boat left the Whitehall Street dock, a gust of wind brought the shrill of distant ships' whistles. In the outer harbor, acres of snow-white canvas billowed as the last British transports headed for the open Atlantic. Minutes passed. The crowd lining the Manhattan shore grew smaller. Suddenly, Washington opened his arms, "embracing" the crowd as he had embraced his officers.

For the common soldier, as for his commander, parting brought mixed feelings. Our old friend Sergeant Martin caught the mood perfectly. To his surprise, he felt "as much sorrow as joy" when his regiment disbanded. One day, the captain handed each man his discharge papers and an IOU for his back pay issued by Congress. Although glad to be leaving, they found it hard to say good-bye. Martin explained:

> We had lived together as a family of brothers for several years, setting aside some little family squabbles, like most other families, had shared with each other the hardships, dangers, and sufferings incidental to a soldier's life; had sympathized with each other in trouble and sickness; had assisted in bearing each other's burdens or strove to make them lighter by council and advice. . . . And now we were to be, the greater part of us, parted forever; as unconditionally separated as though the grave lay between us. . . . Ah! It was a serious time.[13]

It was a serious time for Washington, too. He rode south, a journey marked at each stop by loud celebrations. December 23 found him in Annapolis, Maryland. Several months earlier, a mob of soldiers, angry over back pay, had driven Congress out of Philadelphia. Until things calmed down, it met in the Maryland State House.

Washington had come to Annapolis to close his military career. That morning, he stood before Congress and returned, "with satisfaction," his commission as commander in chief. Onlookers said his hand trembled as he took the paper from his pocket. Then, after a brief ceremony, he walked into the pale sunshine. There, at the foot of the white marble steps, Billy Lee waited with his horse. They reached Mount Vernon by Christmas Eve, 1783.

· · ·

Silhouette of George Washington after the war.

A free man at last, Washington felt as if a heavy load had fallen from his shoulders. Now in his fifty-first year, he had come through the war in very good shape. Apart from his teeth, which gave no end of trouble, he had not been sick a day in eight years. Yet the war had left him physically and mentally tired. He wished only to spend the rest of his life quietly, as a private citizen minding his own business. Early in 1784, he wrote Lafayette:

> At length, my Dear Marquis, I am become a private citizen on the banks of the Potomac, & under the shadow of my own Vine & my own Fig tree, free from the bustle of a camp & the busy scenes of public life. . . . I am not only retired from all public employments, but I am retiring within myself. . . . Envious of none, I am determined to be pleased with all. And this, my dear friend, being the order for my march, I move gently down the stream of life, until I sleep with my Fathers.[14]

Martha Washington in middle age.

He tried to have a "normal" life. He and Martha enjoyed little Nelly and Wash, pampering them as they had done their father. Yet Washington found it hard to pay for all the things he thought his family should have. Like other plantation owners, he was "land poor"; that is, he had plenty of land but little cash. Many people owed him money since before the war. Yet Lund Washington had not collected tenants' rent for years, a serious error; others had borrowed hard cash at low interest rates. Now they paid off in near-worthless paper money. Although Washington tried to increase farm production by planting potatoes and different varieties of wheat, he found it increasingly difficult to make ends meet.

Try as he might, Washington could not

retire within himself. He was not allowed to. He had become our first celebrity and, like a modern movie star or sports idol, he attracted attention. People would not leave him alone. Travelers constantly imposed on his hospitality, inviting themselves for a night and a meal at Mount Vernon. Americans found the place magnificent, a palace. French noblemen, used to real palaces, described the big house as "simple" and thought its mistress "somewhat fat, but fresh and with a pleasant face."[15]

French sculptor Jean-Antoine Houdon made this "life mask" of George Washington in 1785. It is now in the Pierpont Morgan Library, New York City.

Artists came to paint Washington's portrait or chisel his image in marble. In 1785, the French sculptor Jean-Antoine Houdon arrived with his tools. Rather than carve the statue on the spot, a tedious job, he decided to work from a plaster "life mask." He had just smeared Washington's face with plaster when six-year-old Nelly Custis came along. She recalled seeing her step-grandfather "as I supposed, *dead*, and laid out on a large table" under a sheet. "Except his face, on which Houdon was engaged in putting on plaster to form the cast, quills were in the nostrils. I was very much alarmed until I was told that it . . . would not injure him." The life mask is our most accurate "portrait" of Washington.[16]

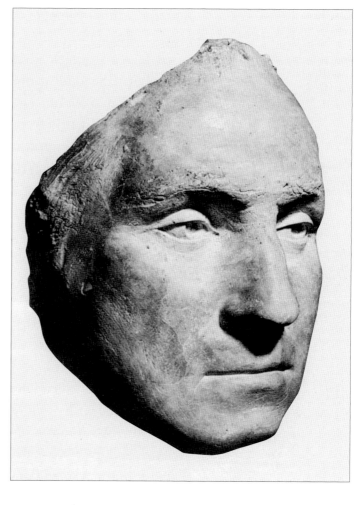

Bulging mailbags arrived at Mount Vernon daily. Letters, Washington told a friend, came from every "Dick, Tom, and Harry who may have been . . . in the Continental service," seeking favors, advice, and loans. Each required an answer, which meant spending hours dictating to his secretary, Tobias Lear.[17]

Those visitors and letters served a useful purpose. They kept Washington informed about current events and public opinion, forcing him to continue to think about his country's future. What was America all about?

What did it stand for? Did it have a mission in the world? How should it reach its goals?

In dealing with these questions, Washington took his cue from a sentence in Thomas Paine's *Common Sense*: "We have it in our power to begin the world over again."[18] Like Paine, he saw the new nation as unique, unlike any in history. It had a chance to break with the past, setting humanity on an entirely different path. Europe's upper classes had always thought ordinary people too stupid to rule themselves without the guidance of kings and nobles. Both Paine and Washington believed America stood for two things. First, it existed to bring its own people happiness with liberty. Second, it must prove that government by the people could succeed, that it would not descend into tyranny. By doing so, it really could begin the world over, giving humanity a fresh start.

Although Washington never used the term "melting pot," he had the idea. He thought of America as a refuge, "an Asylum for the poor and oppressed of all nations and religions." The nation should welcome everyone, he said, for each had something to contribute. He only asked that immigrants not settle as a group in one place, forming tiny nations within the nation. Instead, they should scatter to every part of the country, living beside and marrying people of different backgrounds. In time, they would stop being Englishmen, Frenchmen, or Germans, and become a blend of all peoples. They would be Americans.[19]

Yet they could never unite unless they rejected religious bigotry. For over a thousand years, people had tormented each other over questions of faith. Europeans killed heretics, those who held "false" beliefs about God. Colonial Americans sought to prevent religious minorities from worshiping freely. Washington, however, denounced "the horrors of spiritual tyranny, and every species of religious persecution."[20]

Washington argued that God, the creator of the universe, must be wise enough and strong enough to punish heretics, if necessary, without human help. Humanity, he believed, lacked the wisdom to play God. Religion was a private matter, and government had no business meddling with it. Government exists to protect people's rights, not save their souls. Thus, a good government "gives to bigotry no sanctions, to persecution no assistance." A good citizen obeys the law and worships as he or she wishes—or does not worship at all. Citizens "may be Mohometans, Jews or Christians of any sect, or they may be Atheists," those who deny the existence of God.[21]

America also needed peace. The Revolution had burned out of Washington any thoughts of military glory. Once a visitor reminded him that he had said he knew of no music so pleasing as the whistling of bullets. The general sat silent for a moment, then replied: "If I said so, it was when I was young." Experience had taught him better. He hated war, calling it "this plague of mankind." War stirs "mad heroism" and "that false ambition which desolates the world with fire and sword for the purposes of conquest and fame." Americans must never fight except in self-defense or to protect "our essential rights."[22]

Peace required national unity; that is, showing a solid front to the world. After winning independence, most Americans still thought of themselves as citizens of their states, not of the United States. They praised their "mother states" and called their state "my country." Not Washington. During his wartime travels, he came to realize that no part of the country could exist without the others. As he told a friend, he had learned "to contemplate the United States as one great whole." He had not fought for Virginia or the South, much as he loved both, but for America.[23]

A weak government had prolonged the war and increased its suffering. To avoid such tragedies in the future, the country needed an unbreakable "Union of states" under one government. In short, Washington saw the United States as one nation indivisible with liberty and justice for all.[24]

As they existed, the Articles of Confederation made this seem an impossible dream. Unable to raise taxes, Congress had to scrap the small navy built during the war—a bad move, since North African pirates constantly seized American ships and sailors. Unable to support an army, Congress stood by while Britain refused to leave its frontier outposts as promised in the peace treaty. Worse, the states acted like thirteen separate and selfish countries. States charged each other for using their waterways, even put tariffs on goods passing though their territory. New York, for example, taxed every New Jersey chicken and Connecticut cabbage that crossed its borders, and vice versa.

Farmers everywhere grumbled. During the war, they had received high prices for their produce. To meet the demand, they borrowed money to buy more land, equipment, and work animals. Prices fell when the war ended, leaving them with their debts. At the same time, states raised taxes to cover the fall in the value of paper money. By 1786, taxes were higher than those the British had imposed on the colonies. People who failed to meet loan payments and tax bills lost their property and went to debtors' prison, where they stayed until a relative paid the money they owed.

In the fall of 1786, a farmer named Daniel Shays stepped into the picture. During the Revolution, Shays had fought in the battles of Lexington, Bunker Hill, and Saratoga. Now he organized mass protests against high taxes in western Massachusetts. Some 1,200 irate farmers closed local courts, emptied debtors' prisons, and prevented sheriff's auctions of farms for unpaid taxes. Finally, state troops drove the farmers off with muskets and cannons. Their leader fled to Vermont, which had not yet entered the Union as a state, and Shays's Rebellion collapsed.

Washington did not take the rebellion lightly. "Are your people getting mad?" he angrily wrote a friend in Massachusetts. "What is the cause of all this? When and how is it to end?" He already knew the "cause" and the "how," but not the "when." America needed a strong central government. If the Articles of Confederation could not give it that, then fix them!

Others shared his concern. Men like Benjamin Franklin, Alexander Hamilton, and James Madison realized that something must be done. Shortly before the rebellion, Congress called a meeting of state delegates to discuss how to improve the Articles. Some delegates favored asking Congress to call a full-scale convention to continue the discussions. Others hesitated, until news from Massachusetts of Shays's Rebellion scared property own-

James Madison, the "father of the Constitution" and fourth president of the United States.

ers all over the country. Their fears tipped the balance in favor of the convention. Virginia's state legislature chose Washington as a delegate.

On May 25, 1787, fifty-five delegates from every state except Rhode Island met at Philadelphia in the Pennsylvania State House, a building later known as Independence Hall. These delegates formed a brilliant array of talent and experience. Most were in their thirties or forties and had fought in the Revolution. As a group, they were wealthier and better educated than the average American citizen. More than half were lawyers by training and had served in the Continental Congress. Nineteen owned slaves. Strong supporters of the Articles of Confederation did not attend, because, said Patrick Henry of Virginia, they "smelt a rat." And they were right.

The convention began by electing Washington its president. Delegates had a special reason for choosing him. Most had already decided that the Articles could not be fixed. These delegates meant to scrap them entirely and create something new, the Constitution of the United States. Yet Congress had called the convention only to *revise* the Articles. In effect, delegates intended an illegal overthrow of the existing system; that is, a revolution. Here was where Washington came in. Everyone trusted him. By electing him president, delegates hoped to use his prestige as a cover for their actions. If Washington favored the change, well, then, people would think it must be all right! He knew their reason for electing him and approved of it.

The Constitutional Convention met every Monday through Saturday from 8:00 A.M. to four o'clock in the afternoon. Meetings began after Washington entered the chamber and sat on a large, high-backed chair set on a raised platform. Apart from a few words on a trivial matter, he gave no speeches; as president, he did not think he should publicly express opinions on matters under discussion. Yet in private gatherings, held after the convention finished the day's business, he let delegates know exactly what he thought and expected.

At such times, Washington was as stiff and formal as he had been with his troops during the war. Gouverneur Morris, a well-known lawyer, once bet a friend that he could get chummy with Washington. Morris walked across the room, slapped him on the back, and said, "My dear General, I

George Washington presided over the Constitutional Convention in Philadelphia in 1787. Although he seldom spoke at the convention, in private he exercised tremendous influence on the delegates.

am very happy to see you look so well!" Washington suddenly stepped back and fixed Morris with an icy stare for several minutes without saying a word. Stunned, Morris retreated into the crowd, glad to get away. "I have won the bet," he said, "but paid dearly for it, and nothing could induce me to repeat it."[25]

It was a typical Philadelphia summer, hot and humid, with swarms of flies and mosquitoes buzzing about. Working behind locked doors, with drapes drawn against insects and street noises, delegates drew up their blueprint for a government based on James Madison's "Virginia Plan." A short, sickly man of thirty-six, Madison was a student of history and politics. Nicknamed the "Father of the Constitution," he became the fourth president of the United States.

Madison proposed a "federal system"; that is, one where the central government shared power with the states. The government would have three branches: legislative, executive, and judicial. Congress would be a bicameral (two-chambered) legislature. Male voters would elect the first chamber, or House of Representatives, with the number of representatives depending on the state's population. To balance representation based on population, each state legislature would also elect two members to the second chamber, or Senate. Acting together, both chambers would pass laws for the entire nation, raise taxes, and declare war. The executive branch, led by a president, would carry out the laws and conduct foreign affairs. The president would not be elected directly by the people, but by an electoral college chosen by the state legislatures. A system of courts crowned by a Supreme Court would rule on whether the government and states acted legally. A system of "checks and balances" guaranteed that no branch grew too powerful.

Progress came slowly, as delegates debated every detail of the Virginia Plan. Slavery, however, threatened to spoil everything. Opposition to it had increased since the end of the war. People from all walks of life demanded its abolition not only for its brutality, but because of the Declaration of Independence. America's charter of liberty declares certain "self-evident" truths needing no proof. The greatest truth is that "all men are created equal." God has given humanity certain "unalienable rights," which nobody can take away. Among them are the right to "life, liberty, and the pursuit of happiness." It followed that all people everywhere, even slaves and women, share these rights simply because they are human beings.

Abolitionist societies formed in the northern states. They met little resistance, because the economy there depended far less on slavery than in the South. In 1780, while the war with England raged, Pennsylvania banned slavery; Massachusetts, Connecticut, New York, and Rhode Island did the same between 1783 and 1786. Their laws did not free the adult slaves themselves, but made their children free—and then not before they became adults. Many southerners also favored abolition. Since slavery was not as profitable as before the war, Virginia and Maryland allowed owners to free their slaves if they wished.

The problem was that Georgia and South Carolina needed *more* slaves to work newly settled farmlands. "Negroes," a South Carolina politician declared, "are our wealth, our only natural resource." If anything, delegates from these states wanted the Constitution to strengthen slavery. Not only must it protect their existing "property," they said, but allow them to import slaves freely. Most important, they wanted slaves counted equally with whites in drawing the lines of election districts, thus giving slave owners more power in Congress. If they lost on any of these points, they threatened to leave Philadelphia and wreck any plan for a united country.[26]

"Am I not a Woman and a Sister?" An abolitionist handbill stressing equality as a human right mentioned in the Declaration of Independence.

To save the Constitution, delegates made three compromises. Under the Three-Fifths Compromise, three-fifths of a state's slave population would be included in deciding the number of seats it had in the House of Representatives. A Fugitive Slave Law forbade anyone to block the return of a runaway slave to his or her owner. Lastly, southerners gained the right to import enslaved Africans for another twenty years, until 1807. As a bonus, the Constitution dropped the word *slave* in favor of "persons held to Service or Labor." No words, however, could change slavery's brutal reality.

Where did Washington stand on the question of slavery? Before leaving Mount Vernon, he wrote Robert Morris, a wealthy Philadelphia merchant and financial expert: "I can only say that there is not a man living who wishes more sincerely than I do to see a plan adopted for the abolition of [slavery]." His words are clear enough, but his true meaning is not.[27]

Washington seems to have had two minds on slavery. Although he claimed to favor abolition, he came down harshly on abolitionists who "tampered" with "happy and contented slaves." Did he really believe anyone could be happy and contented in bondage? We cannot say. If so, he never explained why house servants, the best treated and most privileged slaves, ran away, even poisoned their owners.[28]

In keeping with his letter to Morris, Washington vowed never to buy another slave unless "compelled" by necessity. Yet that vow did not stop him from selling nine slaves to pay taxes during the war. Afterward, he saw nothing wrong with taking five slaves instead of cash from a planter who owed him money. He also bought a bricklayer, since "I have much work in this way to do this Summer." Principle always gave way before economic need. Washington was no hypocrite; he believed what he said. Yet he simply could not get along without slave labor.[29]

Washington's opposition to slavery remained low-key and private. Perhaps he felt speaking out would do more harm than good. America's future depended on having a permanent Union under a strong central government. By denouncing slavery openly, surely he would have outraged public opinion in the Deep South, wrecking the convention. So he kept quiet and welcomed the compromises. Delegates approved the Constitution on September 17, 1787.

Those compromises only stored up trouble for the future. True, they allowed the United States to be born. Yet they also meant that black people paid for white people's freedom with their continued bondage. Abraham Lincoln understood this terrible trade-off. In 1854, he said the Constitution hid slavery away, "just as an afflicted man hides away . . . a cancer, which he dares not cut out at once, lest he bleed to death." The bleeding came anyhow, as we shall see.[30]

The Constitution would not take effect until nine state legislatures voted to ratify, or adopt, it. The debate over ratification, however, was not limited to legislatures. It raged in the country's many newspapers and wherever people gathered.

Opponents charged that the framers gave too much power to the federal government at the expense of the states. Worse, they claimed the Constitution failed to protect the individual citizen from the government. Federalists, or supporters of the Constitution, argued that the Constitution alone could prevent economic chaos and bloodshed. Leading Federalists—James Madison, Alexander Hamilton, John Jay—made their case in *The Federalist*, an influential series of essays printed in newspapers and later in book form. After ratification, they promised to add ten amendments, called the Bill of Rights, to the Constitution. These would guarantee the individual the right to a jury trial, protection against un-reasonable searches, freedom of the press, free speech, and freedom of religion.

Although Washington did not campaign for the Constitution openly, he worked for it tirelessly behind the scenes. He arranged for a printer to reissue *The Federalist* in Richmond and told the authors to use his name freely. At every opportunity, he urged influential people to support ratification.

In June 1788, New Hampshire became the ninth state to adopt the Constitution, making it the law of the land. What an achievement! For the first time in history, a nation changed its system of government without an upheaval, without the loss of even a single life. Much of the credit went to the master of Mount Vernon. "Be assured," James Monroe wrote Thomas Jefferson, "his influence carried this government."[31]

Ratification gave Washington another reason to worry. Many legislators voted for the Constitution not because of what it said, but because they believed he would become the first president. That was not what Washington wanted. He yearned for the peace and quiet of family life. Besides, he doubted his abilities. He knew how to farm and to fight, not how to be a politician and statesman.

Everyone he trusted and respected urged him to serve. The first years under the Constitution, they knew, would be difficult. Getting the system to work required a person with leadership ability equal to the fine words on paper. Only he, Washington, had the skill and moral authority to give government by the people a fair chance of success. As early as January

Ratification of the Constitution. In this drawing, eleven columns—states—are in place, while two others are still unsure about how to vote.

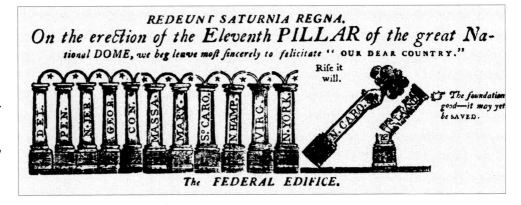

REDEUNT SATURNIA REGNA.
On the erection of the Eleventh PILLAR of the great National DOME, we beg leave most sincerely to felicitate " OUR DEAR COUNTRY."

Rise it will.

The foundation good—it may yet be SAVED.

The FEDERAL EDIFICE.

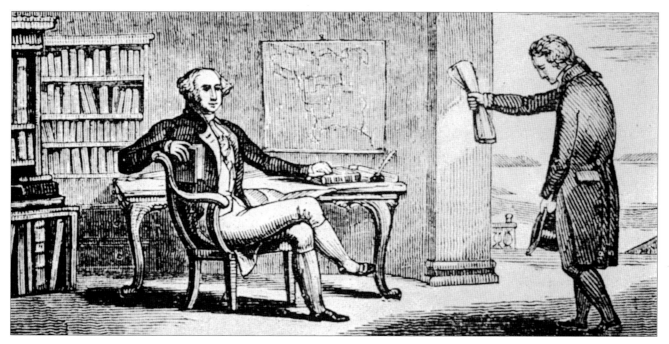

George Washington gets official notification of his unanimous election as the first president of the United States. From John Frost's *History of the United States,* 1836.

1788, Lafayette told him so in a passionate letter. "In the name of America, of mankind at large, and of your own fame, I beseech you, my dear General, not to deny your acceptance of the office of President for the first years. You only can settle that political machine."[32]

Such pleas did not ease Washington's mind. Yet he knew his duty and promised to serve if the nation wished.

It did. On April 14, 1789, the secretary of Congress brought official notice of his unanimous choice as president by the Electoral College; John Adams would be vice president. Two days later, he left for New York City, which Congress had made the temporary capital until it could select a permanent site. Before setting out, he told his diary that he left home "with a mind oppressed with more anxious and painful sensations than I have words to express."[33]

THE SACRED FIRE
OF LIBERTY

"The preservation of the sacred fire of liberty, and the destiny of the republican model of government are...finally staked on the experiment entrusted to the hands of the American people."

—WASHINGTON, FIRST INAUGURAL ADDRESS, APRIL 30, 1789

Elizabeth Town, New Jersey, April 23, 1789. It was a sparkling spring morning with a brisk wind blowing from the Atlantic Ocean to the south. Whitecaps dotted the waters of New York Bay. The air, fresh and cool, tickled one's nostrils with a hint of salt. It was a glorious day to be alive, and to be American.

The town's main street lay silent and deserted, but for a few stray dogs. Every shop was locked and shuttered, every school closed. Townspeople wore their finest clothes because they wanted to look their best on a day future generations would remember, they said, "until the ending of the world."

Everyone had gathered at the town dock before sunrise. Parents held up their small children, pointing to the soldiers who lined the dock, each man shouldering a musket with a silvery bayonet. A red carpet covered the rough wooden planks leading to a flight of stone steps scrubbed clean as a whistle. A barge bobbed in the water at the foot of the stairs, decorated with colored streamers and flags. Specially built for the occasion, it had thirteen oarsmen dressed in white, each representing a state. Their mission: Row the first president of the United States across the harbor to his inauguration in New York City.

As the town clock struck noon, a drumroll sounded in the distance. The honor guard snapped to attention. A hush fell over the crowd. Suddenly, riders appeared with a tall man on a big white horse leading the way. As he came forward, the crowd broke into cheers.

Before setting out from Mount Vernon a week earlier, Washington had told aides that he hoped people would not make a fuss over him. He just wanted to get to New York as quietly as possible. Yet the American people had other ideas.

Every town Washington passed through welcomed him with clanging church bells, wildly cheering crowds, and long-winded speeches by local dignitaries. In some towns, he rode under flower-covered arches, while women and girls threw flowers in front of his horse. Relays of riders escorted him along the roads between towns—so many riders that he rode for hours amid clouds of dust. The dust made his eyes water and crackled between his teeth.

Those receptions were sedate compared to what awaited him today. Washington stepped into the barge and, at the shrill call of a boatswain's whistle, the rowers set to work. As the barge slid away from the New Jersey shore, dozens of small craft decorated with flags and pennants followed in its wake.

The procession came out of the Kill van Kull into New York Bay. Passing Bedloe's Island, the future site of the Statue of Liberty, it headed for the southern tip of Manhattan Island.

Now other, larger craft joined the procession. A Spanish warship, the *Galveston*, raised the flags of twenty nations. *Galveston*'s crew lined its spars, the crossbars used to support the sails, cheering as the barge passed. Two sloops—small, swift vessels—took up positions behind and beside the barge. Aboard one sloop, a choir of twenty-five men and women sang patriotic songs; aboard the other, a twelve-man glee club sang a song of welcome. Meanwhile, every cannon aboard every ship thundered its salute.

The barge tied up at Murray's Wharf at the foot of Wall Street. Nearly the entire city had turned out to see Washington's arrival. In addition, thousands of visitors had come for the event—so many that late arrivals could not find a room for love or money. Friends or relatives took in the lucky ones. The unlucky ones camped in the fields on either side of Bowery Lane, later the city's most heavily populated area. "We shall remain here if we have to sleep in tents, as many have to do," a determined visitor wrote her friend in Philadelphia.[1]

New York's civic leaders met Washington as he stepped ashore. After greeting him formally, they escorted him up Broadway toward President's House, a rented house at number 3 Cherry Street used as the first official home of the president of the United States, near what is today the Manhattan side of the Brooklyn Bridge. There he would receive well-wishers and meet with government officials until his inauguration on April 30.

Crowds lined both sides of Broadway, the city's chief thoroughfare, an unpaved road that rain turned into a muddy stream and dry spells into a desert of windswept dirt. Glancing upward, Washington saw people leaning out of windows, perched on rooftops, or clinging to high tree branches. Every mouth seemed open, every arm waving.

"I have seen him!" a young woman cried. "I never saw a human being that looked so great and noble as he does. I would fall down on my knees before him." Some said they could die happy at last, having seen Washington with their own eyes. This outpouring of affection touched him deeply, although not in the way we might expect. Washington's smiles seemed, well, "formal"—hardly expressions of joy. He did not wave to the crowd. Instead, he made a little bow at each outburst of cheering and touched his hat as a polite salute. Nobody who saw him that day, and wrote about it, mentioned that he smiled even once.[2]

After reaching President's House, Washington sank into a chair to catch his breath. Then the next wave of well-wishers swarmed around him until late in the evening. Before going to bed, he took his diary from its leather case. "The loud acclamations of the people," he wrote, "filled my mind with sensations as painful . . . as they are pleasing." Pleasing because he liked being liked, as we all do. Painful because he felt that Americans expected too much of him. Of course, everyone loved him—now. Would they love him after he made the necessary, if unpopular, decisions every leader must make? Only time would tell.[3]

Thursday, April 30, 1789. Inauguration Day. Every church bell in New York City began ringing at 9:00 A.M. on this cool, crystal-clear morning. People crowded the houses of worship, forcing latecomers to stand on the sidewalks, while congregations inside prayed for the nation and its leader.

At noon, a butler opened the front door of 3 Cherry Street. An honor guard of soldiers lined the sidewalk between the doorway and the street, where a cream-colored coach waited with a cavalry escort.

Washington came out alone; Martha did not like crowds, so she planned to arrive a month later with Nelly and Wash. His carriage rolled through the narrow streets, between lines of cheering onlookers. Its destination was the old City Hall in Wall Street, near where the New York Stock Exchange stands today. Congress had recently taken over the building and given it a new name: Federal Hall.

Leaving the coach, Washington went upstairs and out onto a balcony. The crowd shouted its greeting when he came to the rail. Men tossed their

Federal Hall in New York City.

hats into the air; women waved handkerchiefs. He thanked them by laying his hand on his heart and bowing slightly. Then, stepping back, he put his right hand on a Bible and solemnly took the same oath each president has taken every four years ever since: "I solemnly swear that I will faithfully execute the office of President of the United States and will, to the best of my ability, preserve, protect, and defend the Constitution of the United States." Although it was not part of the required oath, Washington added "So help me God!" and then kissed the Bible.[4]

"So help me God!" George Washington took the oath of office on the second-floor balcony of Federal Hall, overlooking Wall Street, in New York City. The tall building in the background is the new Trinity Church, built after the fire of 1776.

The moment he finished, sailors aboard ships in the harbor heard shouts from the direction of Wall Street. "Long live George Washington!" "God bless our Washington!" "Long live our beloved President!"[5]

When the cheering stopped, Washington read his inaugural speech, at 1,200 words the shortest in our history. In it he asked God to help the American people find happiness and liberty under the Constitution. His voice did not carry very far in the open, and hardly anyone in the crowd made out more than a few phrases. To those who stood with him on the balcony, the president did not seem very confident. The fearless battle commander had stage fright. What is more important, he dreaded the huge job that lay ahead. When he finished, he said to no one in particular, "I greatly expect that my countrymen will expect too much from me."[6]

After a brief service in a nearby church, Washington went home to prepare for the evening celebrations. It was a night to remember. Candles lit every window in town. Crowds at the Battery marveled at a fireworks show lasting two hours. The president watched the display with a group of dignitaries several streets away. He was still tense, and his face seemed set in stone. Catherine Boudinot, age eight, stood with them in a bright yellow dress. When her father, Elias, a government official, wanted to take her home and she protested, Washington's face lit up with a smile. "No, you pretty little yellow bird," he said, "you shall see as well as anybody," and hoisted her on his shoulder. That broke the ice; he enjoyed the rest of the celebration. There would be few such happy moments in the next eight years.[7]

Nowadays, we know what to expect when a new president comes into office. He automatically takes over the government, a vast organization with hundreds of thousands of employees and a budget of hundreds of billions of dollars. Not the first president. In 1789, the federal government barely existed; it had only seventy-five post offices, a few clerks, and an army of 718 soldiers. As for money, Washington always thought in thousands and millions; like most Americans then, he could not imagine a billion of anything. You can search his writings and not find the word *billion*.

The First Congress under the Constitution set up the machinery of government. As the Federalists had promised, it approved the Bill of

Rights. It also passed a tariff on imported goods and created the Departments of State, Treasury, War, and Justice. The Judiciary Act organized the federal court system.

Washington had to shape the president's office, defining its relations with the other branches of government. "I walk on untrodden ground," he said, meaning that he had nothing to draw on for experience and example. Knowing that every decision he took might influence the future, he had to move with extreme caution.[8]

Washington believed that the president was a role model, the person who set the tone for the nation. Success, therefore, not only involved getting the job done, but doing it in the right spirit. Character, for him, counted as much as ability. A president must *be*, and must be *seen* to be, a good person. People must not think of him as a shrewd operator serving his own ends, but as a moral person devoted to the public welfare. Everything the president did, however great or trivial, must reveal his moral character—his decency, truthfulness, and sense of honor. "A good moral character is the first essential of man," said Washington. "I hope I shall always possess firmness and virtue enough to maintain the character of an honest man, as well as prove that I am."[9]

John Adams supported Washington's appointment as commander of the Continental Army. Later, he became the second president of the United States. Painting by Charles Willson Peale.

Our first president was a "hands-on" leader. No detail was too small not to deserve his personal attention. He began by hiring every government employee, nearly a thousand people. These included everyone from high officials to the lighthouse keeper at Portland, Maine; he even bought the oil for the lamp, haggling over the price. Vice President John Adams said Washington sought only the best men (not women), who "would give dignity and luster" to the government.[10]

Yet there was never any doubt about who was in charge. During the war years, Washington had learned that nothing got done, or got done correctly, unless he stayed on top of things always. Now he applied that principle to running the government. Washington tracked the doings of each department by reading and commenting on all official papers, an impossible task today. He met with his Cabinet, or department heads, to seek their advice on special problems whenever necessary. Cabinet members were: Secretary of State Thomas Jefferson, Secretary of the Treasury Alexander Hamilton, Secretary of War Henry Knox, and Attorney General Edmund Randolph.

Not only must Washington run the government, he had to decide how to behave toward others, and how they should behave toward him. Just what should Americans call him? Congress spent days debating his official title. Vice President Adams favored this one: "His Elective Highness the President of the United States of America and Protector of the Rights of the Same." Others suggested several shorter but equally pompous titles like: "Majesty," "His Mightiness," and "His Exalted High Mightiness." Washington, practical as always, ignored such windy nonsense. America was a republic, not a monarchy, and should not use royal titles. He insisted

President Washington and his Cabinet. Left to right: Washington, Secretary of War Henry Knox, Secretary of the Treasury Alexander Hamilton, Secretary of State Thomas Jefferson, and Attorney General Edmund Randolph. A Currier & Ives print dated 1876.

that people just call him "President of the United States." That was soon shortened to "Mr. President."[11]

Washington earned a salary of $25,000 a year. This sum, worth about $1 million in today's money, made him the highest-paid employee, public or private, in the land; Cabinet members received $3,500 a year and members of Congress $6 daily, during sessions. All the president's expenses came out of his own pocket. He bought his food and drink, kept his horses in a stable he built, bought a cow for fresh milk, and entertained guests; he spent about $1,000 a year on wine alone. After moving to larger quarters at 39–41 Broadway, he hired fourteen white servants and brought seven slaves from Mount Vernon to do the chores. It cost $115 a week to run the president's house; that is, more than an unskilled laborer earned in a year.[12]

As a Virginia planter, Washington had always lived in style. Now, as president, this also became a matter of "image." Since the president represented the nation, having the proper lifestyle built respect for the office he held. Washington kept his distance to stress the dignity of his office. Tuesday afternoons he held "levees," or receptions, for anyone choosing to visit his house; he only asked that they be "clean and polite." Thursday evenings he gave dinners for members of Congress, high government officials, and visiting dignitaries. These were not like relaxed gatherings at Mount Vernon. At the proper time, a servant would call out "The President of the United States." Then President Washington entered the room and bowed to each guest but did not shake hands even with friends. Stiff and formal, he sat at the dinner table, hardly saying a word. "Today I dined with the President," a guest wrote, "and as usual the company was as grave as a funeral." At 9:00 P.M. sharp, he left his guests and went upstairs with Martha to bed.[13]

For the lady from rural Virginia, New York came as a shock. Then, as now, people of different backgrounds rubbed shoulders in its bustling streets and spoke a babble of languages. English, Dutch, German, and French competed with the brogue of Ireland and the dialects of West Africa. (One in ten New Yorkers was a slave.) Since Broadway was the main wagon route into the city, it was also the noisiest street. Creaking wagons and mooing cattle streamed passed the president's house at all hours of the day and night. Lacking proper sanitation, the streets stank of horses and "corporation pudding," a polite term for human waste. After dark, slaves collected it in buckets from the houses. They emptied the buckets into the gutters to attract nature's scavengers, the pigs that roamed about freely.[14]

"I live a dull life here," Martha complained to relatives in Virginia. "I never go to any public place. Indeed, I am more like a state prisoner than anything else . . . and as I cannot do as I like, I am obstinate and stay at home a great deal." Yet she did her duty and in doing so created the role of First Lady. She supervised the president's household and served as his hostess, a familiar role at Mount Vernon. She must have heard plenty of political talk, but she kept it to herself. Martha always avoided official business; there is no evidence that she ever discussed politics with her husband. First Ladies would follow her example until far into the twentieth century.[15]

Martha's greatest worry was the president's health. His teeth, always a problem, made life miserable. Even as a young man, he had sprinkled his diary with complaints about "aching teeth and inflamed gums." Over the years, dentists pulled one bad tooth after another. To handle the pain, he used laudanum, a blend of opium and alcohol; he grew opium poppies in his garden at Mount Vernon. Most plantation owners grew opium poppies, and some may have become addicted to the drug. Nobody ever mentioned that the first president was an addict. Washington had countless sets of dentures made of hippopotamus ivory and the teeth of cows, pigs, and elk. Sometimes dentists bought "live" ones from poor people willing to sacrifice healthy teeth for a few dollars each. One set of false teeth was set in lead, weighed three pounds, and had steel springs. No wonder portraits show Washington tight-lipped and with jaws clenched.[16]

In June 1789, the president developed a painful growth on his left thigh, possibly cancer. He lay in bed wide awake and very still while two surgeons removed the "violent tumor" without anesthetic of any sort. "Cut deeper," the chief surgeon told his assistant. "Cut deeper." The tumor never returned. By October, Washington was well enough to go on a month-long tour of New England to learn firsthand people's attitudes toward the new government. He traveled in a hired coach with two secretaries and six servants. Since then, hundreds of places have boasted that "Washington slept here." Martha stayed in New York with her grandchildren.[17]

A year later, the president came down with pneumonia. He tossed and turned, gripped by a raging fever. To allow him to rest quietly, Martha had straw laid in the gutter outside the house to dull the sound of carriage wheels and had chains stretched across Broadway to divert the traffic. Although few people knew about his operation, everyone learned about the pneumonia from the newspapers. Until the danger passed, the nation held its breath, fearing both for him and itself. "You cannot conceive the public alarm," Thomas Jefferson wrote a friend. "It proves how much depends on his life." Without Washington's guiding hand, the Constitution had little chance of succeeding.[18]

Americans agreed that they needed the president, but on little else. Before long, men who had firmly supported ratification of the Constitution began quarreling over government policies. These quarrels led to the formation of two political parties: the Federalists led by Alexander Hamilton, and the Republicans led by Thomas Jefferson. Washington disliked parties; he called them "factions," selfish cliques that cared nothing for the general welfare. Yet, whether he liked it or not, they became a permanent part of American life.

Alexander Hamilton, the first secretary of the treasury, did more than anyone else to lay the economic foundations of the new nation. Painting by Charles Willson Peale.

The party leaders were natural enemies, as different as day and night. Hamilton was born to an unmarried woman in the West Indies in 1755. Sent to college in New York by a family friend, he joined Washington's staff at the outset of the Revolution, becoming a trusted aide. A brave fighter and brilliant staff officer, he quickly rose to the rank of colonel. Next to Lafayette, he was Washington's favorite officer. The general called him "my boy."[19]

Hamilton had no faith in ordinary men and women. The mass of the people the world over, he said, "is a great beast." Ignorant and violent, this monster could never govern itself. Government, Hamilton insisted, must be left to "the rich and the well-born." Although a fiery patriot, he still admired the British system, where the king and nobility ruled. In America, a republic, he wanted a government controlled by wealthy merchants and bankers who would keep the masses in line. This elite, the country's "natural rulers," lived mainly in the cities of the northeast: New York, Philadelphia, Boston. For America to enjoy peace and prosperity, he said, the government must put their interests first.[20]

Jefferson disagreed. Although he was a wealthy slaveowner, he understood the needs of ordinary white Americans. He accused Hamilton and his "British party" of trying to turn the nation into a mirror-image of the former enemy. Jefferson despised kings and nobles as stupid people who fought stupid wars with other people's blood. He also despised "money men," those who grew rich by managing money but produced nothing; and he considered cities to be sewers of human corruption. In Jefferson's vision of America, people were neither rich nor poor, but had enough to live comfortably. That meant having a democracy of small-town people and independent farmers. As to the central government, he had a simple rule: Less is best. Since he hoped to keep government close to the people, he favored states' rights, limiting federal power to allow the greatest possible self-rule by the states.

Thomas Jefferson, the first secretary of state and third president of the United States. Painting by Charles Willson Peale.

Five months after taking office, Washington asked Hamilton to design a plan to restore economic prosperity. In January 1790, the treasury secretary sent Congress his *Report on the Public Credit*. The Continental Congress had borrowed $84 million in the form of bonds purchased by bankers and wealthier citizens during the Revolution. At the same time, state governments had borrowed another $25 million to cover all their wartime expenses. Hamilton urged Congress to repay the entire debt, federal and state, with an excise, or tax on the manufacture, sale, and use of certain products. Paying both debts would establish the nation's credit, thus strengthening the nation by tying the money men closely to the government.

Republicans, and particularly James Madison, attacked Hamilton's plan. Madison reminded Congress that, when the war ended, Washington's soldiers had received IOUs for their back pay. The majority had sold them, often at ten cents on the dollar, to speculators for ready cash. If Congress paid off now, at face value plus interest, the money men stood to make a fortune at public expense. That was unfair. Equally important, most southern states had already repaid their debts by taxing their citizens. So, if the federal government took over the remaining state debts, southerners would end up paying double taxes, since northerners had not met their responsibilities.

Yet each side needed the other. If northerners favored Hamilton's debt plan, southerners wanted the national capital built in their part of the country, because they thought it would give them more influence over the government. Knowing that, in July 1790, Jefferson arranged the "dinner-table bargain" in his New York house. Over dinner with Hamilton, he and Madison agreed to persuade Virginia members of Congress to pass the tax plan. In return, Hamilton would use his influence to get the Federalists to agree to put the capital in the South. Congress voted to return to Philadelphia until the year 1800, then transfer to the District of Columbia, a ten-square-mile area along the Potomac River donated by Virginia and Maryland. The president would supervise the planning and construction of the "Grand Columbian Federal City." That mouthful soon became "Washington City"—or Washington, D.C., for short.

In 1792, Washington turned sixty. In passing that milestone, he compared life to a hill, which we slowly climb until we reach the top, then quickly go down the other side. Well, said Washington, he was "descending the hill." Time had become an enemy. He felt himself growing old. Already hard of hearing, he also developed rheumatism; sometimes it hurt so badly he could hardly move his hands or turn himself in bed. Visitors noticed that the soldier who had always stood ramrod-straight now stooped, and his hair had turned snow white. The squabbling of Federalists and Republicans still made him miserable; sometimes, he said, it made his head swim. Perhaps he should retire at the end of his term as president?[21]

His just mentioning the word *retirement* alarmed people. Leaders of both parties begged him to reconsider. Only Washington stood above the bitter party disputes, they said. Without his leadership, the country might break apart, igniting a civil war. "This is the event at which I tremble," Jefferson wrote him in panic. "The confidence of the whole Union is centered in you. Your being at the helm will be more than an answer to . . . violence or secession. North and South will hang together if they have you to hang on [to]. . . . "[22]

Washington changed his mind for the sake of the country. When it came to deciding between his public duty and his private wishes, duty always came first. Yet the decision to seek a second term did not come easily or without pain. When he told Martha of his decision, her temper flared. After calming down, she apologized for the outburst. She would never leave his side, she said. The president put his arms around his wife. She put his head down on her shoulder. "Poor Patsy," he said. "Poor Patsy."[23]

Another election. Another unanimous vote in the Electoral College. On March 4, 1793, Washington took the oath of office again. He had bound himself to another term of what he sadly called "slavery." Few people have ever *not* wanted to be president so badly.[24]

The second term got off to a bad start and kept going downhill. To understand the reason, we must go back four years.

On July 14, 1789, ten weeks after Washington's first inauguration, 20,000 people stormed the Bastille, a hated royal fortress in Paris, starting the French Revolution. King Louis XVI had borrowed heavily to pay for the war against Britain. He went so far into debt that he could not even keep up with the interest payments. When he tried to raise taxes, the Estates General, or national legislature, blocked the move. If the king wanted higher taxes, members said, he must agree to rule under a constitution. Similarly, the nobility and clergy, who did not pay taxes, would have to pay their fair share.

GEORGE WASHINGTON

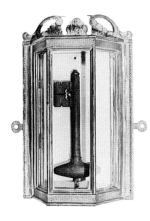

Lafayette sent Washington the key to the Bastille, the great prison-fortress in Paris, as proof that American ideals of liberty were changing Europe. Washington hung the gift on the wall of Mount Vernon, where it is today.

The roots of the French Revolution lay deep in American soil. Our revolution fired the imaginations of countless Europeans. For those who dreamed of a better world, the Declaration of Independence had become their Bible, George Washington their hero. This was especially true of the French officers who had served in America. Mainly noblemen, they returned to their homeland inspired by the experience of fighting for liberty. "We were all dreaming of Liberty," the Count de Ségur recalled years later. Referring to his friends, another officer wrote: "Each of them thought he would be called upon to play the part of Washington."[25]

None had that feeling stronger than the Marquis de Lafayette. After the war, he became an outspoken champion of American ideals. In the entrance to his Paris mansion, he placed a large framed copy of the Declaration of Independence. Next to it he left a space for, he said, the future "Declaration of French Rights." French people so identified him with the American leader that they dubbed him *le Washington français*, "the French Washington." Lafayette honored his old chief by sending him the key to the Bastille as a tribute "which I owe as a son to my adopted father." The key still hangs on a wall at Mount Vernon, just where Washington put it.[26]

Most Americans welcomed the French Revolution as part of the world-wide struggle for liberty begun at Lexington, Concord, and Bunker Hill. In New York, city leaders changed the name King Street to Liberty Street; Boston's Royal Exchange Alley became Equality Lane. President Washington, however, did not welcome the revolution blindly or expect it to work miracles. Experience had taught him that people may do evil while aiming to do good. In return for the key, he sent Lafayette a stern warning. "I caution you," he wrote, "against running into extremes"—that is, allowing mob violence to spin out of control. If that happened, he feared a bloodbath that would make the American Revolution seem tame.[27]

Washington's worst fears became reality. France experimented with various forms of government, each failing after a short time. Finally, in 1792, fighting broke out between the revolutionaries and the king's supporters. To make matters worse, the revolutionaries called for "a war of all peoples against all kings," a crusade to spread their cause world-wide. Violence met violence. Led by Britain, Austria and several German states launched a full-scale assault on revolutionary France. Defeated by foreign armies while civil war raged at home, France faced disaster. In turn, mob violence spread like an epidemic disease. Fearing a royalist plot to force open the capital's crowded jails, mobs of Parisians invaded the prisons and slaughtered over two thousand people in three days during September.

Another government took over in Paris, led by a political party called

the Jacobins. To rally the nation, the Jacobins began the Reign of Terror. Those who served the Reign of Terror became known as "terrorists." The words *terrorist* and *terrorism* have become part of our vocabulary, terms for those willing to use any means, including mass murder, to paralyze or destroy the opposition.

Terrorists became a law unto themselves. Those suspected of disloyalty, even in their thoughts, faced a ten-minute trial before a jury of Jacobin fanatics. Anyone found guilty went to the guillotine, or "national razor," a machine for cutting off heads with a heavy iron blade that slid

Washington was right to fear that the French Revolution would grow ever more violent. This engraving shows the September 1792 massacre of "traitors" in the Paris prisons. Over two thousand people died in a single day.

Before and after. The French revolutionaries used the guillotine, a machine for chopping off heads quickly and, they thought, painlessly, to execute opponents.

between two wooden uprights. From 1792 to 1795, the guillotine claimed 2,794 victims in Paris alone; in other cities, as many as 200 people lost their heads each day. Victims came from all walks of life. They included nobles and farmers, priests and workers, lawyers and merchants. On January 21, 1793, King Louis XVI went to the guillotine; members of the mob dipped handkerchiefs in his blood as a memento. Queen Marie Antoinette followed her husband a few weeks later. France became a republic where everyone was supposed to be equal. People no longer used terms like "sir" or "madame," but called one another "citizen" and "citizeness."

The French Revolution divided Americans, too. Federalists came to oppose it for the same reasons Tories had resisted our own Revolution. Horrified at the violence, they urged the president to side with Britain against the "enemies of Christian civilization." Republicans took the opposite view. Since France had helped America win independence, they insisted America should return the favor. Diners in Philadelphia celebrated Louis XVI's death by passing a roasted pig's head around the table on a silver platter; each said "tyrant" as he handed it to his neighbor. Even the mild-mannered Jefferson showed a bloody-minded streak. He glorified the French cause. "Rather than it should have failed, I would have seen half the earth desolated," he wrote in January 1793. "Were there but an Adam and an Eve left in every country, and left free," it would have satisfied him.[28]

Washington took the Reign of Terror personally. It hurt him to learn that so many officers who had once fought at his side were dying by the hundreds under the guillotine. Terrorists executed Admiral d'Estaing and imprisoned the Counts de Rochambeau and de Grasse. Although they jailed Lafayette, he escaped into exile in Austria. Fearing the worst, his wife sent their fifteen-year-old son, George Washington Lafayette, to safety across the Atlantic. The president loved the son as he had loved his father. Washington paid his tuition at Harvard College, where he studied

The execution by guillotine of King Louis XVI in Paris.

for a year. After that, he stayed at Mount Vernon as a guest for nearly two more years.

Kindness to friends, however, did not solve the president's chief problem. What to do about France and the war raging in Europe?

Bombarded by advice from all sides, he held to his own ideas on foreign policy. Washington believed independence meant more than freedom from British rule. It meant America's taking charge of its affairs both at home and abroad. The president believed that a nation's first obligation was to itself. Every nation has special interests, goals it must achieve for its own benefit. America, he said, must expand its trade by avoiding foreign conflicts. "My ardent desire," he wrote, "[is] to keep the U States free from *political* connections with *every* other country." In other words, he hoped to convince foreign nations that "we act for *ourselves* and not for *others*."[29]

Thus, in April 1793, Washington issued a Neutrality Proclamation, forbidding Americans to take part in any war not declared by Congress. That proclamation would become the cornerstone of our foreign policy for over a century and a half. Only with the creation of NATO—the North Atlantic Treaty Organization—in 1949 would the United States join a permanent military alliance. Instant communications, ballistic missiles, and nuclear weapons have created a world far different from any the first president could have imagined.

Washington's proclamation failed to calm the storm. Friends and enemies of France traded insults on the streets of every town. Fistfights erupted in taverns. Angry crowds heckled and stoned opposition speakers. Federalists called Republicans "filthy Jacobins," brothers to those "frog-eating, man-eating, blood-drinking cannibals" across the sea. Republicans denounced Federalists as "British boot-lickers," traitors to the ideals of the Declaration of Independence. Republican newspapers damned the proclamation as "a royal edict" that betrayed an old friend, France, in favor of an old enemy, England.[30]

France's minister to America, "Citizen" Edmond Charles Genêt, began to turn up the heat. In the spring of 1793, this fast-talking man demanded that America allow his country to use its seaports for attacks on the British West Indies. He even licensed privately owned American ships to capture British merchantmen in the name of France, activities bound to bring reprisals from the world's leading naval power. When American officials protested, Genêt organized a network of Democratic and Republican Societies, encouraging their members to oppose their elected government.

Vice President Adams described "the terrorism" unleashed by Genêt's societies. Adams told how, day after day, "ten thousand people in the streets of Philadelphia . . . threatened to drag Washington out of his house." Yet Washington had the last word. After he demanded Genêt's recall, the minister learned that the Jacobins planned to cut off his head the moment he landed. He threw himself on the president's mercy. Washington allowed him to stay in the United States, saving his life. Genêt married a wealthy woman and became a loyal American.[31]

No sooner had Genêt left the scene when yellow fever struck Philadelphia in the summer of 1793. Since nobody knew the disease's cause, a virus transmitted by mosquitoes, it was impossible to treat it or prevent its spread. To move the "bad air," doctors advised burning gunpowder and firing cannons every hour on the hour. People stayed at home, behind

A silhouette of Edmond Charles Genêt, better known as "Citizen" Genêt. His job was to persuade the United States to allow French warships to use its seaports for attacks on the British West Indies.

locked doors; those who ventured out chewed garlic and doused their clothes with vinegar to ward off infection. Family members abandoned dying loved ones; friends avoided each other for fear of infection. Nothing worked. Free black people, however, acted heroically during the epidemic. For many weeks, members of the Free Africa Relief Society risked their lives by volunteering to nurse the sick and take bodies to common graves outside town.[32]

Over five thousand Philadelphians died of yellow fever; nearly half the population fled to safety in the country or to other towns. The president wished to stay; it was his duty, he said. Martha wished to go but refused to leave her husband's side. So, rather than "hazard her," as he put it, they returned to Mount Vernon. From the comfort of his study, he did the government's business. Yet it was not all shuffling papers and consulting Cabinet members. Often he met with experts to discuss his pet building project: the nation's future capital.

To direct the project, Washington hired a former army engineer, Major Pierre Charles L'Enfant. "Langfang," as he called him, laid out a city of long, wide avenues radiating from a hub, the Capitol, like spokes of a wheel. The president, however, ruled on the smallest details. For example, he approved the plans for every street, even chose the paving stones, and passed on the design of every government building. He decided how many workers to employ, mostly slaves rented from Virginia planters; they would get a pound of meat a day and all the cornmeal they could eat.

Plan for the east front of the Capitol of the United States. President Washington supervised every detail of work on the new city that would bear his name.

East Front of the Capitol of the United States as originally designed by William Thornton and adopted by General Washington President of the United States

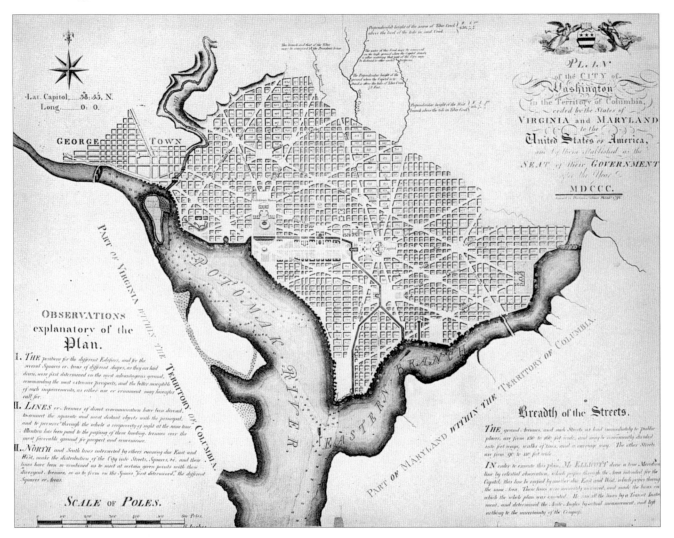

An 1800 plan of the city of Washington.

In this way, the sweat of unfree people became part of America's temples of freedom, the Capitol and the White House.

Washington once lost his temper with David Burns, the owner of a farm where the White House stands today. "Had not the Federal City been laid out here, you would have died a poor tobacco planter," he growled. The farmer growled back in a thick Scotch accent. "Ay, mon!" he replied, "an' had ye nae married the widow Custis, w'a' her naugurs, you would have been a land surveyor today, an' a mighty poor ane at that." Washington changed his tone.[33]

The First Family returned to Philadelphia early in 1794, after cold weather ended the epidemic and just as the "Whiskey Rebellion" flared across western Pennsylvania. Hamilton's excise tax had cut demand for the corn whiskey farmers sold to shopkeepers for the things they needed. Angry over the excise, they compared it to the old British Stamp Act. Again tax collectors met sizzling tar and white feathers. Again farmers took out their muskets. Seven thousand armed "Whiskey Boys" met in Braddock's Field outside Pittsburgh—where Colonel Washington had fought nearly forty years earlier—to force an end to tax collections.

President Washington dug in his heels. He understood their grievances, he said. The issue, however, was not about money. It was about the rule of law. Britain had tried to impose the Stamp Act without the colonies' consent. That was wrong. Now the American people, acting through Congress, had passed the excise tax. In a republic, the only way to unmake a law is by the same method that made it; that is, a vote of the people's elected representatives. The president insisted that no minority could dictate to the whole Union. If it did, then say good-bye to self-government, for anyone could obey or disobey any law for any reason. Rather than see that happen, he ordered fifteen thousand militiamen into action; if necessary, he would personally lead them. The rebellion collapsed at the first show of force.

Washington scarcely had time to relax after the Whiskey Rebellion. Britain still refused to give up seven forts built on American soil, as it had promised in the Treaty of Paris. Used as bases for arming the Indians, these forts blocked settlement of the lands south of the Great Lakes, allowing Britain to control the fur trade. Moreover, London was angry over the antics of Citizen Genêt and ignored American neutrality. In November 1793 alone, the Royal Navy seized 250 American ships bound for France with "materials of war," including food. British Navy captains also arrested many of the American sailors on board these ships as deserters, forcing them to serve on British warships. Some sailors *were* deserters. Yet the majority were American-born or naturalized citizens. Outraged members of Congress demanded retaliation.

Words are not bullets or warships or fighting men. Washington knew the country was unprepared to fight. Desperate to avoid war, he sent John

John Jay was the first chief justice of the United States Supreme Court. A skilled diplomat, he also negotiated the Jay Treaty with Great Britain. From an engraving in Washington Irving's *Life of George Washington*.

Jay, a leading Federalist whom he had appointed chief justice of the Supreme Court, to London. King George's ministers were not in a generous mood, and the envoy won few concessions. By the terms of Jay's Treaty, the United States agreed to close its ports to French shipping. In return, Britain agreed to abandon the forts and repay American shipowners a small part of their losses.

President Washington did not like Jay's Treaty because it did not ban future captures of American ships and seamen. Yet he could not object too strongly. Rejecting the treaty would probably ignite the very war with Britain he hoped to prevent. Similarly, supporting it would bring criticism for "surrendering" American interests to an old enemy at the expense of an old friend, France.

Republicans argued that the 1778 Treaty of Alliance with France was still in effect. Washington, however, agreed with Hamilton, who said it was not. That treaty had been made with the French monarchy. Well, times had changed. When the revolutionaries abolished the monarchy and killed Louis XVI, the treaty also died. The United States had no legal obligations toward France. Thus, Washington recommended that the Senate, which must pass on all treaties, give its approval to Jay's Treaty. So it did, but only after a bruising debate.

Public reaction to Jay's Treaty took the president by surprise. He had expected some rough going, but nothing like the storm of abuse that broke. "The cry against the Treaty," Washington wrote Hamilton, "is like that against a mad-dog." Hamilton knew that only too well. While he was speaking in its favor in New York, a Republican mob pelted him with stones, bloodying his head.[34]

Washington also became a target. All presidents have had their share of abuse, but few, if any, faced worse than the first. Thomas Jefferson sniped

at him behind his back; in private letters he said England had captured the president's mind. People who had once adored Washington as the nation's savior turned on him with rage and disgust. Republican speakers called him "Emperor George," a "tyrant," and Martha "Our Gracious Queen." The Republican press lambasted him as a fraud, a false patriot who had "labored to prevent our independence." Thomas Paine also turned against him. The author of *Common Sense* branded Washington "treacherous in private friendship . . . and a hypocrite in public life."[35]

All this was nonsense spouted by people who had let their emotions take over their reason, Washington thought. Yet it hurt. Never had Washington experienced such vicious insults; even the British had not stooped so low during the Revolution. Rather than reply, he kept the pain inside, refusing to lower himself to the level of his critics. Those nearest to him knew how

An anti-Republican cartoon showing President Washington driving the federal chariot against French "cannibals" while Thomas Jefferson (right) tries to hold it back.

much he despised the press. He thought most newspaper writers peddlers of lies and rubbish. They were, he snapped, a "bad and diabolical" lot of "infamous scribblers." While trying to rise above party bickering, he found himself agreeing more often with Hamilton's than Jefferson's followers.[36]

Despite the personal attacks, Washington could have won reelection easily. Most Americans still adored him as "the Father of His Country" and "the Man Who Unites All Hearts." Yet he yearned for retirement, yearned for peace and quiet in the years left to him. After Senate passage of Jay's Treaty in 1795, he decided enough was enough. This time, nothing would shake his determination to retire. That decision pleased Martha no end. It also began a tradition. Until Franklin D. Roosevelt's election to a third term in 1940, no president served more than two terms. In 1951, the Twenty-Second Amendment to the Constitution made the two-term tradition the law of the land.[37]

Washington's decision was a milestone in human history. In the past, men fought to gain and hold power. Washington deliberately walked away from power. He did so for personal reasons, but also for the good of the new country. The first president wanted to get the American people used to the idea that their leaders, even if they could do so, did not seek power for life, were not emperors or dictators. His retirement soothed some old wounds. George III was flabbergasted when he learned of the president's decision. Washington's action, the king said, made him "the greatest character of the age." The twentieth-century poet Robert Frost agreed. "George Washington was one of the few in the whole history of the world who was not carried away by power."[38]

On September 19, 1796, the country learned of Washington's decision. That morning, the Philadelphia *Daily American Advertiser* printed an article under the title "To the PEOPLE of the United States." The article appeared on page 2, filling it and half the next page with small type. Other newspapers quickly copied the *Advertiser* article. A New Hampshire paper, the *Courier*, reprinted it with a different title: "Washington's Farewell Address."

With Hamilton's help, the president had updated the notes for his original farewell address, four years earlier. The reason for printing it, instead

George Washington in 1796, three years before his death. Gilbert Stuart painted this classic picture, perhaps the most famous of all Washington portraits.

of delivering it in person, was that Washington wanted to reach the largest number of people in the shortest time. Washington's Farewell Address is one of America's great public documents, ranking alongside the Declaration of Independence, Constitution, Bill of Rights, and Lincoln's Gettysburg Address. It is Washington's testament to the nation he loved, a summary of the experience and wisdom gained over a lifetime of service. Until the 1970s, both houses of Congress had it read aloud on the anniversary of his birth.

The Farewell Address stressed the two themes closest to Washington's heart. At home, he warned Americans against the harmful effects of "the Spirit of Party." That spirit, he said, always "agitates the community with ill-founded jealousies and false alarms, kindles the animosity of one part against another, [and] foments occasionally riot and insurrection." If left unchecked, party conflicts would tear the Union apart and lead to disaster. A strong Union, however, would bring peace at home and prevent the growth of "overgrown military establishments"—large and expensive standing armies.[39]

Abroad, Washington advised Americans to stay out of other nations' affairs. He said:

> The great rule of conduct for us, in regard to foreign nations is in extending our commercial relations to have with them as little political connection as possible . . . Europe has a set of primary interests, which to us have none, or a very remote relation. Hence she must be engaged in frequent controversies, the causes of which are essentially foreign to our concerns. . . . 'Tis our true policy to steer clear of permanent alliances with any portion of the foreign world. . . . Taking care always to keep ourselves . . . on a respectably defensive posture, we may safely trust to temporary alliances for extraordinary emergencies.[40]

Federalists and Republicans tore into each other in the November presidential race. Federalist John Adams narrowly beat Republican Thomas Jefferson. Since Jefferson got the next highest vote in the Electoral College, he became vice president.

The outcome pleased Washington. He was even happier when he stood near Adams while he took the oath of office on March 4, 1797. Next morning, the new president wrote his wife that Washington really enjoyed the ceremony. "Methought I heard him say, 'Ay! I am fairly out and you fairly in! See which of us will be happiest.' "[41]

THE FIRST
AND THE LAST

*" I was the first and the last of my father's children by the second marriage.
When I will be called upon to follow is known only by the Giver of Life.
When the summons comes, I shall endeavor to obey with good grace."*
—GEORGE WASHINGTON, SEPTEMBER 1799

*I*n May 1797, barely two months after leaving office, Washington expressed his hopes for the future. "Retired from public employment," he wrote a friend, "my hours will glide smoothly on." He was too optimistic. The last two and a half years of his life would be as bumpy as any.[1]

Back at Mount Vernon, he easily took up his old routines. He still awoke at dawn to inspect his farms on horseback until noon. Sometimes he sat for artists who came to paint his portrait; French artist Charles de Saint-Mémim painted the last portrait of him from life in November 1798. Evenings found him and Martha dining with guests, mostly tourists eager to pay their respects or simply gawk at America's great man.

The year 1798 also found Washington worrying about the continued feuding between Federalists and Republicans. Things got so bad that two members of the House of Representatives went at each other with coal tongs and a club. That summer the old soldier also took out his general's

uniform again. Enraged by the neutrality policy, France had begun to seize American merchant ships. Washington agreed to help President Adams prepare the army for war. Fortunately, the crisis passed, as France decided it had all the enemies it needed in Europe.

Washington was relieved, both for his country and himself. The master of Mount Vernon was not getting any younger. He marked the passage of time by the passing of his brothers and sister; the last, Betty, died in 1797. Although still in good health, he had no energy for favorite activities like dancing and foxhunting. In the evening, after dinner, he tried to write pri-

The Washington family at home, Mount Vernon, 1796. "Wash" Custis and his sister, Nelly, stand by their grandparents. The unidentified black man behind Martha may be Billy Lee. Painting by Edward Savage.

vate letters; his secretary, Tobias Lear, answered the routine mail. Yet he never seemed to get very far. "When the lights are brought," he told a friend, "I feel tired and disinclined to engage in this work, conceiving that the next night will do as well. The next comes, and with it the same causes of postponement, and effect, and so on. . . . I have not looked into a book since I came home."[2]

One thing worried him more than ever. We recall that he favored abolishing slavery but needed forced labor to work his estate. Washington continued to have two minds on the subject. During his presidential years, critics had accused "the great champion of American freedom" of hypocrisy for holding black people in "unchristian bondage and ignorance." That kind of talk embarrassed him but did not stop him from demanding his property rights.[3]

Washington wished to have it both ways. In 1795, for example, he tried to avoid embarrassment by removing his name from ads for a runaway slave circulated north of Virginia. The next year, he located a fugitive

Politics gets violent. A fight broke out in the House of Representatives in 1798 between Matthew Griswold and Matthew Lyon over Lyon's criticism of policies of President John Adams.

named Oney Judge in Portsmouth, New Hampshire. A wizard with the sewing needle, she had been a favorite of Martha's. Washington asked a treasury official, Joseph Whipple, to persuade her to return by promising she would not face punishment. Oney, however, did not fear punishment, or even death. She told Whipple "she should suffer death rather than return to slavery." Furious at "the ingratitude of the girl," Washington asked Whipple to kidnap her and bring her to Virginia by ship. When Whipple said that might cause a riot, he let the matter drop. This willingness to use force against a young woman shows him at his worst. It also shows him as a human being, not a spotless figure carved in white marble.[4]

The last life portrait of Washington, November 1798. An engraving after a painting by French artist Charles de Saint-Mémim.

Washington remained torn after leaving office. He needed money—*badly*. His years as president had not entitled him to a pension; ex-presidents and members of Congress would not receive pensions until the twentieth century. Unfortunately, his account books showed a steady loss of income. Despite his best efforts, Mount Vernon's soil continued to lose fertility, bearing ever-smaller crops. Washington also found that he had more "hands" than he needed. In every year since 1789, the upkeep of his slaves cost more than the value of all they produced for the market. Slaves were slowly eating their master into bankruptcy.

Washington was in a bind. He could have sold the surplus slaves had his conscience allowed it. It did not. Although eager to recapture runaways, he had grown to hate "this kind of traffic in the human species," as he called the slave trade. Without selling lands in the Ohio Valley, he could not have supported his comfortable lifestyle. Yet that could not go on forever. "What then is to be done?" he asked a friend. "Something must or I shall be ruined."[5]

Money troubles were bad enough. One incident, however, shows that Washington thought these minor beside the disaster he feared slavery might bring in the future. During the summer of 1798, he met an English actor, John Bernard, on the road from Alexandria. He immediately liked the fellow and invited him to spend the day at Mount Vernon. It was a glorious day, and they sat on the veranda overlooking the Potomac. Bernard asked about the Revolution.

Washington described it as a crusade for liberty. As he spoke, a servant set a jug of water on the table. Bernard smiled. His host knew what *that* meant; the Englishman was mentally comparing Washington's glowing words about liberty with the fact of slavery. Washington fell silent, the corners of his mouth tightening into a frown. When he spoke again, his eyes, Bernard recalled, "burned with a steady fire." Yes, Washington said, he owned black people—always had. Yet it made him miserable. Now he saw slavery as the chief threat to his life's work. Washington's next words left a deep impression on his guest: "I can clearly foresee that nothing but the rooting out of slavery can [save] our Union."[6]

The rooting out of slavery! These were strong words, spoken with great emotion. Still, Washington could never bring himself to say them in public. As before, in the Constitutional Convention, he did not want to inflame tempers North and South. Surely, that was good politics. Sometimes, however, leaders need to go beyond politics for the sake of principle. By playing it safe, Washington lost a historic chance to put his prestige behind the cause of black freedom.

Already times were changing. Five years earlier, in 1793, Eli Whitney had invented the cotton gin, a machine for separating cotton fiber from the seeds, which are like barbed fishhooks. Until then, few planters raised cotton as a cash crop, since a worker needed a day to clean a pound of fiber by hand. Whitney's invention cleaned a thousand pounds in a few hours. Washington never mentioned it in his letters and diaries, possibly because he had never heard of it. Nevertheless, the cotton gin changed everything.

The gin made cotton growing profitable. Prices soared, increasing demand for slave labor and for land to plant larger crops. This sharpened the national debate, as southerners tried to expand slavery into the western territories. A half century later, by the 1850s, each side in the debate claimed Washington as its own. John C. Calhoun, the fiery senator from South Carolina, explained the southern position best. The first president, he said, "was one of us—a slaveholder and a planter." Just as Washington had resisted British tyranny, Calhoun favored secession, a state's leaving the Union, to protect the southern way of life.[7]

Abraham Lincoln knew better. "Honest Abe" had idolized the figure of Washington since boyhood. As an adult, Lincoln studied the first president's writings and speeches, particularly the Farewell Address, with its fervent support for the Union. Lincoln had harsh words for those who used his hero "to unsay what Washington said, and undo what Washington did." The first president did not want slavery to spread, Lincoln insisted, correctly. Washington denounced secessionists as he had denounced the Whiskey Rebels: both were minorities dictating to the nation rather than changing its laws by the methods of the law. Lincoln vowed to halt the spread of slavery and hold the Union together at all costs.[8]

After winning the presidential election of 1860, Lincoln linked God and Washington to his own mission. South Carolina had already seceded from the Union, with more states preparing to follow. Before leaving his home in Springfield, Illinois, for the inauguration, Lincoln said: "I now leave, not knowing when, or whether ever, I may return, with a task before me greater than that which rested upon Washington. Without the assistance of that Divine Being, who ever attended him, I cannot succeed. With that assistance I cannot fail."[9]

Eleven southern states eventually formed a separate country. Although some southern leaders wanted to name their country Washington, they chose the Confederate States of America instead; yet its postage stamps bore his likeness. For four terrible years, from 1861 to 1865, Union and Confederacy fought the Civil War. That struggle ended with the total "rooting out of slavery," but at a cost of 620,000 lives.[10]

The first president's family played an important, if indirect, role in the Civil War. Both sides declared Mount Vernon neutral ground, claiming Washington as the sacred symbol of their cause. "Wash" Custis had built Arlington House directly across the Potomac from the capital on land given by his adoptive father. Ironically, his daughter, Mary, married Robert E. Lee, son of Light-Horse Harry Lee, Washington's gallant cavalryman. As a Confederate general, "Bobby" Lee brought death to thousands of Union soldiers. When the capital's cemeteries filled, Lincoln sent the overflow to Arlington House, turning its grounds into our first national cemetery.

In 1799, the Civil War lay three generations into the future. Meanwhile, Washington still wrestled with the question: "What then is to be done?" Finally, he found the answer.

In July, he wrote his will in a firm, clear hand. Washington began by declaring that, upon his death, "my dearly beloved wife Martha" should have the use of his property for the rest of her life. That meant everything: money, land, buildings, livestock, slaves. When she died, all would go to various relatives; all, that is, except the slaves. Washington freed Billy Lee immediately in gratitude "for his faithful services during the Revolutionary War." As for the others, he declared they "shall receive their freedom." To give them fair starts in the world, he ordered instruction in reading, writing, and "some useful occupation" for any who wished to leave Mount Vernon. For those who chose to remain, he set up a fund to support them for life. Thus, in the end, Washington did the only sensible thing he could think of, easing his conscience and making amends for the past. No other founder of our country freed all his slaves.[11]

Finally, Washington left each of his nephews one of his swords. He asked only that they use the weapons in self-defense "or in the defense of their Country and its rights."

Tobias Lear, Washington's secretary, urged him to take medicine when he got sick after going out in bad weather. He refused, preferring to let the sickness leave in its own good time.

The former president lived less than six months after making his will. On December 12, he set out as usual to inspect his farms. It was a nasty day. A mixture of wind-driven snow and freezing rain began to fall. In the afternoon, he went to dinner without changing his wet clothes, a fatal error. Next day, December 13, he had chills but trudged through five inches of snow to mark dead trees for cutting. Upon his return to the house, Tobias Lear urged him to take some medicine. "No," he replied. "You know I never take anything for a cold. Let it go as it came."[12]

Washington awoke before dawn on December 14 with a painful sore throat. The pain worsened, until he had trouble breathing. Gradually, his skin took on a bluish color, a sign of oxygen deprivation. At Martha's urging, Lear sent for Dr. James Craik, a lifelong friend of Washington's, and two other physicians from nearby Alexandria. Given the medical knowledge of the day, they did their best.

Today, we might think their "best" a form of torture. First, they made their patient gargle a mixture of tea and vinegar, which nearly choked him. Next, they dosed him with calomel, a laxative to "flush" the sickness out of his system. They followed this with a drug that raised large blisters on his neck, to "draw out" the infection. He grew worse.

Finally, they tried bleeding, a favorite treatment for most illnesses in the eighteenth century. They bled him four times, taking a total of ninety-six ounces, well over half the blood in his body. After his death, critics claimed they took too much blood, further weakening his resistance. Loss of blood did him no good, but it did not cause his death, either. Medical historians believe Washington had an infection caused by a microbe that makes the lining of the throat swell and destroys oxygen-carrying red blood cells. Without antibiotics, a twentieth-century discovery, he was doomed the moment the infection took hold.[13]

James Craik, Washington's friend and doctor since they had served together in the French and Indian War. Dr. Craik stood at Washington's bedside when he died.

Although slowly suffocating, Washington remained logical and clear-headed. He knew the end was coming. While still able to speak, he gave final instructions about his will. As the hours passed, Martha, Lear, the doctors, and Christopher, a black butler, gathered in the sickroom. Martha sat at the foot of his bed throughout the ordeal, showing little emotion. She had seen so many loved ones die before and had mentally prepared for this loss.

Her husband lingered throughout the day and into the night. "I find myself going," he whispered, gasping for air. A little later, Dr. Craik came to his bedside. "Doctor," he murmured, "I die hard, but I am not afraid to go. . . . My breath cannot last long."[14]

Nor did it. Death came at ten o'clock in the evening. He was two months shy of his sixty-eighth birthday.

"Is he gone?" Martha asked in a firm but calm voice.

Lear nodded, then began to cry.

" 'Tis well," she sighed. "All is now over. I shall soon follow him. I have no more trials to pass through."[15]

On December 18, Martha watched from a window of the house as the funeral procession went the short distance to the family tomb. She wanted a simple funeral; there were no high officials present, only neighbors and some militiamen from Alexandria. Eight veterans of the Continental Army carried the heavy coffin. It was made of mahogany wood lined with lead and had a lead cover soldered in place. After a brief service, the mourners left.

News of Washington's death brought an outpouring of grief not seen again until Abraham Lincoln's murder in 1865. (Popular pictures showed Washington welcoming Lincoln into heaven.) Every city held a ceremony to mourn the great man. Yet those ceremonies were more than expressions of sorrow. By coming together in mourning, people of all classes affirmed their love of the nation Washington had done so much to create and preserve.

George Washington's last moments of life.

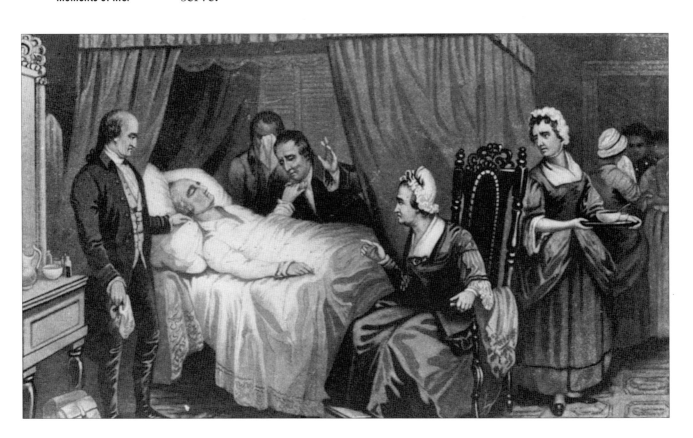

The Washington family's tomb. Since the tomb was in poor condition, in 1831 the bodies of the master of Mount Vernon and his wife were moved to a new tomb, where they lie today.

A day after the funeral, the House of Representatives voted to build a monument in his honor—the Washington Monument—in the capital. The House then passed a resolution offered by Light-Horse Harry Lee. It pays tribute "To the memory of the MAN, first in war, first in peace, and first in the hearts of his countrymen."[16]

Notes

PROLOGUE *A Man for His Times*

1. Thomas Paine, *Collected Writings* (New York: The Library of America, 1995), 101.
2. Richard Norton Smith, *Patriarch: George Washington and the New American Nation* (Boston: Houghton Mifflin, 1993), 37.
3. Christopher Duffy, *The Military Experience in the Age of Reason* (New York: Atheneum, 1988), 23.
4. James Morton Smith, ed., *George Washington: A Profile* (New York: Hill & Wang, 1996), 37.
5. Howard Zinn, *A People's History of the United States* (New York: HarperPerennial, 1995), 50.
6. Norman Gelb, *Less than Glory* (New York: G. P. Putnam's Sons, 1984), 28.
7. Evarts B. Greene, *The Revolutionary Generation, 1763–1790* (Chicago: Quadrangle Books, 1971), 181.
8. *Ibid.*, 181.
9. Edmund S. Morgan, *The Meaning of Independence: John Adams, Thomas Jefferson, George Washington* (New York: W.W. Norton, 1978), 6.
10. Gelb, *Less than Glory*, 22–23.
11. Morgan, *The Meaning of Independence*, 15.
12. Gelb, *Less than Glory*, 140.
13. Wallace Brown, *The King's Friends* (Providence: Brown University Press, 1966), 124.
14. Marcus Cunliffe, *George Washington: Man and Monument* (Boston: Little Brown, 1958), 13.
15. Barry Schwartz, *George Washington: The Making of a Symbol* (New York: The Free Press, 1987), 41, 194; P.M. Zall, ed., *George Washington Laughing: Humorous Anecdotes by and about Our First President from Original Sources* (Hamden, Conn.: Archon Books, 1989), 20; Charles Royster, *A Revolutionary People at War: The Continental Army and American Character, 1775–1783* (New York: W.W. Norton, 1981), 257; Cunliffe, *George Washington*, 71.
16. Smith, *Patriarch: George Washington and the New American Nation*, 4.
17. John C. Fitzpatrick, ed., *The Writings of George Washington from the Original Manuscript Sources, 1745–1799*, 39 vols. (Washington, D.C.: U.S. Government Printing Office, 1931–1944), XI, 291.
18. *Ibid.*, XXII, 34; XXVI, 486.
19. Roy P. Basler, ed., *The Collected Works of Abraham Lincoln*, 9 vols. (New Brunswick, N.J.: Rutgers University Press, 1953–1955), IV, 235–36.

1. *A Man of Good Quality*

1. Washington continued to celebrate his birthday on February 11. But when he retired as president, Americans began to observe the modern date, February 22, in his honor.
2. W. E. Woodward, *George Washington: The Image and the Man* (Garden City, N.Y.: Garden City Publishing Co., 1942), 15.
3. George Washington Parke Custis, *Recollections and Private Memoirs of Washington by His Adopted Son, George Washington Parke Custis* (New York: Derby and Kackson, 1860), 131.
4. W. B. Allen, ed., *George Washington: A Collection* (Indianapolis: Liberty Fund, 1988), 6–14.
5. Thomas Jefferson, *Writings* (New York: The Library of America, 1984), 1319.
6. John C. Fitzpatrick, ed., *The Diaries of George Washington*, 4 vols. (Boston: Houghton Mifflin, 1925), I, 5.
7. *Ibid.*, I, 9.
8. *Ibid.*, I, 17–19.
9. *Ibid.*, I, 25.
10. John E. Ferling, *The First of Men: A Life of Washington* (Knoxville: University of Tennessee Press, 1988), 16.
11. Fitzpatrick, *The Writings of George Washington*, I, 107.
12. Eric Robson, "Purchase and Promotion in the British Army in the Eighteenth Century," *History* XXXVI (1951), 58.

2. *The World on Fire*

1. Originally, Native Americans did not call themselves Indians, a term used by the early explorers. Native people always identified themselves by their tribal names.
2. William Bradford, *Of Plymouth Plantation, 1620–1647* (New York: Alfred A. Knopf, 1952), 295–96; John E. Ferling, *A Wilderness of Miseries: War and Warriors in Early America* (Westport, Conn.: Greenwood Press, 1980), 33–34, 52–53; Carl Van Doren, *Benjamin Franklin* (New York: Viking, 1938), 247.
3. English people named these wars after their rulers at the time: King William's War (1689–97), Queen Anne's War (1702–13), King George's War (1739–48).

4. Willard Sterne Randall, *George Washington: A Life* (New York: Henry Holt, 1997), 74.

5. Fitzpatrick, *The Diaries of George Washington*, I, 44.

6. *Ibid.*, I, 44.

7. *Ibid.*, I, 55.

8. *Ibid.*, I, 63.

9. *Ibid.*, I, 65.

10. *Ibid.*, I, 65.

11. *Ibid.*, I, 65.

12. Charles Cecil Wall, *George Washington: Citizen Soldier* (Charlottesville: University Press of Virginia, 1980), 13.

13. Washington, *Writings*, 48.

14. Thomas A. Lewis, *For King and Country: The Maturing of George Washington, 1748–1760* (New York: HarperCollins, 1993), 152.

15. Washington, *Writings*, 613.

16. Duffy, *The Military Experience in the Age of Reason*, 89, 90.

17. T. H. McGuffie, ed., *Rank and File: The Common Soldier at Peace and War, 1642–1914* (New York: St. Martin's Press, 1964), 42; Sylvia R. Frey, *The British Soldier in America: A Social History of Military Life in the Revolutionary Period* (Austin: University of Texas Press, 1981), 57.

18. H. C. B. Rogers, *Weapons of the British Soldier* (London: Seeley Service & Co., 1960), 94.

19. McGuffie, *Rank and File*, 95.

20. Benjamin Franklin, *Writings* (New York: The Library of America, 1987), 1441.

21. Reginald Hargreaves, *The Bloodybacks: The British Serviceman in North America and the Caribbean, 1655–1783* (New York: Walker & Co., 1968), 124.

22. Lee McCardell, *Ill-Starred General: Braddock of the Coldstream Guards* (Pittsburgh: University of Pittsburgh Press, 1958), 180.

23. *Ibid.*, 230, 236; Charles E. Hamilton, ed., *Braddock's Defeat* (Norman: University of Oklahoma Press, 1959), 45.

24. Washington, *Writings*, 55.

25. Noemie Emery, *Washington: A Biography* (New York: G.P. Putnam's Sons, 1976), 86.

26. Paul E. Kopperman, *Braddock at the Monongahela* (Pittsburgh: University of Pittsburgh Press, 1977), 26, 30.

27. *Ibid.*, 176.

28. Washington, *Writings*, 58.

29. McCardell, *Ill-Starred General*, 251.

30. *Ibid.*, 252.

31. Randall, *George Washington*, 136; Kopperman, *Braddock*, 170.

32. Washington, *Writings*, 59.

33. Kopperman, *Braddock*, 130.

34. Washington, *Writings*, 58.

35. Kopperman, *Braddock*, 171.

36. Francis Parkman, *France and England in North America*, 2 vols. (New York: The Library of America, 1983), II, 997.

37. Samuel G. Drake, *Tragedies in the Wilderness: An Account of the Remarkable Occurrences in the Life and Travels of Col. James Smith* (Boston: Antiquarian Bookstore, 1841), 184–85.

38. Washington's notes are in David Humphreys, *Life of General Washington* (Athens: University of Georgia Press, 1991), 18.

39. Emery, *Washington*, 91.

40. Charles E. Hamilton, ed., *Braddock's Defeat* (Norman: University of Oklahoma Press, 1959), 32.

41. Randall, *George Washington*, 141.

42. Washington, *Writings*, 58, 59.

43. Randall, *George Washington*, 150.

44. Ralph K. Andrist, ed., *George Washington: A Biography in His Own Words* (New York: Newsweek, 1972), 58.

45. Andrist, *George Washington*, 65.

46. Randall, *George Washington*, 151; Washington, *Writings*, 74, 75.

47. Ferling, *The First of Men*, 46.

48. Louis Knott Koontz, "Washington on the Frontier," *Virginia Magazine of History and Biography*, XXXVI (1928), 315.

49. *Ibid.*, 315.

50. Humphreys, *Life of Washington*, 22.

51. Kopperman, *Braddock at the Monongahela*, 92.

52. Schwartz, *George Washington*, 150.

3. *A Kind of Destiny*

1. Randall, *George Washington*, 176; George W. Nordham, *George Washington's Women: Mary, Martha, Sally and 146 Others* (Philadelphia: Dorrance & Co., 1977), 33–34.

2. Miriam Anne Bourne, *First Family: George Washington and His Intimate Relations* (New York: W. W. Norton, 1982), 198; Nordham, *George Washington's Women*, 22.

3. Washington, *Writings*, 146.

4. Emery, *Washington*, 142; Paul Leland Haworth, *George Washington, Country Gentleman* (Indianapolis: Bobbs-Merrill Company, 1925), 226.

5. Woodward, *George Washington*, 225.

6. Richard B. Morris, *Seven Who Shaped Our Destiny: The Founding Fathers as Revolutionaries* (New York: Harper & Row, 1973), 50; Smith, *Patriarch*, 18; Zall, *George Washington Laughing*, 50.

7. Nordham, *George Washington's Women*, 4; Emery, *Washington*, 295.

8. Nicholas Cresswell, *The Journal of Nicholas Cresswell, 1774–1777*, ed. Nicholas MacVeagh (New York: Dial Press, 1924), 270.

9. Ferling, *The First of Men*, 83.

10. Washington, *Writings*, 107.

11. William S. Baker, ed., *Early Sketches of George Washington* (Philadelphia: J.B. Lippincott, 1894), 13–14.

12. Philip S. Foner, *History of Black Americans: From Africa to the Emergence of the Cotton Kingdom* (Westport, Conn.: Greenwood Press, 1975), 220.

13. George H. Mazyck, *George Washington and the Negro* (Washington, D.C.: The Associated Publishers, 1932), 1–2.

14. Randall, *George Washington*, 207; Fitzpatrick, *The Diaries of George Washington*, I, 278.

15. Ferling, *The First of Men*, 68; George Washington, *Letters from George Washington to Tobias Lear* (Rochester, N.Y.: The Genesee Press, 1905), 94, 51; James T. Flexner, *George Washington: Anguish and Farewell, 1793–1799* (Boston: Little, Brown, 1972), 437.

16. Morgan, *The Meaning of Independence*, 30.

17. Julian Ursyn Niemcewicz, *Under Their Vine and Fig Tree, Travels through America in 1797–1799* (Elizabeth, N.J.: Grossman Publishing Co., 1965), 100–01.

18. Mazyck, *George Washington and the Negro*, 16; Fritz Hirschfeld, *George Washington and Slavery: A Documentary Portrayal* (Columbia: University of Missouri Press, 1997), 30.

19. Ferling, *The First of Men*, 478.

20. Emery, *Washington*, 143–44.

21. Manfred S. Guttmacher, *America's Last*

King: An Interpretation of the Madness of George III (New York: Scribner's, 1941), 122–23.

22. Washington, *Writings*, 116.

23. *Ibid.*, 130.

24. John Ferling, *A Life of John Adams* (New York: Henry Holt, 1996), 70.

25. Randall, *George Washington*, 258; Fitzpatrick, *Writings of Washington*, III, 232.

26. John C. Miller, *The Origins of the American Revolution* (New York: Atlantic Monthly Press, 1943), 291.

27. John S. Pancake, *1777: Year of the Hangman* (University, Ala.: University of Alabama Press, 1977), 79.

28. Hughes, *Washington*, I, 200.

29. Washington, *Writings*, 155–56.

30. Haworth, *George Washington*, 221; Hirschfeld, *George Washington and Slavery*, 110.

31. Washington, *Writings*, 160.

32. Bruce Ingham Granger, *Political Satire in the American Revolution* (Ithaca, N.Y.: Cornell University Press, 1960), 42.

33. Harry M. Ward, *The American Revolution: Nationhood Achieved, 1763–1788* (New York: St. Martin's Press, 1995), 263.

34. John W. Fortescue, *A History of the British Army*, 13 vols. (London: Macmillan, 1899–1930), III, 168, 170.

35. Royster, *A Revolutionary People at War*, 136.

36. James Thomas Flexner, *George Washington: The Forge of Experience, 1732–1775* (Boston: Little, Brown, 1965), 343.

37. Washington, *Writings*, 167–69.

38. *Ibid.*, 173.

4. War and Washington

1. Pancake, *1777: The Year of the Hangman*, 10.

2. George F. Scheer & Hugh F. Rankin, eds., *Rebels and Redcoats* (Cleveland: World Publishing Co., 1957), 67; Burke Davis, *George Washington and the American Revolution* (New York: Random House, 1975), 44.

3. Stuart Bernath, "George Washington and the Genesis of American Military Discipline," *Mid-America* 49 (1967): 86; Davis, *George Washington*, 6; Scheer & Rankin, *Rebels and Redcoats*, 82.

4. Ferling, *A Wilderness of Miseries*, 115; Royster, *A Revolutionary People at War*, 60.

5. Andrist, *George Washington*, 115–16.

6. Randall, *George Washington*, 292; Davis, *George Washington*, 44–45.

7. Rev. E. B. Hillard, *The Last Men of the Revolution* (Barre, Mass.: Barre Publishers, 1968), 37.

8. Fitzpatrick, *Writings of George Washington*, IV, 81; XXVI, 39.

9. Mazyck, *George Washington and the Negro*, 42–43. For the story of the Ethiopian Regiment, see Chapter VI, "Washington's Advance."

10. Frank Moore, *Songs and Ballads of the American Revolution* (New York: D. Appleton & Co., 1856), 101.

11. Thomas Paine, *Collected Writings* (New York: The Library of America, 1995), 25, 29, 35.

12. Washington, *Writings*, 206.

13. Scheer & Rankin, *Rebels and Redcoats*, 108.

14. Flexner, *George Washington*, II, 82.

15. Pancake, *1777: The Year of the Hangman*, 26.

16. Elisha Bostwick, "A Connecticut Soldier under Washington: Elisha Bostwick's Memoirs of the First Years of the Revolution," *William and Mary Quarterly* 6 (1949): 102.

17. Gelb, *Less than Glory*, 161; Ray W. Pettengill, ed., *Letters from America, 1777–1779, Being Letters of Brunswick, Hessian, and Waldeck Officers with the British Armies during the Revolution* (Port Washington, N.Y.: Kennikat Press, 1964), 166.

18. Thomas Jones, *History of New York During the Revolutionary War*, 2 vols. (New York: Arno Press, 1968), I, 101–02.

19. Scheer & Rankin, *Rebels and Redcoats*, 148.

20. Ambrose Serle, *The American Journal of Ambrose Serle, Secretary to Lord Howe, 1776–1778* (San Marino, Calif.: The Huntington Library, 1940), 71.

21. Ferling, *The First of Men*, 102.

22. Joseph Plumb Martin, *Private Yankee Doodle: Being a Narrative of Some of the Adventures, Dangers and Sufferings of a Revolutionary Soldier* (Boston: Little, Brown, 1962), 24.

23. *Ibid.*, 26.

24. Rupert Hughes, *George Washington*, 3 vols. (New York: William Morrow, 1926–30), II, 444.

25. *Ibid.*, 445.

26. Pettengill, *Letters from America*, 154.

27. Ferling, *The First of Men*, 98.

28. Martin, *Private Yankee Doodle*, 33.

29. *Ibid.*, 33.

30. *Ibid.*, 34.

31. Douglas Southall Freeman, *George Washington: A Biography*, 7 vols. (New York: Scribner's, 1948–59), IV, 493.

32. Davis, *George Washington*, 125.

33. *Ibid.*, 126.

34. Edwin G. Burrows and Mike Wallace, *Gotham: A History of New York City to 1898* (New York: Oxford University Press, 1999), 241; Thomas J. Wertenbaker, *Father Knickerbocker Rebels: New York City during the Revolution* (New York: Scribner's, 1948), 101.

35. John Bakeless, *Turncoats, Traitors and Heroes* (Philadelphia: J. B. Lippincott, 1959), 120.

36. Burrows & Wallace, *Gotham*, 242.

37. Martin, *Private Yankee Doodle*, 82–83.

38. Richard Brookhiser, *Founding Father: Rediscovering George Washington* (New York: The Free Press, 1996), 26.

39. Emery, *Washington*, 204.

40. William S. Stryker, *The Battles of Trenton and Princeton* (Boston: Houghton Mifflin, 1898), 107.

41. *Ibid.*, 5; James Thacher, *Military Journal of the American Revolution* (New York: The New York Times and Arno Press, 1969), 67.

42. Scheer & Rankin, *Rebels and Redcoats*, 212.

43. Davis, *George Washington*, 164.

44. Stryker, *The Battles of Trenton and Princeton*, 147.

45. Randall, *George Washington*, 325.

46. J. G. Seume, "Memoirs of a Hessian Conscript: J. G. Seume's Reluctant Passage to America," *William and Mary Quarterly* 5 (1948): 553.

47. Scheer & Rankin, *Rebels and Redcoats*, 215–16.

48. *Ibid.*

49. Davis, *Washington*, 183.

50. Scheer & Rankin, *Rebels and Redcoats*, 217.

51. *Ibid.*, 217.

52. *Ibid.*, 219.
53. *Ibid.*, 219.
54. *Ibid.*, 210. To give a fig for something is to give it little value.

5. *Pounds of Sorrow*

1. Scheer & Rankin, *Rebels and Redcoats*, 208–09.
2. Randall, *George Washington*, 356.
3. Hirschfeld, *George Washington and Slavery*, 120.
4. Scheer & Rankin, *Rebels and Redcoats*, 233.
5. *Ibid.*, 233; Linda G. DePauw, "Women in Combat: The Revolutionary War Experience," *Armed Forces and Society* 7 (1981): 209–26.
6. Scheer & Rankin, *Rebels and Redcoats*, 413–14.
7. Davis, *George Washington*, 221–22; Freeman, *George Washington*, IV, 484.
8. Davis, *George Washington*, 222.
9. Van Doren, *Benjamin Franklin*, 585.
10. Alfred H. Bill, *Valley Forge: The Making of an Army* (New York: Harper & Brothers, 1952), 83.
11. Davis, *George Washington*, 255, 264.
12. Albigence Waldo, "Valley Forge Diary, 1777–1778," *Pennsylvania Magazine of History and Biography* XXI (1897): 308.
13. Martin, *Private Yankee Doodle*, 77; Charles K. Bolton, *The Private Soldier Under Washington* (Port Washington, N.Y.: Kennikat Press, 1964), 85.
14. Waldo, "Valley Forge Diary," 306–07.
15. Martin, *Private Yankee Doodle*, 110–11.
16. Gelb, *Less than Glory*, 106; Fitzpatrick, *The Writings of George Washington from the Original Manuscript Sources, 1745–1799*, X, 195–96.
17. Randall, *George Washington*, 352–53.
18. Schwartz, *Washington*, 27–28.
19. Scheer & Rankin, *Rebels and Redcoats*, 305; North Callahan, *George Washington: Soldier and Man* (New York: William Morrow & Co., 1972), 127.
20. William A. Bryan, *George Washington in American Literature, 1775–1865* (New York: Columbia University Press, 1952), 31; Emery, *Washington*, 282.
21. Smith, *Patriarch*, 13–14.
22. Hilliard, *The Last Men of the Revolution*,

70.
23. *Ibid.*, 70; Bill, *Valley Forge*, 144–45.
24. Royster, *A Revolutionary People at War*, 220.
25. John MacAuley Palmer, *General von Steuben* (Port Washington, New York: Kennikat Press, 1966), 149.
26. Royster, *A Revolutionary People at War*, 221.
27. Palmer, *General von Steuben*, 157.
28. Scheer & Rankin, *Rebels and Redcoats*, 308.
29. Moore, *Songs and Ballads of the American Revolution*, 211.
30. Bill, *Valley Forge*, 170.
31. *Ibid.*, 180.
32. *Ibid.*, 19.
33. Broadus Mitchell, *The Price of Independence: A Realistic View of the American Revolution* (New York: Oxford University Press, 1974), 236; DePauw, "Women in Combat," 215.
34. Martin, *Private Yankee Doodle*, 123–24.
35. Bill, *Valley Forge*, 214.
36. Custis, *Recollections and Private Memoirs of Washington*, 217.
37. Martin, *Private Yankee Doodle*, 127; Custis, *Recollections and Private Memoirs of Washington*, 413–14. Washington later had Lee put on trial for disobeying orders and cowardice in the face of the enemy. A jury of officers convicted Lee on all charges, and he left the army.
38. Bill, *Valley Forge*, 219.
39. Martin, *Private Yankee Doodle*, 127; Davis, *George Washington*, 293.
40. Martin, *Private Yankee Doodle*, 132–33. Molly Pitcher served to the end of the war. Afterward, she received a government pension, dying at the age of seventy-eight.
41. Bill, *Valley Forge*, 227. The Guards and Grenadiers were the best units in the British army.

6. *Great Washington's Advance*

1. Martin, *Private Yankee Doodle*, 134.
2. Fitzpatrick, *Writings of George Washington*, XIV, 484.
3. Gelb, *Less than Glory*, 196.
4. Elswyth Thane, *Potomac Squire* (New York: Duell, Sloan and Pearce, 1963), 193.

5. Thomas J. Fleming, *Beat the Last Drum: The Siege of Yorktown, 1781* (New York: St. Martin's Press, 1963), 36–37.
6. Sylvia R. Frey, "The British and the Black: A New Perspective," *The Historian* 39 (1976): 229; Benjamin Quarles, *The Negro in the American Revolution* (Chapel Hill: University of North Carolina Press, 1961), 144.
7. Mazyck, *George Washington and the Negro*, 71; Foner, *A History of Black Americans*, 330–35.
8. Callahan, *George Washington*, 193.
9. Randall, *George Washington*, 385; Scheer & Rankin, *Rebels and Redcoats*, 388.
10. Randall, *George Washington*, 381.
11. *Ibid.*, 387.
12. Gelb, *Less than Glory*, 129.
13. Scheer & Rankin, *Rebels and Redcoats*, 376.
14. Callahan, *George Washington*, 207.
15. John C. Dann, ed., *The Revolution Remembered: Eyewitness Accounts of the War for Independence* (Chicago: University of Chicago Press, 1980), 188; Mitchell, *The Price of Independence*, 18.
16. Scheer & Rankin, *Rebels and Redcoats*, 465.
17. Davis, *George Washington*, 362. Arnold served his British masters well. In September 1781, he burned New London, Connecticut, and slaughtered the defenders of Fort Griswold outside the town after they surrendered. He survived the war and went to England. Even the English scorned him as a traitor, and he grew ever more bitter. Arnold died in London in 1801, after losing his money in bad business deals.
18. Wall, *George Washington*, 160–61.
19. Davis, *George Washington*, 435; William Feltman, *The Journal of Lieut. William Feltman, of the First Pennsylvania Regiment, 1781–82* (Philadelphia: The Historical Society of Pennsylvania, 1853), 5.
20. *Ibid.*, 30; Hector St. John de Crèvecœur, *Letters of an American Farmer* (London: J. M. Dent & Sons, 1912), 172–73.
21. Davis, *The Campaign That Won America*, 56.
22. Emery, *Washington*, 269–70; Fleming, *Beat the Last Drum*, 91.
23. Stephen Bosnal, *When the French Were Here* (New York: Kennikat Press, 1968), 92–93.

24. Burke Davis, *The Campaign That Won America: The Story of Yorktown* (New York: Dial Press, 1970), 6; Abbé Claude Robin, *Travels Through North America* (New York: Arno Press, 1969), 35.

25. Fleming, *Beat the Last Drum*, 74.

26. Bosnal, *When the French Were Here*, 121.

27. Fleming, *Beat the Last Drum*, 73.

28. Bosnal, *When the French Were Here*, 38.

29. Emery, *Washington*, 28.

30. Robin, *Travels Through North America*, 35.

31. Davis, *The Campaign That Won America*, 21.

32. *Ibid.*, 21.

33. *Ibid.*, 385.

34. *Ibid.*, 170.

35. Thacher, *Military Journal of the American Revolution*, 277–78.

36. Davis, *George Washington*, 404.

37. Scheer & Rankin, *Rebels and Redcoats*, 475; Custis, *Recollections and Private Memoirs of Washington*, 236.

38. Martin, *Private Yankee Doodle*, 228.

39. Fleming, *Beat the Last Drum*, 256.

40. Martin, *Private Yankee Doodle*, 241.

41. Thacher, *Military Journal of the American Revolution*, 280.

42. *Ibid.*, 285.

43. *Ibid.*, 284, 286.

44. Scheer & Rankin, *Rebels and Redcoats*, 491.

45. *Ibid.*, 491.

46. Davis, *George Washington*, 435.

47. Custis, *Recollections and Private Memoirs of Washington*, 248.

48. Davis, *The Campaign That Won America*, 265.

49. Scheer & Rankin, *Rebels and Redcoats*, 494.

50. Martin, *Private Yankee Doodle*, 242.

7. *The Thing Is Done*

1. Benson Bobrick, *Angel in the Whirlwind: The Triumph of the American Revolution* (New York: Simon & Schuster, 1997), 466.

2. *Ibid.*, 466.

3. *George Washington: A Collection*, 203–04.

4. Davis, *George Washington*, 449.

5. *Ibid.*, 451.

6. Brookhiser, *Founding Father*, 44.

7. Scheer & Rankin, *Rebels and Redcoats*, 502.

8. Wertenbaker, *Father Knickerbocker Rebels*, 256; Gelb, *Less Than Glory*, 223.

9. Donald Barr Chidsey, *The Loyalists: The Story of Those Americans Who Fought Against Independence* (New York: Crown Publishers, 1973), 172.

10. Scheer & Rankin, *Rebels and Redcoats*, 503.

11. *Ibid.*

12. *Ibid.*

13. Martin, *Private Yankee Doodle*, 280.

14. Washington, *Writings*, 553–54.

15. Fleming, *Beat the Last Drum*, 106.

16. Richard M. Ketchum, *The World of George Washington* (New York: American Heritage Publishing Company, 1974), 254.

17. Tebbel, *George Washington's America*, 438.

18. Paine, *Collected Writings*, 52.

19. Smith, *Patriarch*, 164.

20. Schwartz, *George Washington*, 85.

21. Brookhiser, *Founding Father*, 147; Smith, *Patriarch*, 164.

22. Zall, *George Washington Laughing*, 15, 59; Matthew Spalding and Patrick J. Garrity, *A Sacred Union of Citizens: George Washington's Farewell Address and the American Character* (New York: Rowman & Littlefield Publishers, 1996), 127.

23. Smith, *Patriarch*, 218.

24. John R. Alden, *George Washington: A Biography* (New York: Wings Books, 1984), 220.

25. Max Farrand, ed., *The Records of the Federal Convention of 1787*. 4 vols. (New Haven, CT.: Yale University Press, 1966), III, 85–86.

26. Foner, *History of Black Americans*, 399.

27. Washington, *Writings*, 594.

28. Smith, *Patriarch*, 188.

29. Mazyck, *George Washington and the Negro*, 103.

30. Roy P. Basler, ed., *The Collected Works of Abraham Lincoln*, 9 vols. (New Brunswick: Rutgers University Press, 1953), II, 274.

31. Spalding & Garrity, *A Sacred Union of Citizens*, 28. James Monroe became the fifth president of the United States, serving between 1817 and 1825.

32. Cunliffe, *George Washington*, 148.

33. *The Diaries of George Washington*, ed. Donald D. Jackson and Dorothy Twohig,

6 vols. (Charlottesville: University Press of Virginia, 1976–79), V, 312.

8. *The Sacred Fire of Liberty*

1. John Tebbel, *George Washington's America* (New York: E. P. Dutton, 1954), 261.

2. Barry Schwartz, *George Washington: The Making of a Symbol* (New York: The Free Press, 1987), 49.

3. Stephen Decatur, *Private Affairs of George Washington, from the Record and Accounts of Tobias Lear* (Boston: Houghton Mifflin Co., 1933), 5.

4. Freeman, *George Washington*, VI, 192.

5. Bobrick, *Angel in the Whirlwind*, 491; Randall, *George Washington*, 448.

6. Bobrick, *Angel in the Whirlwind*, 491.

7. Tebbel, *George Washington's America*, 267.

8. Flexner, *George Washington: Anguish and Farewell*, 25.

9. Spalding & Garrity, *A Sacred Union of Citizens*, 11–12.

10. Smith, *Patriarch*, 219; Randall, *George Washington*, 453.

11. Randall, *George Washington*, 453.

12. Ferling, *The First of Men*, 390.

13. Schwartz, *George Washington*, 6.

14. Smith, *Patriarch*, 36.

15. Decatur, *Private Affairs of George Washington*, 46.

16. Smith, *Patriarch*, 24.

17. Tebbel, *George Washington's America*, 273; Decatur, *Private Affairs of George Washington*, 27–28. Washington toured the Southern states from April to June, 1791. John Tebbel's book has a complete description of the presidential tours.

18. Randall, *George Washington*, 462–63.

19. Smith, *Patriarch*, 51.

20. *Ibid.*, 199; Smith, *Patriarch*, 199.

21. Ferling, *The First of Men*, 343.

22. Jefferson, *Writings*, 988–89.

23. Nordham, *George Washington's Women*, 102.

24. Flexner, *George Washington: Anguish and Farewell*, 17.

25. Bosnal, *When the French Were Here*, 242–43.

26. Smith, *Patriarch*, 20, 164.

27. Louis Martin Sears, *George Washington & The French Revolution* (Detroit: Wayne State

University Press, 1960), 33.

28. Jefferson, *Writings*, 1004.

29. Washington, *Writings*, 918.

30. Smith, *Patriarch*, 210–11; Tebbel, *George Washington's America*, 343.

31. Flexner, *George Washington: Anguish and Farewell*, 63.

32. Smith, *Patriarch*, 182.

33. Zoll, *George Washington Laughing*, 46–47.

34. Washington, *Writings*, 914.

35. Spalding & Garrity, *A Sacred Union of Citizens*, 105; Schwartz, *George Washington*, 67, 68; Harry Hayden Clark, ed., *Thomas Paine: Representative Selections*, (New York: Hill & Wang, 1961), 408.

36. Randall, *George Washington*, 491.

37. *Ibid.*

38. Brookhiser, *Founding Father*, 103; Smith, *Patriarch*, 359.

39. Washington, *Writings*, 970.

40. *Ibid.*, 974–75.

41. James Bishop Peabody, ed., *John Adams: A Biography in His Own Words* (New York: Newsweek, 1973), 358.

9. *The First and the Last*

1. Washington, *Writings*, 995.

2. *Ibid.*, 996–97.

3. Hirschfeld, *George Washington and Slavery*, 191.

4. *Ibid.*, 112–17.

5. Washington, *Writings*, 1047.

6. Hirschfeld, *George Washington and Slavery*, 72–73.

7. Bryan, *George Washington in American Literature*, 75–76.

8. Basler, *The Collected Works of Abraham Lincoln*, III, 550.

9. *Ibid.*, IV, 190.

10. Merton E. Coulter, *The Confederate States of America, 1861–1865* (Baton Rouge: Louisiana State University Press, 1950), 60, 127.

11. Washington, *Writings*, 1023–1024. The fund made its last payment in 1833, with the death of the last freedman.

12. Flexner, *George Washington: Anguish and Farewell*, 457.

13. J. Worth Estes, "George Washington and the Doctors: Treating America's First Superhero," *Medical Heritage*, 12, no. 1 (1985), 54.

14. Flexner, *George Washington: Anguish and Farewell*, 460.

15. Smith, *Patriarch*, 355. Mrs. Washington died at Mount Vernon on May 22, 1802, ten days before her seventy-first birthday. She spent her last days in fear of her slaves. Mrs. Abigail Adams visited her in December 1800. She said Martha "did not feel as tho her life was safe in their hands," since they might kill her to hasten their freedom. (Hirschfeld, *George Washington and Slavery*, 214.)

16. Brookhiser, *Founding Father*, 199.

More Books About
Washington and His Times

Alden, John R. *The American Revolution, 1775–1783*. New York: Harper Torchbooks, 1962.

———. *George Washington: A Biography*. New York: Wings Books, 1984.

Anderson, Troyer Steele. *The Command of the Howe Brothers During the American Revolution*. New York: Oxford University Press, 1936.

Andrist, Ralph K., ed. *George Washington: A Biography in His Own Words*. New York: Newsweek, 1972.

Atwood, Rodney. *The Hessians: Mercenaries from Hessen-Kassel in the American Revolution*. New York: Cambridge University Press, 1980.

Bakeless, John. *Turncoats, Traitors and Heroes*. Philadelphia: J. B. Lippincott, 1959.

Baker, William S., ed. *Character Portraits of Washington As Delivered by Historians, Orators, and Divines*. Philadelphia: Robert Lindsay, 1887.

———. *Early Sketches of George Washington*. Philadelphia: J. B. Lippincott, 1894.

Bellamy, Francis Rufus. *The Private Life of George Washington*. New York: Thomas Y. Crowell, 1951.

Bill, Alfred H. *The Campaign of Princeton*. Princeton: Princeton University Press, 1948.

———. *Valley Forge: The Making of an Army*. New York: Harper & Brothers, 1952.

Billias, George Athan. *George Washington's Opponents: British Generals and Admirals in the American Revolution*. New York: William Morrow, 1969.

Bliven, Bruce, Jr. *The Battle for Manhattan*. New York: Henry Holt, 1956.

———. *Under the Guns: New York, 1775–1776*. New York: Harper & Row, 1972.

Blumenthal, Walter Hart. *Women Camp Followers of the American Revolution*. New York: Arno Press, 1974.

Boardman, F. W. *Against the Iroquois: The Sullivan Campaign of 1779 in New York State*. New York: David McKay, 1975.

Bobrick, Benson. *Angel in the Whirlwind: The Triumph of the American Revolution*. New York: Simon & Schuster, 1997.

Bolton, Charles K. *The Private Soldier Under Washington*. Port Washington, N.Y.: Kennikat Press, 1964. Reprint of a 1902 book.

Bosnal, Stephen. *When the French Were Here*. New York: Kennikat Press, 1968. First published in 1945.

Bostwick, Elisha. "A Connecticut Soldier Under Washington: Elisha Bostwick's Memoirs of the First Years of the Revolution," *William and Mary Quarterly* 6 (1949): 94–107.

Bourne, Miriam Anne. *First Family: George Washington and His Intimate Relations*. New York: W. W. Norton, 1982.

Bowen, Catherine Drinker. *Miracle at Philadelphia: The Story of the Constitutional Convention, May to September 1787*. Boston: Little, Brown, 1966.

Brookhiser, Richard. *Founding Father: Rediscovering George Washington*. New York: The Free Press, 1996.

Brown, Richard Maxwell. *Strain of Violence: Historical Studies of American Violence and Vigilantism*. New York: Oxford University Press, 1975.

Bryan, William A. *George Washington in American Literature, 1775–1865*. New York: Columbia University Press, 1952.

Burrows, Edwin G. and Mike Wallace. *Gotham: A History of New York City to 1898*. New York: Oxford University Press, 1999.

Busch, Noel R. *Winter Quarters: George Washington and the Continental Army at Valley Forge*. New York: Liveright, 1974.

Callahan, North. *George Washington: Soldier and Man*. New York: William Morrow, 1972.

————. *Henry Knox: George Washington's General*. New York: Rinehart & Co., 1958.

————. *Thanks, Mr. President: The Trail-Blazing Second Term of George Washington*. New York: Cornwall Books, 1991.

Chidsey, Donald Barr. *The Loyalists: The Story of Those Americans Who Fought Against Independence*. New York: Crown Publishers, 1973.

Chinard, Gilbert. *George Washington as the French Knew Him*. Princeton: Princeton University Press, 1940.

Cresswell, Nicholas. *The Journal of Nicholas Cresswell, 1774–1777*. Edited by Nicholas MacVeagh. New York: Dial Press, 1924.

Crow, Jeffrey J., and Larry E. Tise, eds. *The Southern Experience in the American Revolution*. Chapel Hill: University of North Carolina Press, 1978.

Cumming, William P. and Hugh Rankin, eds. *The Fate of a Nation: The Revolution Through Contemporary Eyes*. London: Phaidon Press, 1975.

Cunliffe, Marcus. *George Washington: Man and Monument*. Boston: Little, Brown, 1958.

Custis, George Washington Parke. *Recollections and Private Memoirs of Washington by His Adopted Son, George Washington Parke Custis*. New York: Derby and Kackson, 1860.

Dalzell, Robert F. Jr., and Lee Baldwin Dalzell. *George Washington's Mount Vernon: At Home in Revolutionary America*. New York: Oxford University Press, 1998.

Dann, John C., ed. *The Revolution Remembered: Eyewitness Accounts of the War for Independence*. Chicago: University of Chicago Press, 1980.

Davis, Burke. *The Campaign That Won America: The Story of Yorktown*. New York: Dial Press, 1970.

————. *George Washington and the American Revolution*. New York: Random House, 1975.

Decatur, Stephen. *Private Affairs of George Washington, from the Record and Accounts of Tobias Lear*. Boston: Houghton Mifflin, 1933.

DePauw, Linda G. "Women in Combat: The Revolutionary War Experience," *Armed Forces and Society* 7 (1981): 209–26.

Dorson, Richard M., ed. *America Rebels: Personal Narratives of the American Revolution*. New York: Pantheon, 1953.

Dunn, Hohn C., ed. *The Revolution Remembered: Eyewitness Accounts of the War for Independence*. Chicago: University of Chicago Press, 1980.

Emery, Noemie. *Washington: A Biography*. New York: G. P. Putnam's Sons, 1976.

Estes, J. Worth. "George Washington and the Doctors: Treating America's First Super-hero." *Medical Heritage* 12, no. 1 (1985): 44–57.

Feltman, William. *The Journal of Lieut. William Feltman, of the First Pennsylvania Regiment, 1781–82*. Philadelphia: The Historical Society of Pennsylvania, 1853.

Ferling, John E. *The First of Men: A Life of Washington*. Knoxville: University of Tennessee Press, 1988.

————. *A Wilderness of Miseries: War and Warriors in Early America*. Westport, Conn.: Greenwood Press, 1980.

Fitzpatrick, John C. *George Washington Himself*. Boston: Houghton Mifflin, 1930.

————. *Washington: Commander in Chief*. Philadelphia: Bobbs-Merrill, 1933.

Fleming, Thomas J. *Beat the Last Drum: The Siege of Yorktown, 1781*. New York: St. Martin's Press, 1963.

Flexner, James Thomas. *George Washington and the New Nation, 1783–1793*. Boston: Little, Brown, 1970.

————. *George Washington: Anguish and Farewell, 1793–1799*. Boston: Little, Brown, 1972.

————. *George Washington in the American Revolution, 1775–1783*. Boston: Little, Brown, 1968.

————. *George Washington: The Forge of Experience, 1732–1775*. Boston: Little, Brown, 1965.

Freeman, Douglas Southall. *George Washington: A Biography*. 7 vols. New York: Scribner's, 1948–59.

Frey, Sylvia R. "The British and the Black: A New Perspective," *The Historian* 39 (1976): 117–31.

————. *The British Soldier in America: A Social History of Military Life in the Revolutionary Period*. Austin: University of Texas Press, 1981.

More Books About Washington and His Times

Gelb, Norman. *Less Than Glory*. New York: G. P. Putnam's Sons, 1984.

Guttmacher, Manfred S. *America's Last King: An Interpretation of the Madness of George III*. New York: Scribner's, 1941.

Hamilton, Charles E., ed. *Braddock's Defeat*. Norman: University of Oklahoma Press, 1959.

Hargreaves, Reginald. *The Bloodybacks: The British Serviceman in North America and the Caribbean, 1655–1783*. New York: Walker & Co., 1968.

Haworth, Paul Leland. *George Washington, Country Gentleman*. Indianapolis: Bobbs-Merrill, 1925.

Hibbert, Christopher. *Redcoats and Rebels: The American Revolution Through British Eyes*. New York: W. W. Norton, 1990.

Higginbotham, Don. *George Washington and the American Military Tradition*. Athens: University of Georgia Press, 1985.

———. *The Glorious Cause: The American Revolution, 1763–1789*. New York: Oxford University Press, 1982.

Hillard, Rev. E. B. *The Last Men of the Revolution*. Barre, Mass.: Barre Publishers, 1968. First published in 1864.

Hirschfeld, Fritz. *George Washington and Slavery: A Documentary Portrayal*. Columbia: University of Missouri Press, 1997.

Holcombe, Arthur N. "The Role of Washington in the Framing of the Constitution." *Huntington Library Quarterly* 19, no. 8 (1956): 317–34.

Hughes, Rupert. *George Washington*. 3 vols. New York: William Morrow, 1926–30.

Irving, Washington. *The Life of George Washington*. Tarrytown, New York: Sleepy Hollow Restorations, 1975.

Jensen, Merrill. *The Founding of a Nation: A History of the American Revolution, 1763–1776*. New York: Oxford University Press, 1968.

Jones, Thomas. *History of New York During the Revolutionary War*. 2 vols. New York: Arno Press, 1968. First published in 1879.

Kaminski, John P., and Jill Adair McCaughan. *A Great and Good Man: George Washington in the Eyes of His Contemporaries*. Madison: Wisc.: Madison House, 1989.

Ketchum, Richard M. *The Winter Soldiers*. Garden City, N.Y.: Doubleday, 1973.

Knox, James H. Mason. "Medical History of George Washington." *Bulletin of the Institute of the History of Medicine* 1, no. 6 (1933): 174–91.

Koontz, Louis Knott. "Washington on the Frontier," *Virginia Magazine of History and Biography* XXXVI (1928), 305–27.

Kopperman, Paul E. *Braddock at the Monongahela*. Pittsburgh: University of Pittsburgh Press, 1977.

Leach, Douglas E. *Arms for Empire: A Military History of the British Colonies in North America, 1607–1763*. New York: Macmillan, 1973.

Lear, Tobias. *Letters and Recollections of Washington*. New York: Macmillan, 1906.

Leckie, Robert. *George Washington's War: The Saga of the American Revolution*. New York: HarperCollins, 1992.

Lewis, Fielding O. "Washington's Last Illness." *Annals of Medical History*, new ser., 4 (1932): 245–48.

Lewis, Taylor, Jr., and Joanne Young. *Washington's Mount Vernon*. New York: Holt, Rinehart & Winston, 1973.

Lewis, Thomas A. *For King and Country: The Maturing of George Washington, 1748–1760*. New York: HarperCollins, 1993.

Lowell, Edward J. *The Hessians*. Port Washington, N.Y.: Kennikat Press, 1965. Reprint of a book first published in 1884.

Martin, Joseph Plumb. *Private Yankee Doodle: Being a Narrative of Some of the Adventures, Dangers and Sufferings of a Revolutionary Soldier*. Boston: Little, Brown, 1962.

Maurer, Martin. "Military Justice Under General Washington," *Military Affairs* 28 (1964): 8–16.

Mazyck, George H. *George Washington and the Negro*. Washington, D.C.: The Associated Publishers, 1932.

McCardell, Lee. *Ill-Starred General: Braddock of the Coldstream Guards*. Pittsburgh: University of Pittsburgh Press, 1958.

McDonald, Forrest. *The Presidency of George Washington*. Lawrence, KS: University Press of Kansas, 1974.

McGuffie, T. H., ed. *Rank and File: The Common Soldier at Peace and War, 1642–1914*. New York: St. Martin's Press, 1964.

Miller, John C. *Origins of the American Revolution*. Boston: Little, Brown, 1943.

————. *Triumph of Freedom, 1775–1783*. Boston: Little, Brown, 1948.

Mitchell, Broadus. *The Price of Independence: A Realistic View of the American Revolution*. New York: Oxford University Press, 1974.

Montross, Lynn. *Rag, Tag and Bobtail: The Story of the Continental Army, 1775–1783*. New York: Harper & Brothers, 1952.

Moore, Charles. *Family Life of George Washington*. Boston: Houghton Mifflin, 1926.

Moore, Frank. *Songs and Ballads of the American Revolution*. New York: D. Appleton & Co., 1856.

Morgan, Edmund S. *The Genius of George Washington*. New York: W. W. Norton, 1981.

————. *The Meaning of Independence: John Adams, Thomas Jefferson, George Washington*. New York: W. W. Norton, 1978.

Morison, Samuel Eliot. *The Young Man Washington*. Cambridge, Mass.: Harvard University Press, 1932.

Morris, Richard B. *Seven Who Shaped Our Destiny: The Founding Fathers as Revolutionaries*. New York: Harper & Row, 1973.

Nettles, Curtis P. *George Washington and American Independence*. Boston: Little, Brown, 1951.

Niemcewicz, Julian Ursyn. *Under Their Vine and Fig Tree: Travels Through America in 1797–1799*. Elizabeth, N.J.: Grossman Publishing Co., 1965.

Nordham, George W. *George Washington's Women: Mary, Martha, Sally and 146 Others*. Philadelphia: Dorrance & Co., 1977.

Norton, Mary Beth. *Liberty's Daughters: The Revolutionary Experience of American Women, 1750–1800*. New York: HarperCollins, 1980.

Palmer, John MacAuley. *General von Steuben*. Port Washington, N.Y.: Kennikat Press, 1966.

Pancake, John S. *1777: Year of the Hangman*. University, Ala.: University of Alabama Press, 1977.

Peckham, Howard H. *The Toll of Independence*. Chicago: University of Chicago Press, 1974.

Pettengill, Ray W., ed. *Letters from America, 1777–1779, Being Letters of Brunswick, Hessian, and Waldeck Officers with the British Armies During the Revolution*. Port Washington, N.Y.: Kennikat Press, 1964.

Quarles, Benjamin. "Lord Dunsmore as Liberator," *The William and Mary Quarterly* XV (1958): 234–507.

————. *The Negro in the American Revolution*. Chapel Hill: University of North Carolina Press, 1961.

Randall, Willard Sterne. *George Washington: A Life*. New York: Henry Holt, 1997.

Rasmussen, William M. S., and Robert S. Tilton. *George Washington: The Man Behind the Myths*. Charlottesville: University Press of Virginia, 1999.

Robin, Abbé Claude. *Travels Through North America*. New York: Arno Press, 1969. First published in 1783.

Royster, Charles. *A Revolutionary People at War: The Continental Army and American Character, 1775–1783*. New York: W. W. Norton, 1981.

Scheer, George F., and Hugh F. Rankin, eds. *Rebels and Redcoats*. Cleveland: World Publishing Co., 1957.

Schwartz, Barry. *George Washington: The Making of a Symbol*. New York: The Free Press, 1987.

Sears, Louis Martin. *George Washington & The French Revolution*. Detroit: Wayne State University Press, 1960.

Smith, James Morton, ed. *George Washington: A Profile*. New York: Hill & Wang, 1996.

Smith, Richard Norton. *Patriarch: George Washington and the New American Nation*. Boston: Houghton Mifflin, 1993.

Spalding, Matthew, and Patrick J. Garrity. *A Sacred Union of Citizens: George Washington's Farewell Address and the American Character*. New York: Rowman & Littlefield Publishers, 1996.

Stryker, William S. *The Battles of Trenton and Princeton*. Boston: Houghton, Mifflin, 1898.

Swiggert, Howard. *The Great Man: George Washington as a Human Being*. Garden City, N.Y.: Doubleday, 1953.

Tebbel, John. *George Washington's America*. New York: E. P. Dutton, 1954.

Thacher, James. *Military Journal of the American Revolution*. New York: The New York Times and Arno Press, 1969. Originally published in 1862.

Thane, Elswyth. *Potomac Squire*. New York: Duell, Sloan and Pearce, 1963.

————. *Washington's Lady*. New York: Dodd, Mead, 1960.

Van Doren, Carl. *The Great Rehearsal: The Story of the Making and Ratifying of the Constitution of the United States*. New York: Viking Press, 1948.

Waldo, Albigence. "Valley Forge Diary, 1777–1778," *Pennsylvania Magazine of History and Biography* XXI (1897): 299–323.

Wall, Charles Cecil. *George Washington: Citizen Soldier*. Charlottesville: University Press of Virginia, 1980.

Ward, Harry M. *The American Revolution: Nationhood Achieved, 1763–1788*. New York: St. Martin's Press, 1995.

Washington, George. *The Diaries of George Washington*. Edited by John C. Fitzpatrick. 4 vols. Boston: Houghton Mifflin, 1925.

———. *The Diaries of George Washington*. Edited by Donald D. Jackson and Dorothy Twohig. 6 vols. Charlottesville: University Press of Virginia, 1976–79.

———. *George Washington: A Collection*. Edited by W. B. Allen. Indianapolis: Liberty Fund, 1988.

———. *Letters from George Washington to Tobias Lear*. Rochester, N.Y.: The Genesee Press, 1905.

———. *Writings*. New York: The Library of America, 1997.

———. *The Writings of George Washington from the Original Manuscript Sources, 1745–1799*. Edited by John C. Fitzpatrick. 39 vols. Washington, D.C.: U.S. Government Printing Office, 1931–44.

Wells, Walter A. "The Last Illness and Death of George Washington." *Virginia Medical Monthly* 53 (1926–27): 629–42.

Woodward, W. E. *George Washington: The Image and the Man*. Garden City, N.Y.: Garden City Publishing Co., 1942.

Wright, Robert K., Jr. *The Continental Army*. Washington, D.C.: U.S. Army Center for Military History, 1984.

Zall, P. M., ed. *George Washington Laughing: Humorous Anecdotes by and about Our First President from Original Sources*. Hamden, Conn.: Archon Books, 1989.

Index

Page numbers in *italics* refer to illustrations.

abolitionism, *74*, 186, 215–17, *216*, 250–52
Acts of Trade and Navigation, 6–7
Adams, Abigail, 143, 247
Adams, John, 8, 9, 79, 80, 91–93, 104, 143, 200, 219, 226, *226*, 238, 246–47, 249, *250*
Africa, 4, 6, 60, *71*, 109
Alexandria, Va., 27, 48, 69, 72, 252, 255, 256
Algonquian Indians, 34
Allegheny Mountains, 50, 57, 59
Allegheny River, 34, 35, 38, *38*, 55, 60, 130
Allen, Ethan, 91
American Crisis, The (Paine), 3
André, Major John, 176–78, *177*, *178*
Appalachian Mountains, 34
Arlington House, 253–54
Arnold, Benedict, 91, 143, 148, 162, 176–79, *176*, *179*, 183, 204
Arnold, Peggy Shippen, 176
Articles of Confederation, 200–1, 211, 212, 213
Atlantic Ocean, 4–5, 29, 32
Australia, 4

Baltimore, Lord, 65
Barbados, 28–29
Bastille, 233, *234*
Beechley, W., *173*
Belvoir, 25–26, 62
Bernard, John, 252
Bible, 17, 66, 71, 224
Bill of Rights, 217–18, 225–26, 246
Blue Ridge Mountains, 26, 34, 35
Boston, Battle of, *98*, 105–9, *107*, 110
Boston, Mass., 5, 8, 14, 62, 79–84, 86–89, 94–98, *98*, 231
  British occupation of, 79–80, 83–84, 88–89, *88*, 91, 95–96, 102, 104–6
  Custom House in, 79, *80*
  liberation of, 106–9, *108*, 110

Boston Massacre, 79–80, *80*, 104, 171
Boston Tea Party, 82–83, *82*, 87
Boudinot, Catherine, 225
Boudinot, Elias, 225
Braam, Jacob van, 35
Braddock, Gen. Edward, 42–43, *43*, 48, *50*, 51–58, *55*, *59*, 60, 61, 83, 129, 164
Brandywine, Battle of, 14, 143–46, *145*
British army, 13, 14, 22, 42–57, 76, 79–80, *80*, 83, 200
  drills and discipline of, 44–48, 53–54, 57, 58, 110
  Ethiopian Regiment of, 103, 174
  fife and drum bands of, 47, 49, 54, 196
  fighting style of, 45–47, 49–57, 95–96, 117–19
  42nd Highlanders of, 124, *124*
  guns and equipment of, 45–47, *46*, 49–50, 95–96, *96*, 116–17
  Hessian soldiers in, 110, *110*, 113, 115, *115*, 117, 118, 120, 122, 127, 129–32, *131*, *132*, 142, 143, 144, 162, 167, 168–69, 196, 198
  life of career soldiers in, 43–57, *50*
  Native American alliances with, 34, 39–41, 48–49, 169–70, *170*, 241
  officers and commissions in, 30–31, 42, 44, 47, 54, 61, 83–84, 88–89, 91, 198
  recruitment and abduction in, 43, 109–10, *110*
  scarlet uniforms of, 30, 43–44, *44*, 46, 52, 56
  Tory regiments in, 204
British Empire, 75, 104, 113, 171
  territories of, 3–4, 6–10, 60, 109
  see also Great Britain; London
British navy, 61, 89, 102, 107–8, 109, 112–13, 115, *115*, 122–23, 140, 142–43, 168–69, 200, 241
British Parliament, 75–79, 171, 200
  colonial trade and taxation regulated by,

6–7, 8–9, 48, 76–79, *77*, *78*, *79*, 81–84, 85–86, *87*, 212, 241
British West Indies, 4, 28–29, 60, 72, 74, 77, 204, 230, 238, *238*
Brooklyn Heights, N.Y., 115–20
Brown Bess musket, 45–46, *46*
Bunker Hill, Battle of, 95–96, *96*, 102, 103, 106, 120, 212, 234
Burgoyne, Gen. John, 91, 142–43, 148
Burns, David, 240

Cadwalader, John, 152–53
Calhoun, John C., 253
Cambridge, Mass., 96, 99, 101
Camden, Battle of, 180
Campbell, Col. Archibald, 172
Canada, 7, 32–33, 34, 60, 61, 108, 109, 112, 142, 204
Carleton, Gen. Guy, 200
Cartagena, City of, 22–23
Chadds Ford, Pa., 143–45
Chappel, Alonzo, *169*, *206*
Charleston, S.C., 5, 172–74, 175
Chesapeake Bay, 17, 18, 142–43, 189, 191–92
Chew, Benjamin, *148*
Christopher (slave), 255
Church of England, 8
Civil War, U.S., 9, 16, *74*, 154, 253–54
Clinton, Gen. Sir Henry, 91, 117–18, 160–66, *161*, 168, 171–72, 174, 176–78, 189–91, 200
Closen, Count Ludwig von, 188
Cobb, David, 195
Coercive Acts, 83, 85–86
colonies, *2*, 3–10, 62
  commerce and trade in, 6–7, 70, 71, *71*, 72, 76–84, 211–12
  government and law in, 6–7, 8–9, 22–24, 25, 30–31, 48, 66, 71, 76–77, 83, 84, 102

population of, 4, 33, 70–71
rivalry and dispute in, 8, 9–10, 102–3
struggle for independence in, 9–10, 16, 48, 76–94, *77*, *90*, 104, *104*
tobacco farming and trade in, 5, 17, 18–19, 20–21, 30, 42, 70, *70*, 73, 77
wilderness and frontier in, 4, 6, 33
Common Sense (Paine), 104, *104*, 210, 243
Concord, Battle of, 88–89, *88*, *89*, 103, 105, 234
Confederate States of America, 253–54
Congress, U.S., 62, 225–26, 231–32, 237, 241
bicameral structure of, 215, 226, 246
see also House of Representatives, U.S.; Senate, U.S.
Connecticut, 4, 91, 215
Constitution, U.S., 10, *212*, 213, 214–18, 225–26, 230, 246
ratification of, 217–18, *218*
Twenty-Second Amendment to, 244
see also Bill of Rights
Continental Army, 91–94, 256
enlistment in, 9, 97–100, 102–3, 133, 138, 174
free blacks in, 103, 174, 188
French volunteers in, 140–41, *141*
hardship, illness, and deprivation in, 11–12, 126–27, 129, 133, 134, 138–39, 149–53, *150*, 187–88, 201–3
officers in, 99, 100, 101, 105–6, *105*, 110, 111, *111*, 135, 230–31
order and discipline in, 96, 99–102, *100*, 123, 156–59, *156*, *158*, 164
uniforms and frontier dress of, 94, 97–98, *99*
Washington as commander of, 10, 13–14, 62, 93–94, *93*, 95–96, *98*, 99–103, *100*, 104–8, *107*, *114*, *120*, *124*, *131*, *132*, *134*, *135*, *136*, *145*, *148*, *154*, *158*, *164*, *165*, 202–7, *205*, *206*, *207*, *226*
Washington's addresses to, 133, 202–3, 204–6, *206*
Washington's farewell to, 204–7, *206*
weapons and equipment of, 96–97, 98–99, *99*, 102, 105–6, *106*
women and children traveling with, 143, 155, 166, *166*
Continental Association, 86–88
Continental Congress, 84–94, 100, 102, 108, 109, 112, 113, 127, 141, 146–47, 152–54, 211–18, 252
first meeting of, 84–88, *85*
functions of, 147, 171, 172, 174, 179–80, 200–2, 211, 231
second meeting of, 86, 88, 90–94, *92*
Washington chosen as president of, 212–18, *214*

Conway, Gen. Thomas, 152–53
Conway Cabal, 152–53, 172
Cornwallis, Lady, 172
Cornwallis, Lord Charles, 117, 125, 127, 129, 133–34, 136, 144, 172, 173, *173*, 181–84, 186, 190–91, 193–97, 199
cotton gin, 252
Craik, James, 54, 255, *255*
Cresswell, Nicholas, 68
Crèvecoeur, Hector St. John de, 185–86
Currier & Ives, *18*, *227*
Custis, Daniel Parke, 63
Custis, Eleanor "Nelly" Calvert, 65, 200
Custis, Eleanor "Nelly" Parke, 200, 208, 209, *249*
Custis, Elizabeth, 192
Custis, George Washington "Wash" Parke, 200, 208, *249*, 253–54
Custis, John "Jacky," 63, 64–65, *66*, 192, 199–200
Custis, Martha "Patsy," 63, 64, 66, *66*

Darley, F.O.C., *100*, *164*
Daughters of Liberty, 89–90
Davies, Thomas, *126*
Declaration of Independence, 3, 10, 77, 109, 113–15, *114*, 140, 215, *216*, 234, 238, 246
de Grasse, François Joseph Paul, Count, 186, 189, 191, 192–93, 236
Delaware River, 142, 143–44, 161–62
Washington's crossing of, 129–30, *131*
Democrat and Republican Societies, 230
Denny, Ebenezer, 196
Dinwiddie, Robert, 30, 34–37, *35*, 39, 53, 57–59
Dolly, Quamino, 174
Dumas, Captain, 52
Dumas, Mathieu, 191
Dunbar, Thomas, 51, 56
Dunmore, John Murray, Lord, 84, 103, 174
Duquesne, Marquis, 34

East India Company, 81
East River, 110, 111, 115, 117, 122, 125
Electoral College, 219, 233, 246
Enfant, Pierre Charles L', 240
Estaing, Charles Hector Théodat, Count d', 160, 168–69, 236
Estates General, 233

Fairfax, Bryan, 84
Fairfax, George William, *25*, 63

Fairfax, Sally Cary, 62–63
Fairfax, Thomas, Lord, 12, 26
Fairfax, William, 25, 26, 35
Fairfax family, 25–26, *25*, 27, 30, 62–63
Federalist, The, 217–18
Federalists, 217–18, 225–26, 230–33, 236, 238, 246, 248
Feltman, William, 185
Ferguson, Patrick, 144
Ferry Farm, 20–21, 24, 30
Fithian, Philip, 119
Fitzgerald, John, 130
Forbes, John, 60–61, 63
Fort Cumberland, 48–49, 51, 56, 57, 58, 60
Fort Duquesne, 39, 41, *43*, *50*, 51–52, 53, 55–56, 57, 60
Fort Le Boeuf, 34, 37
Fort Lee, 111, 125, *126*
Fort Necessity, 40–41, 42, 56
Fort Niagara, 170
Fort Pitt, 61
Fort Presque Isle, 34
Fort Ticonderoga, 91, 105, 142
Fort Venango, 37, 60–61
Fort Washington, 111, 125
France:
American rebel cause supported by, 10, 140–41, 148, 159, 168–69, 175–76, 186–93, 236
British wars with, 7, 10, 32, 34–43, 48–61, 69, 75, 76, 109, 140, 233, 234–35
Native Americans allied with, 7, 33, 34, *43*, 48–57, *55*, 76
territories controlled by, 32–33, 61, 140, 169, 186
see also French Revolution; Paris
Franklin, Benjamin, 10, 34, 48, *49*, 79, 147, 156, 159, 160, 200, 212
Fredericksburg, Va., 21, 26
Free Africa Relief Society, 239
French and Indian War, 10, 34–43, 48–61, 69, 159, 180–81, 187, *255*
French army, 187–90, *188*, 198, 201
French navy, 160, 168–69, 186, 191–93, 238, *238*
French Revolution, 233–38, *235*, *236*, 242
Reign of Terror in, 235–36
French West Indies, 61, 140, 169, 186
Frost, John, *219*
Frost, Robert, 244
Fugitive Slave Law, 216

Gage, Gen. Thomas, 83–84, 88–89, 95–96
Galveston, 221
Gates, Gen. Horatio, 143, 148, *149*, 152, 172–73, 180

Genêt, Edmond Charles, 238, *238*, 241
George II, King of England, 48, 61
George III, King of England, 74–77, *75*, 79,
    81–84, 86, 89, 102, 104, 109, 110, *112*,
    113, *114*, 115, 126, 129, 141, 171, 174,
    200, 201, 204, 242, 244
George Washington, 12
Georgia, 4, 84, 172, 216
Germantown, Battle of, 14, 147–48, *148*
Germany, 109–10, 234–35
Gettysburg Address, 246
Gipson, William, 181
Gist, Christopher, 35, 37–39, *38*
Gowanus Creek, *118*, 119
Graves, Thomas, 191
Grayson, Alexander, 124
Great Britain, 3–4, 21, 26, 75–79
    crime and punishment in, 43, 76, 171
    disdain for American fighting men in, 80,
        83, 84, *84*, 95, 117
    see also British Empire; British Parliament;
        London; Revolutionary War
Great Lakes, 32, 76, 170, 201, 241
Greene, Gen. Nathanael, 123, 153–54, 162, 172,
    180–83, *181*
Grenville, George, 76, 77
Griswold, Matthew, *250*
guillotine, 235–36, *236*, 237

Hale, Nathan, 125
Half-King, Chief, 39–41
Hamilton, Alexander, 81, 174, 212, 217–18, 227,
    227, 230–32, *230*, 241, 242, 244
Harlem Heights, Battle of, 14, 123–25, *124*
Harvard College, 108, 236–37
Harvey, William, 89
Hayes, Mary Ludwig (Molly Pitcher), 166,
    166
Henry, Edward L., *132*
Henry, Patrick, 213
Hickey, Thomas, 112, *113*
History of the United States (Frost), *219*
Holland, 81, 171
Honeyman, John, 129
Houdon, Jean-Antoine, 209, *209*
House of Representatives, U.S., 215, 216, 248,
    250, 257
Howe, Adm. Sir Richard "Black Dick," 109,
    113, 122, 142, 191
Howe, Robert, 180
Howe, Gen. Lord William, 91, 95–96, *97*, 109,
    112–13, 115–20, 125, 129, 136, 139–40,
    142, 144–49, 152, 160–62, *161*
Hudson River, 105, 109, 110, 111, 123, 125, 142,
    168, 176, *177*, 187, 206–7

Huntington, Daniel, *38*
Huntington, Ebenezer, 179–80
Huron Indians, 34, 52

India, 4, 60, 109, *173*
Iroquois Indians, 34, 39–41, 169–70, *170*
Irving, Washington, *25*, *28*, *59*, *97*, *141*, *156*,
    175, *242*

Jacobins, 235, 238
Jakes, Francis, *23*
Jamestown, Va., 18, 70
Jay, John, 200, 217–18, 241, *241*
Jay's Treaty, 242, *242*, 244
Jefferson, Thomas, 10, 25, 79, 113–14, 218, 227,
    227, 230–31, *231*, 233, 236, 242–43, *243*,
    246
Journal of Major George Washington, The
    (Washington), 39, *39*
Judge, Oney, 250–51
Judiciary Act, 226
Jumonville, Joseph Coulon de, 40, 41

Kimberley, Denison, *38*
Knox, Gen. Henry, 105–6, *105*, 130, *148*, 206,
    227, *227*

Lafayette, George Washington, 236–37
Lafayette, Marquis de, 140–41, *141*, 143,
    145–46, 149, 152, 162, 163, 165, 166,
    175, 177, 183, 186, 191–93
    Washington's relationship with, *141*, 143,
        146, 166, 192–93, 197–98, 201, 208,
        218–19, 230, 234, *234*, 236
Lake Champlain, 105, 142
Lake Erie, 34
Laurens, Henry, 200
Lear, Tobias, 209, 250, 254–55, *254*
Lee, 102
Lee, Billy, 84–85, *100*, 101, 155, 166, 192, 207,
    249, 254
Lee, Charles, 110, 111, *111*, 161, 163–64, *164*,
    167
Lee, Gen. "Light-Horse" Harry, 181, 254, 257
Lee, Mary Custis, 254
Lee, Robert E., 254
Leutze, Emanuel, *131*
Lexington, Battle of, 89, 103, 105, 212, 234
Life and Memorable Actions of Washington
    (Weems), 15–16
Life of George of Washington (Irving), *25*, *28*,
    59, *97*, *141*, *156*, *175*, *242*

Lincoln, Abraham, ix, 15–16, 154, 246, 253, 254,
    255, 256
Little Hunting Creek Plantation, 20, 24
London, 4, 5, 8, 18, 34–35, 39, 43, 61, 70, 75, *78*,
    81, 109, 147, 171, 183, 241
Long Island, 111, 115, *115*, 116
Long Island, Battle of, 14, 115–20, *115*, *118*,
    120, 144, 172
Loring, Elizabeth, 139–40, 142, 160
Loring, Joshua, 139, 160
Louis, Joe, 13
Louis XV, King of France, 61
Louis XVI, King of France, 140, 148, 175, 233,
    236, *237*, 242
Louisiana, 32
Lyon, Matthew, *250*

McCurtin, Daniel, 112
McKean, Thomas, 199
McRae, John C., *15*
Madison, James, 212, *212*, 214–15, 217–18, 232
Manhattan, 110–12, 122–26, 168, 221–25
Martin, Joseph Plum, 119, 122–23, 126, 151–52,
    163, 168–69, 193, 198, 207
Maryland, 4, 34, 65, 97, 215
Mason, George, 79
Massachusetts, 4, 8, 83, 97, *102*, 215
Mayflower, 70
Mercer, George, 69
militias, 22–24, 89, 102, 241
Mingo Island, 39–41
minutemen, 89, 103
Mississippi River, 32, 35, 201
Mittelberger, Gottlieb, 4–5
Mohawk Indians, 82, *82*
Monmouth, Battle of, 14, 163–67, *164*, *165*, *166*
Monongahela River, 35, 51–52, 54
Monroe, James, 218
Montreal, 61
Morgan, Gen. Daniel, 180–81, *182*, 183
Morris, Gouverneur, 213–14
Morris, Robert, 216–17
Morristown, N.J., 136, 138–39, 141, 143
Mount Vernon, 22, *23*, 24, *24*, 27, 29, 30, 39, 84,
    199–200, 229, 236, *236*, 253
    daily life at, 66–68, *67*, 72–74, 248
    hospitality at, 68, 209, 237, 248, 252
    slaves at, 6, 12, 16, *67*, 70–74, *74*, 77, 78,
        84–85, *100*, 101, 184–85, 216–17, 228,
        250–54
    Washington as master of, 42, 56, 61, 62, *63*,
        64, 66–68, *67*, 69–74, 77–79, 102,
        170–71, 184–85, 192, 207–9,
        248–54
Munsell, Hezekiah, 119

Nancy, 102
Native Americans, 114
    colonial decimation, 5, 33–34, 57
    English alliances with, 34, 39–41, 48–49,
        169–70, *170*, 241
    French alliances with, 7, 33, 34, *43*, 48–57,
        55, 76
    raids and scalping by, 8, 27, 37, 40–41, 48–
        49, 51, 54–55, 57–59, 60, 169–70, *169*
    religion of, 33, 49, 54, 57
    in Revolutionary War, 97, 169–70, *170*
Neutrality Proclamation, 237–38
Newburgh Address, 202
New England, 4, 6, 8, 59–89, 92, 229–30
New Hampshire, 4, 102, 218
New Jersey, 4, 8, *13*, 125–36, *126*, *127*, *134*,
    162–67
Newport, R.I., 5, 6, 169, 175, 187
New York, 4, 7, 8, 215
New York, N.Y., 5, *11*, *13*, 81, 109–15, *114*,
    116, 125–26, 129, 139, 142, 170–72,
    175–77, 186, 203–7
    British occupation and evacuation of, 177,
        177, 203–4, *205*
    Broadway in, 222, 228–29, 230
    Federal Hall in, 223–25, *223*, *224*
    as first U.S. capital, 219, 221–25,
        228–31
    Fraunces Tavern in, 204–7
    Trinity Church in, 124–25, *224*
Nicola, Lewis, 201
North, Frederick, Lord, 81–83, *81*, 200
North Atlantic Treaty Organization (NATO),
    238

O'Hara, Gen. Charles, 197–98
Ohio country, 34, 35–42, *35*, *39*, 49–50, 60, 69,
    251
Ohio River, 34, 35–37, 39
Oliver, Peter, 86–88
Otis, James, 8
Ottawa Indians, 34, 52, 76

Paine, Thomas, 3, 104, *104*, 210, 243
Paoli Massacre, *146*, 147
Paris, 147, 185
Peale, Charles Willson, *64*, 69, *226*, *230*, *231*
Pennsylvania, 4, 7, 8, 34, 97, 129–30, 149–53,
    215
Pequot War, 33–34
Philadelphia, Pa., 5, 8, 57, 81, 84–85, *85*,
    94–95, 102, 104, 131–32, 142–49,
    213–18, 232

British capture of, 147–49, 160–61, 176
    State House (Independence Hall) in, *92*,
        213
    yellow fever epidemic in, 238–39
Phoenix, 122
Pilgrims, 70
Pitt, William, 60, 61
Polk, Charles Peale, *136*
Polson, William, 53
Pontiac, Chief, 76
Poor, Salem, 103
Potomac River, 17, 18, 20, *23*, 24, 26, 42, 78,
    184, 192, 232, 252
Powhatan Confederacy, 33
Princeton, Battle of, 14, 134–37, *135*, *136*,
    140
Protestantism, 8
Puritans, 8, 33–34
Pyle, Howard, *134*

Quebec, 61

racism, 72–74, 103, 250–51
Rall, Johann, 129, 131
Randolph, Edmund, 227, *227*
Rappahannock River, 21, 26
Report on the Public Credit (Hamilton), 231
Republicans, 230, 232–33, 236, 238, 242–43,
    246, 248
Revere, Paul, *80*, 88–89
Revolutionary War, 9–10, 12–14, 62, 68, *81*,
    252, 254
    casualties and destruction of, 10, 89, *89*,
        95–96, *96*, 118–22, *121*, 125, 131, 135,
        145, 151, 167, 168–69
    courage and valor in, 9, 12–13, 133–36
    events leading to, 76–94
    Native Americans in, 97, 169–70, *170*
    patriotic women in, 84, 89–90, *90*
    political differences during, 102–3
    slogans and songs of, 95, 98, 112, *113*, 130,
        137, 160, 162, 168, 196–97, 199
    see also British army; Continental Army;
        specific battles
Reynolds, Joshua, *184*
Rhode Island, 4, 215
Robertson, Alexander, *23*
Robin, Claude, 188–89
Rochambeau, Count de, 175–76, 186, 187, 189,
    190, 194, 198, 236
Rockingham, Lord, 200
Roebuck, 122
Roosevelt, Franklin D., 154–55, 244

*Rules of Civility and Decent Behaviour in
    Company and Conversation*, 21–22, 25

Saint-Mémim, Charles de, 248, *251*
Salem, Peter, 103
Saratoga, Battle of, 148, *149*, 162, 172, 176, 212
Savage, Edward, *249*
Scott, Charles, 163–64
secessionists, 253–54
Ségur, Count de, 188, 234
Senate, U.S., 215, 242, 244
Seven Years' War, 60, 140, 156
Shawnee Indians, 34, 52
Shays's Rebellion, 212–13
Shenandoah Valley, 26, 40, 58, 59
Shipp, John, 44
slaves, 215–17, 228–29, 240
    classes of, 73
    colonial population of, 70–71
    escape and uprising of, 8, *74*, 103, 174,
        184–85, 193, 198, 250–51
    freeing of, *74*, 103, 114, 174, 186, 215–17,
        239, 250–52, 254
    legal status of, 71, *72*
    living conditions of, *71*, 72–74, 185
    "middle passage" of, 4, *71*
    national debate on, 250–53
    punishment and restriction of, 71, 74,
        185–86
    trade in, 6, 70, 71, *71*, 72, *72*, 74, 77, 174–75,
        217
    Washington's ownership of, 6, 12, 16, *67*,
        70–74, *74*, 77, 78, 84–85, *100*, 101,
        184–85, 216–17, 228, 250–54
Smith, James, 55–56
Sons of Liberty, 77, 81–82, *82*, 83, 86–88, *88*
South Carolina, 4, 172–74, 216, 253
Spain, 22–23, 159
Stamp Act, 76–78, *77*, *78*, 241
Staten Island, 113, 115, 126
Stearns, Junius Brutus, *55*, *65*, *67*
Stephen, Adam, 57
Steuben, Baron von, *154*, 155–59, *156*, *158*,
    162, 164, 187
Stockbridge Indians, 97
St. Pierre, Legardeur de, 37
Stuart, Gilbert, *107*, *245*
Sullivan, John, 169–70, *170*
Supreme Court, U.S., 101, 215, 242, *242*

Tallmadge, Benjamin, 205–6
Tarleton, Gen. Banastre, 183, *184*
Tea Act, 81–83

Thacher, James, 191–92, 195–96
Three-Fifths Compromise, 216
Tories, 102, 105, 106–8, 109, 111–12, *112*, 117, 122, 125, 126, 147, 153, 160, 161, *169*, 172, 176, 181, 191, 203–4, 236
Townshend, Charles, 78–79
Townshend Acts, 78–79, *79*
Treaty of Alliance, 242
Treaty of Paris, 61, 200, 201, 203–4, 211, 241
Trenton, Battle of, 14, 127–33, *131*, *132*, 140, 203
Trumbull, John, *197*

United States of America, 3
    birth of, 9, 16, 137, 213–19
    economic foundations of, 230–32, *230*, 241
    foreign policy of, 237–38, 242
    see also Congress, U.S.; Constitution, U.S.

Valley Forge, Pa., 149–59, *150*, *154*, *156*, *158*, 162, 164, 179, 180
Vietnam War, 9
Ville de Paris, 186, 192–93
Villiers, Captain Coulon de, 41–42, 51
Virginia, 4, 5, 7, 8, 17–28, *18*, 30, 34, 57–62, 66, 76, 86, 97
Virginia Assembly, 19, 39, 58
Virginia Company, 18
Virginia House of Burgesses, 61, 66, 84
Virginia militia, 22–24, 30–31, 39–43, 48, *64*, 69, 86, 92
Virginia Plan, 214–15
Virginia Regiment, 39–43, 48–62, *55*, *60*
"Virginia's Hearts of Oak," 7

Wakefield plantation, 17–18, 24
Waldo, Albigence, 151
Walpole, Horace, 32
Washington, Anne Fairfax, 25, 28, 29, 42
Washington, Anne Pope, 18
Washington, Augustine, Jr., 19, 21, 24
Washington, Augustine "Gus," 15, *15*, 17, 19–21, 71, 72
Washington, Bushrod, 101
Washington, Charles, 20
Washington, D.C., 232, 239–40
    Capitol in, 239, *239*
    Washington Monument in, 257
Washington, Elizabeth "Betty," 20
Washington, George:

aging and decline of, 232–33, 249–50, 254–55
ancestry of, 17–19, *19*
assassination plot against, 111–12, *113*
birth of, 17–18, 19–20, 32
Cabinet of, 227, *227*, 239
character and personality of, 12, 14–15, *15*, 16, 21–22, 25–26, *28*, 39, 43, 54, 58–61, 62–63, 66, 67–68, 69, 72–74, 91–94, 101–2, 108, 119, 123, 133, 139, 153, 202–3, 213–14, 216–17, 226–28, 233, 244, 250–52
childhood and adolescence of, 5, 6, 12, 15–16, *15*, 20–30, *22*, *24*, *25*, *28*, 34, 71
death of, 72, 255–57, *256*
dentures of, 229
earnings and income of, 27, 39, 69–70, 72–73, 228
education and training of, 21–22, 24–25
explosive temper of, 101, 119, 123, 133, 152, 240
Farewell Address of, 244–46, 253
as "Father of Our Country," 3, 10–12, 16, 109, 244
favorite reading of, 66
first battle experience of, 40–42
frontier experience of, 26–27, *28*, 35–39, *38*, 43, 48, 59–60
funeral and burial of, 256–57, *256*
honors accorded to, 108, 257
horsemanship of, 24–25, 26, 54, *55*, 69, 85, 155
hunting and fishing of, 24, *25*, 26, 69, 85
illnesses of, 29, 51, 57, 64, 69, 229–30, 232, 254–55, *254*
inaugurations of, *11*, *13*, 24, 220–25, *224*, 233
inoculation of troops by, 139, 193
last will of, 254, 255
life mask of, 209, *209*
marriage and family life of, 14, 62–68, *63*, *65*, *66*, 199–200, 208–9
military career of, 10, 12–14, 30–31, 35–43, 47–62, *55*, *59*, *60*, 91–96, *93*, *98*, 99–103, *100*, 104–98, *107*, *114*, *120*, *124*, *131*, *132*, *134*, *135*, *136*, *145*, *148*, *154*, *158*, *164*, *165*, 202–7, *205*, *206*, *207*, *226*
military skills and strategy of, 51–52, 53–54, 57–61, *60*, 91, 94, 105–6, 117, 127–30, 134–35, 143–46
money problems of, 208, 251–52
physical appearance and stature of, 63, 68–69, 155
political criticism of, 242–44

political philosophy of, 14, 77, 79, 80, 81, 84, 85–86, 104, 108, 210–11, 237–38, 241–43, 246, 249
portraits and drawings of, 10–11, *11*, 12, *13*, *15*, *25*, *28*, *38*, *64*, *65*, *67*, 69, *98*, *100*, *107*, *131*, *132*, *134*, *136*, *154*, *158*, *164*, *165*, *205*, *206*, *207*, *214*, *219*, *224*, *227*, *243*, *245*, *248*, *249*, *251*, *255*, *256*
presidency of, *11*, *13*, 14, 24, 218–48, *219*, *227*, *240*, 250, 251
press hated by, 244
racist beliefs of, 72–74, 103, 250–51
on religious liberty, 210–11
reputation and fame of, 10–12, 15–16, *15*, 54, 91, 108–9, 170, 188–89, 190–91, 199, 209, 220–22, 234
retirement of, 244–56
secret agents of, 94, 110, 125, 129, 142, 161, 178
siblings and half-siblings of, 19, 20
on slavery, 216–17
smallpox contracted by, 29, 64, 69
social skills of, 26, 67–68, 69, 102
statesmanship of, 10, 14, 16, 212–18
surveying skills and jobs of, 24, *24*, 26, 27, *28*, 30, 48, 240
writings of, 14, 17, 20, 21–22, 26–27, 29, 37–39, *39*, 40, 62, 73, 77, 79, 102, *108*, 129, 154, 170–71, 208, 209, 216–17, 222, 248, 249–50, 253
Washington, Jane Butler, 19
Washington, John, 18, 19
Washington, John, Jr., 18–19
Washington, John Augustine "Jack," 20, 129
Washington, Lawrence (George's grandfather), 18–19
Washington, Lawrence (George's half-brother), 19, 21, 22–26, 30
    George Washington's relationship with, 22, *22*, 23, 24–26, 28–29, 141
    illness and death of, 28–30
Washington, Lund, 70, 170–71, 184–85, 208
Washington, Martha Dandridge Custis, 20, *63*, *65*, *208*, *249*
    character and personality of, *63*, 64, 84, 90, 155, 239
    children of, *63*, 64–65, *66*, 192, 199–200
    correspondence of George Washington and, 62, 64, 94, 102, 154
    as First Lady, 228–29, 233
    first marriage of, 63
    marriage of George Washington and, 62, *63*, 64, *65*, 72
    patriotism of, 84, 90, 155
    personal fortune of, 63, 72, 90, 251

physical appearance of, 63, 209
   Washington's relationship with, 14, 63–64,
      66, 68, 94, 155, *158*, 208, 229–30, 232,
      233, 239, 244, 248, 254–56
Washington, Mary Ball, 17, 19–20, *19*, 24, 30
Washington, Mildred, 20
Washington, Samuel, 20
Washington, Sarah, 28, 29, 42
Washington, William, 181
Washington Life Guard, 112, *113*

Wayne, "Mad" Anthony, 167
Weems, Mason Locke "Parson," 15–16, *15*
West Point, 176–78, *177*, 180, 183
Whipple, Joseph, 251
Whiskey Rebellion, 241, 253
White, G. G., *15*
White House, 240
Whitemarch, Pa., 148–49
White Plains, Battle of, 14, 125, 168
Whitney, Eli, 252

Williamsburg, Va., 19, 35, 61, 62, 66, 67, 69, 84,
   192–93
Woodford, William, 101
World War II, 9, 154–55

"Yankee Doodle," 162, 198
Yohn, F. C., *145*
Yorktown, Battle of, 14, *173*, 189, 193–98, *197*,
   199, 201